Copyright 2009 by ABC-CLIO, LLC

Library of Congress Cataloging-in-Publication Data
Peimani, Hooman, 1957-
    Conflict and security in Central Asia and the Caucasus / Hooman Peimani.
        p. cm.
    Includes bibliographical references and index.
    ISBN 978-1-59884-054-4 (hard copy : acid-free paper)—ISBN 978-1-59884-055-1 (e book)
1. Asia, Central—History—1991–   2. Asia, Central—Politics and government—1991–
3. Caucasus—Politics and government.   4. Caucasus—History—1991–   5. Post-communism—
Asia, Central.   6. National security—Asia, Central. I. Title.

    DK859.5.P44 2009
    958'.043—dc22

                                                                    2009010382
13 12 11 10 9   1 2 3 4 5

This book is also available on the World Wide Web as an eBook.
Visit www.abc-clio.com for details.

ABC-CLIO, LLC
130 Cremona Drive, P.O. Box 1911
Santa Barbara, California 93116-1911

This book is printed on acid-free paper ∞
Manufactured in the United States of America

To my son, Justin

Contents

Acronyms and Abbreviations

AP	Associated Press
bpd	barrels per day
BTC	Baku-Tbilisi-Ceyhan oil pipeline
CIS	Commonwealth of Independent States
CPT	Communist Party of Turkmenistan
CST	CIS Collective Security Treaty
CSTO	Collective Security Treaty Organization
ECO	Economic Cooperation Organization
EEC	Eurasian Economic Community
EU	European Union
EURASEC	Eurasian Economic Community
GUAM	Organization for Democracy and Economic Development–Georgia, Ukraine, Azerbaijan, and Moldova
GUUAM	Organization for Democracy and Economic Development–Georgia, Ukraine, Uzbekistan, Azerbaijan, and Moldova
HRW	Human Rights Watch
IMU	Islamic Movement of Uzbekistan
IPAP	Individual Partnership Action Plan
IRNA	Islamic Republic News Agency
ISAF	International Security Assistance Force
JPF	Joint Russian, Georgian, and Ossetian Peacekeeping Forces
JCC	Joint Control Commission
NATO	North Atlantic Treaty Organization
OCU	Organized Crime Unit
OSCE	Organization for Security and Cooperation in Europe
PFP	Partnership for Peace Program (NATO)
RCD	Regional Cooperation for Development
SCO	Shanghai Cooperation Organization

SCP	South Caucasus Pipeline
TAEFOS	Trans-Asian European Fiber Optic System
THF	Turkmen Helsinki Foundation
UN	United Nations
UNECE	United Nations Economic Commission for Europe
UNESCAP	United Nations Economic and Social Commission for Asia and the Pacific
UNIS	United Nations Information Service
UNOCHA	United Nations Office for the Coordination of Humanitarian Affairs
UNODC	United Nations Office on Drugs and Crimes
UPI	United Press International
USSR	Union of Soviet Socialist Republics
WREP	Western Route Export Pipeline

Tables

Introduction

The fall of Communism in the Soviet Union not only ended the Cold War, but it also resulted in the disintegration of the Soviet Union. Being a multinational country, its collapse led to the rise of 15 newly independent states, all of which hosted various ethnic and religious minority groups, although each state was identified with a single ethnic group that accounted for the majority of its population. By force, all these states began the process of transition from a highly centralized political system based on a command economy to a form of free enterprise having a political system consistent with the emerging new economy. None of them was prepared to embark on this gigantic political and economic project alone. Unsurprisingly, with few exceptions—mainly the small Baltic states of Estonia, Latvia, and Lithuania—the others have thus far failed to end this process of transition, or even to build the foundations of a democratic political system based on a corresponding economic system. To expect success from their attempts to achieve this objective in the foreseeable future is simply unrealistic.

Today, despite differences, these nations' economies are neither capitalist nor socialist, although they have just about all the negative aspects of these economic systems. Their political systems represent a spectrum of authoritarianism, retaining many aspects of the Soviet totalitarian system, including repression and human rights abuses. They are run almost exclusively by former Soviet elites turned nationalist. In fact, during the 18 years since the Soviet Union's fall, transition involving these economic and political characteristics has become a permanent feature instead of a passing phenomenon. This is especially evident in the Caucasus and Central Asia. As the least-developed, least-industrialized, and least-prosperous regions of the Soviet Union, these regions' transitional process has been especially agonizing, with significant short-term and long-term social, political, and economic implications for their constituent countries as well as for their neighboring regions.

Because of their failure to complete the transition, the distorted economies of Central Asia and the Caucasus are unable to provide the basic needs of their populations, in most cases unlike the Soviet economy. Their weaknesses have left many people unemployed with no realistic hope of long-term, well-paid employment in the foreseeable future and have contributed to expanding poverty in urban and rural areas alike. The rapidly widening gap in income between the overwhelming majority of the population and the small fraction of affluent people benefiting from the post-independence economy has polarized these societies, a recipe for internal instability and conflict. Added to this, rampant corruption in all the Central Asian and Caucasian governments and the high-handed policy toward opposition groups and individuals of just about all of them have created a suitable ground for the rise and expansion of popular dissatisfaction with the status quo, and thus internal conflict and instability in one form or another. Civil wars in Azerbaijan, Georgia, and Tajikistan; the operation of armed extremist groups in Uzbekistan, Tajikistan, and Kyrgyzstan; and revolutions in Georgia and Kyrgyzstan have reflected their social fragility and internal vulnerability.

Although the internal situation of the Caucasian and Central Asian states makes them prone to instability and conflict, many factors create grounds for interstate conflicts. In fact, some of them have already experienced major external conflicts, including devastating armed ones. In the Caucasus, conflict that began in 1988 between Azerbaijan and Armenia over the Azeri region of Nagorno-Karabakh outlived the Soviet Union and developed into a bloody civil war in Azerbaijan. It ended in 1994, not as the result of a peace treaty settling their disputes but because of a cease-fire agreement that left all outstanding issues unsettled. The two sides could well resort to a new war to end the existing deadlock. Georgia, another Caucasian state, has had highly volatile relations with neighboring Russia, especially since the ascension to power of pro-U.S. president Mikhail Saakashvili as a result of the Rose Revolution of 2003. His military bid to restore Tbilisi's control over the breakaway republic of South Ossetia quickly developed to a short yet devastating war with Russia in August 2008. In its aftermath, Georgia severed ties with Russia and the CIS in the same month. The two neighbors are now sworn enemies, a situation conducive to major conflicts, including armed ones. Azerbaijan has experienced fluctuation in its ties with neighboring Iran that at one point (2001) had the potential to escalate into military confrontation. Over time, Azerbaijan has also experienced difficulties with its neighbor Russia because of the pro-U.S. orientation of the Azeri government with its expanding military ties with Washington and America's European allies and its alleged hosting, tolerating, and outright backing of Chechen separatists fighting in Chechnya. Lacking normal and peaceful relations with Azerbaijan because of its unsettled dispute over the status of Nagorno-Karabakh—and its having sided with the Kharabakhis in their bloody war with Azerbaijan—Armenia has yet to establish normal relations with its western neighbor, Turkey, a historical enemy that is now backing Azerbaijan.

In Central Asia, there are many potential sources of interstate conflict, including border or territorial disputes as well as real or perceived interferences in one regional state's internal affairs by another. For example, the border disagreements and territorial disputes between Kyrgyzstan, Tajikistan, and Uzbekistan that revolve mainly but not exclusively around the potentially rich Ferghana Valley could well ignite a military conflict between any two of them. Conflicts between Uzbekistan and its neighboring Turkmenistan have the potential to escalate should the current course of relations continue. The death of Turkmen president Saparmurad Niyazov in December 2006 and subsequent ascension to power of President Gurbanguly Berdimuhammedov in February 2007 have not settled the dividing issue in their nations' bilateral relations, although tensions have subsided significantly. Moreover, war and instability could well expand from one regional country to another, owing to the existing ripe situation. For the same reason, instability in the form of the ongoing and expanding "low-intensity" war in Afghanistan, in its ninth year today (June 2009), could well spill over into the three neighboring Central Asian states of Turkmenistan, Tajikistan, and Uzbekistan. Furthermore, the secessionist movement of Uyghurs (Uighurs) in China's Xinjiang (Sinkiang) Province, although not very strong and active today, has the potential to cross the border into neighboring Kazakhstan, where a few million Uyghurs reside.

In short, many factors make the Caucasus and Central Asia susceptible to a variety of internal and external military conflicts, including inter-wars and civil wars. In light of the extensive ties of various natures between the Caucasian and Central Asian countries and neighboring (Iran, Turkey, China, and Russia) and non-neighboring (the United States) states, including a regional grouping of states (the European Union) with long-term interests in these regions, at least some of these conflicts could even lead to regional conflicts, involving these states in support of their regional friends and allies in some form. In the case of Georgia, military conflict with Russia in the near future seems to be a distinct possibility in early 2009, which, if it occurs, will certainly involve the aforementioned states, possibly even directly. Such conflicts could range from skirmishes along the Georgian-Russia common borders and their cease-fire line near the breakaway republics of Abkhazia and South Ossetia to another full-scale war. Consequently, war and instability in Central Asia and the Caucasus would have implications not just for the immediate affected states but also for others and potentially for their respective regions, for they could expand to the neighboring regional powers while indirectly affecting the nonregional power, the United States. Furthermore, war and instability could also pit these powers against each other, either through proxy wars or through some sort of direct military conflict.

Apart from their importance to their constituent states, Central Asia and the Caucasus are important regions from a global strategic point of view. Among other things, their importance lies in their significant oil and gas resources. In particular, the United States and the European Union are interested in these resources for the operation of their economies, which are now heavily dependent on the Persian Gulf for fuels. These regions are important notwithstanding that their oil and gas resources are far less than those of the Persian Gulf. In fact, they will only be able to be large suppliers for the Western economies for 15 to 20 years and are thus by no means a substitute for the Persian Gulf. Furthermore, China is becoming increasingly interested in the oil and gas resources of neighboring Central Asia, desiring to feed its own fast-growing economy, and Russia is bidding to expand its control over the oil and gas industries of Central Asia and the Caucasus, hoping to turn itself into the largest player in the global energy market. Moscow, so far (2009), has been very successful, particularly in the case of Central Asia's gas resources and pipelines. Iran and Turkey have sought to secure a share of these regions' fossil energy industries, but for different reasons, their success in this regard has been limited.

Energy significance aside, the strategic importance of Central Asia and the Caucasus is a function of their geopolitical characteristics. These regions border two major nuclear states, one of which (Russia) is in the process of restoring its lost global preeminence and the other (China) aspires to just such a status, enjoying a seemingly unstoppable economic growth in what is now the world's third-largest economy. Those regions also neighbor a non-nuclear regional power (Iran) not only staking claims to a higher status but having the potential to achieve it in the future because of its many favorable characteristics. These include enormous oil and gas reserves, substantial mineral resources, strong financial capabilities, a sizable and expanding industrial base, a huge land area, a large and growing educated population, and prior experience in achieving such a status over its long history. To this should be added its large and well-trained military, with the capability to project its power beyond its borders (mainly but not exclusively through its missile capabilities), backed by a burgeoning homegrown space program now capable of deploying satellites in Earth orbit. What is more, Central Asia and the Caucasus are in close proximity to two other nuclear states (India and Pakistan), which, of course, have much smaller nuclear arsenals than China and Russia—but which also have claims to globally eminent status. These states house about 20 percent of the world's population and occupy a major chunk of its surface. In sum, all these characteristics and factors make Central Asia and the Caucasus important to many countries and regions beyond its borders.

For obvious reasons, against this background, peace and stability in these two regions are one of the primary concerns not only of their member states but of many other states having political, economic, and military or security stakes in those regions. The outbreak of armed conflicts of various forms and durations in Central Asia and the Caucasus could simultaneously affect, in one form or another, faraway regions as well as close neighbors. Because of this, it is important that all those interested in these regions have a clear idea of the internal and external security challenges that face these regional countries, challenges that may develop into conflicts if the current pace of events continues. This book aims to shed light on these challenges by focusing on the factors contributing to the rise and expansion of intra- and interstate conflicts in Central Asia and the Caucasus.

In offering a comprehensive conflict profile of Central Asia and the Caucasus, this book is divided into four parts. In each part's treatment of its specific topics, it concentrates on the conflict-charged situation of the Central Asian and Caucasian states since their independence in 1991 while paying attention to the conflict-related issues occurring before to that date that even now have a bearing on the current and future pace of events in Central Asia and the Caucasus. Wherever appropriate, the scenarios of conflict in the foreseeable future, whether likely or merely possible, are discussed.

Part 1, Regional Essays, deals with issues of regional significance. In its attempt to shed light on factors affecting the security of the Caucasian and Central Asian countries and the stability of their respective regions, it tackles five major-issue areas having short- and long-term implications for Central Asia or the Caucasus.

Furthermore, two chronological timelines are presented that cover the main conflict-related events in the Caucasus and Central Asia. For each region, the period since independence is emphasized and certain major events are also covered that occurred before independence but that are significant for the regional pace of events.

Part 2, Country Profiles, focuses on the history of intra- and interstate conflict of the nations of these regions since 1991. Each of its eight sections is dedicated to the specifics of the situation in a particular Caucasian or Central Asian country. In this regard, the roles or potential roles not only of state actors but also of nonstate actors are analyzed.

Part 3, Geopolitical Organizations, concentrates on the organizations of significance to Central Asia and the Caucasus. Even though many regional and international organizations operate within those regions, six organizations are selected for their particular relevance to this book's focus on conflict, as well as for their significant impact on the regional countries. Each of the six sections deals with one of these organizations, whose mandates range from economic matters to military and security concerns.

Part 4, What the Future Will Hold for Central Asia and the Caucasus, concludes the book. Summarizing the major conflict-related issues of importance to Central Asia and the Caucasus, this part offers insights on the major trends and tendencies in these regions that display potential for developing into conflicts—including armed conflicts—that may affect the regions' peace and security in the foreseeable future.

To these parts are added discussions of specific issues of political, economic, and military and security relevance, presented in 21 sidebars. Each provides analytical information on a topic of general significance for conflict in Central Asia and the Caucasus.

Maps

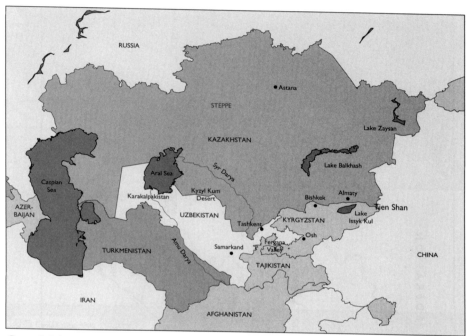

Central Asia

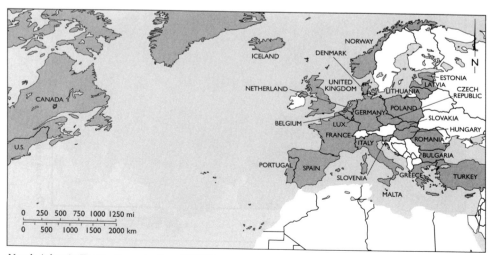

North Atlantic Treaty Organization (NATO)

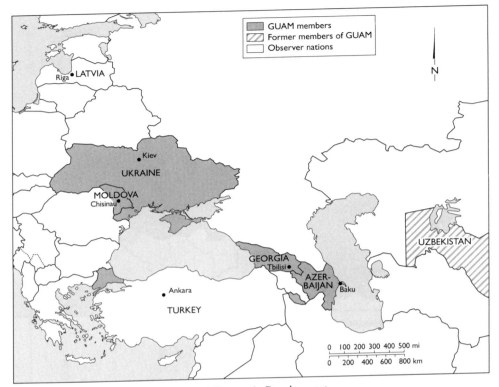

GUAM Organization for Democracy and Economic Development

Part I
REGIONAL ESSAYS

Chapter I

Central Asia as a Transitional Region: Destabilizing Factors since Independence (1991–2009)

The collapse of the Soviet Union in 1991 led to the creation of 15 independent states and the formation of the Commonwealth of Independent States (CIS), a mainly unsuccessful regional organization meant to tie most of the former Soviet republics together under Russian leadership. Like the majority of the CIS countries, the Central Asian countries' post-independence era has been characterized by mounting political, economic, social, and human rights problems against a background of a declining economy, although the extent and intensity of such problems have varied from one country to another. The Central Asians' hope that the enormous social and economic difficulties of the independence era would be only a passing phenomenon, and that all these countries would soon initiate a more prosperous life, has proven to be mainly unrealistic, although each Central Asian country has developed a small stratum of prosperous people. It is clearly evident, 18 years after independence, that the overall situation in Central Asia is not improving significantly and irreversibly. Rather, it is worsening in many respects (aside from progress in overcoming ills of the period immediately following independence, such as the disappearance of the chaotic situation and the eradication of severe shortages of essential goods). Since independence, negative trends in the political, economic, social, and military/security spheres have not only affected the social and economic development of the Central Asian countries but also contributed to the creation of a fragile social and political situation. In addition to internal factors, the unintended effect of the "War on Terror" has contributed to the deterioration of this fragile situation in Central Asia, rendering the region prone to instability in various forms. Within the context of five major areas of activity (i.e., politics, economics, society, military/security, and human rights), and taking into consideration the impact of the "War on Terror," the following account delineates factors that have significantly contributed to political fragility in Central Asia since independence.

POLITICS

The collapse of the Soviet Union was a phenomenal shock to all its forming republics. The sudden development weakened all Central Asian institutions inherited from the Soviet era. The only exception was the political system, which seemed unchallenged and stable. Unlike most other former Soviet republics, such as the Baltic ones, the Central Asian republics' independence was not the result of long and widespread mass anti-government activities demanding fundamental changes. The Central Asian political systems survived independence and remained almost intact, giving these countries' leaders the ability to run their countries with a more or less functional state apparatus. In the post-independence era, Soviet political, economic, and military elites dominated practically all aspects of life in all these countries.

Excluding Tajikistan, which experienced a civil war from 1992 to 1997, and Kyrgyzstan, which experienced the Yellow (Tulip) Revolution in March 2005, the Central Asian states have faced no significant challenges to their authority and have enjoyed internal stability. Nevertheless, to different extents, the potential for instability has existed in all the Central Asian countries. In Tajikistan, a peace treaty ended five years of civil war in June 1997. However, as of 2009, the two sides to the conflict (the Muslim-Democratic coalition and the Tajik government) have not yet fully achieved the goals set in the peace treaty. The civil war is over, but the country still suffers from political uncertainty, partly because of the destructive efforts of anti–peace treaty forces on both sides of the Tajik conflict and the alleged intervention of the Uzbek government in Tajikistan's internal affairs. Allegedly, Tashkent masterminded the abortive 1999 coup in Tajikistan, which was staged mainly by Tajikistan's Uzbeks (Hiro 1998).

Persistent economic problems are also partly responsible for the current unstable situation. The main social and economic causes of the civil war—for example, severe regional disparities, underdevelopment, and clan politics—are still present (Peimani 1998, 28–30, 32–33, 66–67). In the absence of substantial foreign assistance, Tajikistan's extensive underdevelopment and poor economy, together with a severe negative impact on the Tajiks' human security, have generated grounds for popular dissent that could potentially reignite violent civil conflict that might not necessarily be led by the 1990s opposition groups. A major—if not the major—factor preventing such a scenario so far has been a strong aversion to war among the Tajiks, whose memories of the civil war are still vivid. The rise in the late 1990s of Hizb ut-Tahrir, a fundamentalist group advocating a regional fanatic Islamic state, and the group's subsequent expansion despite its illegal status, indicate widening popular dissent.

The other Central Asian countries have avoided civil wars but nonetheless have become increasingly concerned about instability in their region and in their own countries. On the one hand, until the removal of the Taliban from the political scene in November 2001, Taliban-ruled Afghanistan was a direct threat to the security of the three neighboring Central Asian states of Turkmenistan, Uzbekistan, and Tajikistan. In general, the spillover of the Afghan civil war into these Central Asian countries has been a feasible scenario since their independence in 1991, with the likely potential of destabilizing the entire region. This threat has remained in place despite the formation

THE EASTWARD EXPANSION OF NATO AND REGIONAL CONCERNS

The eastward expansion of NATO has been a source of concern for Iran, China, and Russia, for it has brought the military alliance to their neighboring Central Asian and Caucasian states. These states joined NATO's Partnership for Peace Program (PFP) in 1994, except for Tajikistan, which joined in 2001. This has legitimized NATO's presence in those states, although on a small scale. More important, it has laid the grounds for their future membership, so long as both sides wish to pursue it. Of course, none of these countries has become a NATO member so far. Nor does NATO favor their rapid inclusion in its ranks for a range of reasons, including the existence of various sources of armed conflict in many of the states, and concerns about the reaction of Iran, China, and, particularly, Russia. Nevertheless, against the background of a significant American military presence in Central Asia and the Caucasus, the existing PFP arrangement has been disturbing enough for Iran, China, and Russia, each of which has reasons to interpret a U.S. military presence as a clear and present challenge to its national security, and also to its claims to eminent international status. There is little, if any, doubt that this will become a factor in the deterioration of relations between these regional powers and the NATO states. NATO's announcement on September 21, 2006, that Georgia's application for Intensified Dialogue with the alliance was approved likely ensured such a scenario. Although this was no approval of its membership bid, it was a major step, effectively setting the stage for the processing of Georgia's membership application. In the aftermath of the Georgian-Russian war of 2008, NATO's condemnation of Russia — to the extent of rejection of the possibility of business-as-usual with Russia, which prompted Russia's cancellation of certain types of cooperation with NATO with no regret expressed over ending ties with NATO in the future — caused a rapid deterioration of Russia-NATO relations. NATO's announcement of continued support for Georgia and its plan for the latter's eventual NATO membership, in addition to the dispatching of NATO naval vessels to the Black Sea, set the two sides on a confrontational track. Even though Georgia is unlikely to be granted membership in NATO soon, with such division within NATO over the issue, these developments have alarmed not only Russia but also Iran and China, which are equally concerned about NATO's eastward expansion. They will certainly reflect their concern in their relationships with NATO and Georgia.

of a new political system in Afghanistan because of the continued low-intensity war against the Taliban and Al Qaeda. As expanding groups, these two pose a major challenge to the Afghan government's survival, as evidenced by the numerous bombings, small-scale attacks on Afghan and NATO forces, and assassination attempts they mounted in 2009. In February 2008, U.S. national intelligence director Michael McConnell warned about the growing Taliban and their control and expansion in part of Afghanistan despite seven years of U.S./NATO-led war against them (McConnell 2008). Additionally, the situation is ripe for another round of civil war among Afghan groups representing different ethnic groups who could be dissatisfied with their share of power in the central government.

On the other hand, poor economic performance and increasing social and economic problems are contributing to the rise of mass political dissent in Central Asia. Known as the most stable Central Asian country, Uzbekistan has experienced political challenges with a long-term impact on its stability. Political opposition has been on the rise in Uzbekistan's Andijan Province, located in the troublesome Ferghana Valley. The growing instability in the valley has the potential to destabilize the three countries (Kyrgyzstan, Tajikistan, and Uzbekistan) that share it while creating grounds for instability in other Central Asian countries. Uzbekistan has also suffered from violent anti-government activities elsewhere. Of these, the major incidents in the pre-2001 era included a series of bombings in early 1999 in the capital, Tashkent, which demonstrated the vulnerability of the Uzbek state (Hiro 1999, 16).

The Kyrgyz government faced no major challenges for most of the post-independence era until the Yellow (Tulip) Revolution of 2005. However, certain factors sharply damaged its legitimacy, including the gradual monopolization of political and economic power by President Askar Akayev and his closed circle of family and allies, and the expanding corruption within the ruling elite, the government, and the civil service. The growing authoritarianism in what was once the most democratic Central Asian country and the increasing restrictions on the activities of political parties and on individual freedoms and rights paved the way for future eruption of popular dissatisfaction. Added to the persistence of popular dissatisfaction in the post-Akayev era—reflected in various types of anti-government activities, including sit-ins and demonstrations, between 2005 and 2008 (AI 2008) that have continued in early 2009—existing low-level instability, in the form of armed conflict waged by armed drug traffickers and the Islamic Movement of Uzbekistan (IMU) in Kyrgyzstan's part of the Ferghana Valley, poses a challenge to the Kyrgyz state.

The other two Central Asian states, Kazakhstan and Turkmenistan, have so far avoided any significant security threat to their respective states. In addition to growing authoritarianism, other factors have helped the Kazakh government prevent major security challenges. The peculiar ethnic makeup of the country has been a major contributing factor. The numeric weakness of the ethnic Kazakhs, who constituted about 40 percent of the population in 1991 and represent about 50 percent today (2009), has inclined them to rally behind their government despite its several weaknesses, including its corruption. The large Russian ethnic minority, which makes up about 40 percent of the population, has also had its own reason for not challenging the administration of President Nursultan Nazarbayev. The unusual ethnic structure of Kazakhstan has motivated the president to observe the rights of minorities to a large extent and to seek their integration into the country, in recognition of his country's need for friendly ties with Russia for economic and political reasons. It is also a clear sign of his concern about the threat of Russia's direct intervention in his country's internal affairs. As a neighbor, Russia has the opportunity and the means to intervene, for Kazakhstan's large Russian ethnic community provides a social basis and an excuse for such an action. Moreover, Kazakhstan's need for the ethnic Russians, who account for most of the educated and skilled population, has created

Honor guards stand by the coffin of Turkmen president Safarmurad Niyazov in December 2006. (AP Photo/Andriy Mosienko)

another incentive for President Nazarbayev to appease them. His accommodating approach has inclined the ethnic Russians, by and large, to support his government. Balancing Kazakh nationalism with the recognition of minority rights has helped the Kazakh government prevent the eruption of opposition movements. Yet, many factors will likely contribute to the emergence of opposition challenges to the Kazakh state, including Kazakhstan's limited economic growth relative to its needs (its booming oil industry notwithstanding), the growing Kazakh nationalism, and Russia's increasing interest in reestablishing itself in the former Soviet republics. As a recent example, the Georgian-Russian war of August 2008 clearly indicated Moscow's determination to preserve its national interests in these republics.

In Turkmenistan, the high-handed policy of President Saparmurad Niyazov, also known as Turkmenbashi ("Father of Turkmens"), left no room for any type of dissent until his death in December 2006. The totalitarian political system, characterized by Niyazov's cult of personality, prevented the emergence of challenges to the Turkmen state. His successor, Gurbanguly Berdimuhammedov, who became president in a practically unchallenged election in February 2007, has pursued an equally intolerant authoritarian system of government, although he did end his predecessor's cult of personality and reversed many of his illogical policies in 2007 and 2008. For example, he abolished the renaming of days and months after President Niyazov and his mother (Stern 2008). There is no sign of mass dissent in Turkmenistan in early 2009, in part owing to the continuity of authoritarianism and President Berdimuhammedov's easing of some of the excessive restrictions of his predecessor and undoing of his unpopular policies. Yet, the continuity of the current stability will require addressing many social and economic ills, such as Turkmenistan's social polarization.

ECONOMICS

Independence devastated the economies of all the Central Asian countries and shook their social fabric. In particular, the paralysis of their economies not only created severe economic problems (high inflation, skyrocketing prices, shortages, etc.) but also paved the way for a weakening of their social order appropriate for the pre-independence economic system that no longer existed. The sudden collapse of the Soviet system severely damaged the already troubled economies of the newly independent countries, which were incapable of meeting the basic needs of their respective peoples. Major shortcomings (e.g., chronic shortages, low-quality products, inefficient industries and agriculture) characterized the Soviet economy. The Central Asian countries inherited this troubled economy at the time of independence. Unsurprisingly, all of them faced an enormous and increasing number of economic difficulties.

The Soviet Union's fall led to the sudden collapse of the highly centralized, state-dominated economies, which initiated a period of transition from a command economy to a type of free-enterprise economy at a time when the Central Asian countries, like other CIS countries, were unprepared for it. Unsurprisingly, the result was a sudden shock to their economies. In the absence of a viable new economic system, the dismantling of the command economy worsened all the inherited economic shortcomings. Massive closure of rural and urban state enterprises created high unemployment and a large decline in the production of industrial and agricultural goods, as shown in Table 1, while damaging the performance of the health, nutrition, education, and social welfare systems. This situation, coupled with the collapse of the Soviet distribution system, further worsened the chronic shortages of basic products, including foodstuffs, that had been a major characteristic of the Soviet economy. As a result of shortages of fuel and

TABLE 1. Average Annual Sectoral Growth (1990–2003)

	Agriculture	Industry	Services
Kazakhstan	−4.5	−3.7	0.9
Kyrgyzstan	2.8	−6.3	−2.2
Tajikistan	−2.2	−5.3	−1.1
Turkmenistan	0.2	1.6	0.8
Uzbekistan	1.5	−1.5	2.3

Source: World Bank Group, 2005, "Table 4.1—Growth of Output," *World Development Indicators 2005,* Washington, D.C.: The World Bank Group, http://devdata.worldbank.org/wdi2005/Section4.htm (accessed September 3, 2008).

spare parts, frequent power, water, and natural gas cuts disrupted the daily lives of people and harmed industrial and agricultural production, resulting in lower output, which in turn created more shortages and reduced exports. Reduced exports contributed to the deterioration of the financial situation of the Central Asian countries, which had already lost their share of Soviet assistance in cash, goods, equipment, and fuel. Moreover, the sudden drop in interrepublic trade and economic cooperation among the former Soviet republics further worsened those countries' economies.

Facing a new reality, the Central Asian countries opted to restructure their economies to replace the crumbling socialist economy with a type of free-enterprise economy through decentralization and creation of a strong private sector. In practice, all the Central Asian leaders have realized that the establishment of a new economic system in the absence of adequate domestic resources is a Herculean task. Two major factors have slowed down the transitional process in their countries: the lack of required resources (e.g., human, raw material, machinery, equipment, funds) and the fear of sudden eruption of political dissent as a result of radical, rapid, and therefore painful economic reforms. Predictably, these reforms would lead to massive unemployment, the sharp lowering of living standards, and widespread poverty, at least in the short run. Not surprisingly, the majority of former Soviet republics, including those of Central Asia, have chosen to keep major aspects of the Soviet economy while encouraging a limited degree of free enterprise that is mainly confined to the service industry and to small-scale industrial and agricultural enterprises.

The Central Asian economies have all experienced serious difficulties since 1991. Their industrial and agricultural production has sharply decreased because of factors that include the collapse of the command economy and central planning and the withdrawal of subsidies and transfers (cash, equipment, machinery, and fuel) from Moscow. They have also experienced severe financial difficulties for lack of adequate domestic resources and a breakdown in interrepublic trade, in addition to the inevitable consequences of the economic transition (e.g., price liberalization, privatization, and closure of nonviable enterprises). The economic decline is evident in the disappointing performance of all the Central Asian economies during the first decade of independence (the 1990s) as reflected in their mainly negative GDP growth for half of that period. As reflected in Tables 2 and 3, during the period 1992–1996 the economies of Kazakhstan, Kyrgyzstan, Tajikistan, Turkmenistan, and Uzbekistan had contraction periods totaling –37.3 percent, –52.5 percent, –79.3 percent, –57.8 percent, and –18.5 percent, respectively.

Note that the World Bank suggests higher GDP rates than those presented in Table 2, especially for the years 2003 and 2004 (The World Bank Group, 2003/2004). Compared to the International Monetary Fund (IMF) statistics, the rates are a few percentage points higher in most cases, such as Kazakhstan (9.3% and 9.4%), Kyrgyzstan (7.03% and 7.8%), Tajikistan (10.2% and 10.6%), and Uzbekistan (4.2% and 7.7%). However, Turkmenistan's rates (16.92% and 17%) are several times the IMF figures, whereas the Turkmen government claims an even larger growth rate for 2004 (21%), which is believed to be highly exaggerated. Checking against other scattered statistics, such as those of the Asian Development Bank, the IMF statistics in Tables 2 and 3 seem to be at least closer to the reality than the others.

TABLE 2. GDP—Constant Prices, Annual Percent Change

	Kazakhstan	Kyrgyzstan	Tajikistan	Turkmenistan	Uzbekistan
1992	–5.3	–13.9	–29.9	–5.3	–11.1
1993	–9.2	–13.0	–11.1	–10.0	–2.3
1994	–12.6	–19.8	–21.4	–17.3	–4.2
1995	–8.3	–5.8	–12.5	–7.2	–0.9
1996	0.4	7.1	–4.4	–6.7	1.6
1997	1.6	9.9	1.7	–11.3	2.5
1998	–1.9	2.1	5.3	7.0	2.1
1999	2.7	3.7	3.7	16.5	3.4
2000	9.8	5.3	8.3	18.0	3.2
2001	13.5	5.4	10.2	20.5	4.1
2002	9.5	0.0	9.1	6.0	3.2
2003	9.5	5.2	10.2	3.0	0.3
2004	8.0	4.1	8.0	3.0	2.2
2005	7.5	4.5	4.0	3.0	2.2
2006	10.7	3.1	7.0	11.0	7.3
2007	8.5*	8.2	7.8	11.6*	9.5

*Estimated figure.
Sources: International Monetary Fund (IMF), 2004, *World Economic Outlook Database* (April), Washington, D.C.: IMF, www.imf.org/external/pubs/ft/weo/2004/01/data/dbcselm. cfm?G=901 (accessed September 20, 2008); International Monetary Fund (IMF), 2008, *World Economic Outlook Database* (April), Washington, D.C.: IMF, www.imf.org/external/ pubs/ft/weo/2008/01/weodata/weoselgr.aspx (accessed October 1, 2008).

As shown in Table 2, the economic contraction period ended, by and large, in 1997. Positive GDP growth rates, which started late in the 1990s, have continued to this day (early 2009), as evident in Tables 2 and 3. Without a doubt, this phenomenon has helped stop the devastating economic free fall of the early 1990s and has improved the economic environment of the Central Asian countries. However, this positive development falls short of addressing Central Asia's economic problems, for a variety of reasons. After years of contraction, the existing rate of GDP growth since independence up to this date (early 2009) has not been significant enough to fully restore the pre-independence economy in the case of Tajikistan (–79.3% and +74.5%) and has been barely large enough to exceed that of pre-independence in the case of Kyrgyzstan (–52.5% and +58.6%). Comparatively, the situation is much better for Uzbekistan (–18.5% and +41.6%), Kazakhstan (–37.3% and +81.7%), and Turkmenistan (–57.8% and +99.6%). The low economic growth since independence is evident in these countries' insignificant average annual growth between 1992 and

although in different forms and to varying extents, as permitted by the realities of their respective societies. Having no threatening or potentially threatening opposition, Kazakhstan and Kyrgyzstan settled for less dictatorial, although not democratic, political systems. Extensive human rights abuses—ranging from intolerance of any form of political opposition (Turkmenistan) to subjection of legal opposition groups and individuals to various restrictions and maltreatment and of illegal ones to brutal suppression (Uzbekistan and Tajikistan)—have been the case in the first group of states.

In the absence of any major threatening political opposition, the second group of states also subjected legal opposition to various maltreatment and restrictions, though to a lesser extent, leaving more room for peaceful dissent. However, this policy began to change when dissatisfaction with the status quo among nationals increased the possibility of that sentiment developing into mass movements as the opposition groups increased their activities. Hence, since the late 1990s, Kazakhstan and Kyrgyzstan have also increased their human rights abuses, showing an eroding tolerance of dissent even though they are still more democratic or, more accurately, less abusive than Tajikistan, Turkmenistan, and Uzbekistan. Major human rights organizations, including Human Rights Watch (HRW 1993–2008), have documented various human rights abuses (e.g., banning opposition activities, closing opposition facilities, harassing opposition members and supporters through arrests, torture, kidnapping, killing, and unfair trials) by the Central Asian governments since 1991, as well as election fraud.

MILITARY/SECURITY

The Central Asian countries have encountered certain military and security challenges since independence. The threat of internal destabilizing forces has been a main source of concern for Tajikistan and Uzbekistan. Tajikistan experienced a bloody civil war, which, apart from heavy human losses, severely retarded its economic growth with a worsening impact on the human security of its population. Because many issues are yet to be addressed—including the share of the political system of former opposition groups now part of the political process, as well as addressing the severe economic and social deprivation of their strongholds, such as the Badakhshan region—the seeds of a second round of civil war are well in place, a serious threat to Tajikistan's stability and economic and social progress.

In its share of the Ferghana Valley, Uzbekistan has experienced a limited, localized, armed insurgency led by the Islamic Movement of Uzbekistan (IMU), a fundamentalist/ extremist group. The valley is a fertile ground for the growth of other extremist groups as well, mainly Hizb ut-Tahrir. Operating also in Tajikistan, which shares the valley with Uzbekistan and Kyrgyzstan, Hizb ut-Tahrir does not advocate armed struggle but does share the IMU program for the overthrow of the Uzbek regime, while supporting the idea of creating a fanatic religious superstate in Central Asia. The two groups have been severely suppressed and for the time being are unable to pose a serious challenge to the Tajik and the Uzbek governments. However, the expanding dissatisfaction in both Tajikistan and Uzbekistan is preparing grounds for their continuity and expansion in some form as well as the rise of other extremist groups. To a much lesser extent, the two groups have also been active in Kyrgyzstan's part of the Ferghana Valley, a source of concern for the Kyrgyz regime. Reports in 2008 and 2009 indicate activities of the IMU in Central Asia as well as its presence as an ally of the Taliban in Pakistan's Waziristan, bordering Afghanistan (e.g., Sidikov 2008).

Turkmenistan and Kazakhstan have not experienced armed opposition or its potential since independence. However, they, like the other regional states, have been concerned about the growing activities of well-armed international drug traffickers based in Afghanistan, who are interested in Central Asia both as a large market for Afghan-produced narcotics and as a transit route to Europe for them via other CIS countries. Over and above the increasing hazard to the health of Central Asians posed by drugs (to be discussed later), drug trafficking is a growing threat to their security.

There are also external sources of threats, including territorial and border disputes between and among the Central Asians. The main disputes are disagreements over each country's share of the Ferghana Valley between Uzbekistan and Tajikistan and between Uzbekistan and Kyrgyzstan, an issue still unsettled in 2009. To this must be added the threat of separatism in Tajikistan, whose ethnic Uzbeks, who dominate the city of Khojand and its adjacent region, have threatened since independence to secede from Tajikistan to join Uzbekistan. Tajikistan has an inactive claim to Uzbekistan's cities of Samarkand and Bukhara. Uzbekistan and Kazakhstan have had territorial disputes leading to small-scale military confrontations along their borders, most of which have been addressed. Because of Soviet-inherited border disputes, China was a source of concern for Kazakhstan, Kyrgyzstan, and Tajikistan, which share a long border with

Prime Ministers of Russia, China, Kazakhstan, Kyrgyzstan, Tajikistan and Uzbekistan meet in Almaty at a summit of the Shanghai Cooperation Organization (SCO) on October 30, 2008. (Alexy Druzhinin/AFP/Getty Images)

that country. However, since 1991, various border agreements have settled most of them. Today, neither sides sees any benefit in endangering the peace and security of their region or their growing trade and cooperation in political and security matters. This cooperation is reflected in the formation of the Shanghai Cooperation Organization (SCO), in which all Central Asian countries except Turkmenistan are members, along with China and Russia. The SCO also reflects diminishing concern about Russia's effort to regain influence in Central Asia among the regional countries, including those hosting Russian bases (Tajikistan and Kyrgyzstan). On the contrary, they are becoming more concerned about the extensive U.S. military and political presence in their region, as reflected in Uzbekistan's closure of the U.S. air base in Karshi-Khanabad (November 2005) and Kyrgyz president Kurmanbek Bakiev's clear expression of his intent in February 2007 to demand that the U.S. government close the Ganca airbase located at Manas Airport in Bishkek (Neweurasia 2008), which was presented as a clear demand to Washington in February 2009.

"THE WAR ON TERROR": ITS IMPACT ON CENTRAL ASIA (2001 ONWARD)

As an unintended effect, the "War on Terror" has contributed to the deteriorating situation in Central Asia. In particular, it has contributed to the consolidation of authoritarianism and the worsening human rights situation. As mentioned earlier, the Central Asian countries were all on the road to authoritarianism in the late 1990s, although at varying speeds and in different forms. The inauguration of the "War on Terror" accelerated this trend, providing the Central Asian governments with an opportunity to consolidate their authoritarian states to ensure the long-term survival of their rule and to prevent the formation of serious popular political movements challenging their authority. This has been reflected in their growing intolerance of any type of political dissent, indicated by an increase in human rights abuses.

The sudden expansion of the U.S. military in Central Asia and the U.S. government's need for these countries' assistance in its "War on Terror" inclined that government and its allies to avoid criticism of human rights abuses in those countries so as to ensure their cooperation. This policy was regarded as a green light for the Central Asian leaders to commit human rights abuses without fear of major international reaction. Fighting terrorism has provided them with an internationally acceptable pretext for suppressing their political opponents as terrorists. As reported by major human rights organizations such as Amnesty International (AI 2002–2008), there has been an evident increase in human rights abuses in the Central Asian countries.

Hence the "War on Terror" has contributed to the worsening of human rights abuses and the consolidation of authoritarianism in the Central Asian countries, all of which sided with the United States when it began its "War on Terror" in late 2001. Yet, about eight years after the initiation of that program, certain developments have affected the pace of events in the region. Chief among them has been an evident shift among the Central Asians, especially those considered Washington's close allies, toward closer relations with Russia. The outbreak of "color revolutions" in Georgia and Ukraine alarmed the Central Asian elites. Rightly or wrongly, they considered those political events a U.S.-backed plan capitalizing on widespread dissatisfaction among the Georgians and the Ukrainians to replace the southern CIS elite with a new elite fully loyal to Washington, a looming threat to their authority (Blank 2005). These color revolutions led to a tightening of security measures and to the intensification of suppression of opposition groups and individuals, and to a spreading suspicion of U.S. NGOs, which were considered a means for contributing to a situation ripe for color revolutions. As a result, all the Central Asian governments have made licensing of NGOs more difficult and have refused to renew some licenses, forcing certain NGOs viewed as major contributors to those revolutions to shut down their operations in Central Asia. A well-known example in this regard is the Soros Foundation, which in April 2004 was forced to cease operation in Uzbekistan (UN Office for the Coordination of Humanitarian Affairs 2005). In 2005, Tajik president Imomali Rahmonov (now known as Imomali Rahmon) accused the Soros Foundation of acting to destroy Tajikistan's unity, while Kazakh officials opened a criminal investigation for the foundation's alleged tax evasion, seen as a prelude to end its operation (ibid.). Closing and restriction of U.S. NGOs have continued to this date (January 2009).

The outbreak in March 2005 of another color revolution, this time in Central Asia (Kyrgyzstan), was especially alarming, for it heralded the expansion to Central Asia of the perceived U.S. plan while revealing the fragility of the seemingly stable Central Asian regimes. This has resulted in further tightening of the Central Asian countries, on the one hand. On the other, it has created a stronger sense of suspicion towards the United States, resulting in a clear tendency on the part of the Central Asians to strengthen their ties with Russia while seeking to limit their relations with the United States. In 2003 and 2004, respectively, Kyrgyzstan and Tajikistan allowed Russian bases in their countries despite their good relations with the U.S. government. Another recent example is Tashkent's interest in expanding relations with Moscow, evidenced in a variety of events, including Uzbekistan's joining the SCO in June 2001 and rejoining the Collective Security Treaty Organization (CSTO) in June 2006 (Fumagalli 2008) and Uzbek president Islam Karimov's visit with then Russian president Vladimir Putin after the Andijan incident. A major development occurred on November 14, 2005, when Russia and Uzbekistan concluded an alliance agreement against terrorist threats that reportedly also commits them to help each other preserve their national security (VOA 2005b).

The outbreak of a reportedly mass and at least partly armed anti-government incident in Andijan, Uzbekistan, in May 2005 alarmed not only the Uzbek government but those of other Central Asian countries. Reported by the Uzbek authorities as an armed insurgency by extremists and the eruption of dissent or a mixture of both by others, the Uzbek government's suppression of those involved prompted criticism for use of excessive force not only by human rights organizations but also by the U.S. government and the European Union (ibid.). The latter demanded a foreign-led inquiry, which was rejected by the Uzbek government as Tashkent viewed such activity as intervention in Uzbekistan's internal affairs. The Uzbek government has hinted at U.S. involvement in the May incident, an allegation which Washington rejected in 2005. Nevertheless, the Uzbek authorities, rightly or wrongly, blamed the United States and requested the closure of the U.S. air base in Uzbekistan before 2006. The U.S. military completed

U.S. BASES IN CENTRAL ASIA AND THE CAUCASUS

The U.S. bases in Central Asia and the Caucasus are becoming a source of conflict between the regional powers (Iran, China, and Russia) and the United States. The former have been concerned since late 2001 about the expanding military presence of the United States in these regions neighboring their countries in the form of military bases and overflight and emergency landing rights. The regional powers have evaluated the American pattern of deployment as inconsistent with the stated objective of supporting the U.S. military operation in Afghanistan as part of Washington's "War on Terror" for many reasons, including the type and number of facilities as well as their increasing capabilities. In one form or another, Iran, China, and Russia have raised their voices to demand a clear timetable for the withdrawal of the American military from Central Asia and the Caucasus, especially since 2005. The closure of the American base in Uzbekistan in November 2005 in response to the demand of the Uzbek government had their implicit and explicit backing. Yet, because of the regional powers' increasing disagreements and conflict of interests with Washington, the closure did not allay their fear of the short- and long-term negative implications of the remaining U.S. forces for their national security, despite having been officially granted exclusive military bases (in the case of Kyrgyzstan) or access to their hosting countries' bases (in the case of Georgia). The August 2008 Georgian-Russian war seems to have involved efforts to address this fear, since the Russians hinted their military operations against the Georgian military facilities, among many other purposes, sought to eliminate their availability to the U.S. military in any future war against Russia and Iran. Accordingly, on September 19, 2008, the Russian envoy to NATO, Dmitri Rogozin, claimed that the United States, with the Georgian government's consent, had a plan to use Georgian military airports in an attack on Iran before such a war. In fact, according to Rogozin, Washington had launched "active military preparations on Georgia's territory" for an air strike on Iran. Some Russian newspapers also claimed that the destruction by the Russian air force of those airports during the Georgian-Russian war of August 2008 disrupted that plan. Although these regional powers (Iran, China, and Russia) have varying types of relations with Washington and their hostility toward the American government takes different forms, there is no question that they are headed toward conflict with the United States — the form of which will be determined by the specifics of their relations with Washington.

the closure of the Karshi-Khanabad air base on November 21, 2005 (VOA 2005a). The September 2005 visit of U.S. Secretary of State Condoleezza Rice to Kazakhstan and her public raising of the issue of democratization in that country made the Kazakhs also dissatisfied with the United States, whose oil companies are the major developers of the Kazakh oil industry. In short, the Central Asians' ties with the Americans have been deteriorating since 2003.

Although as of this date (early 2009) the Central Asians, especially those geared to the oil and gas industry (Kazakhstan and Turkmenistan), have retained some political ties and economic relations with Washington, they have all been suspicious of American objectives in their region, and this suspicion has prompted their growing ties with the regional powers—Iran, China, and Russia. The Russians have been expanding their influence and presence in the region, as partly reflected in the growing influence of the SCO, in which Iran has observer status but aims at full membership. In its July 2005 meeting, the SCO demanded a clear timetable for the withdrawal of all U.S. forces from Central Asia (Blank 2005). This demand was backed by all the members, including Kyrgyzstan, which has a U.S. Air Force base in its territory, and Kazakhstan and Tajikistan, which have granted overflight and emergency landing rights to the U.S. military. Kazakhstan also hosts a group of U.S. Air Force personnel in Almaty.

CONCLUSION

From the ruins of the Soviet Union, the emergence of the five independent Central Asian states brought about for their people the possibility of building a future better than their unsatisfactory past. However, the Soviet Union's collapse also put those countries on the path of instability in various forms, with predictably devastating impact, weakening if not undermining the basic conditions for achieving that prospect. Luckily enough, major conflicts and political upheavals have so far affected mainly two countries of Central Asia. Yet, this reality should not be a reason for joy in the region, for all its countries are prone to conflict and instability, as reflected in the 2005 incident in Uzbekistan. Today, the Central Asian countries are susceptible to conflicts because of their distorted transition, whose end is anyone's guess.

BIBLIOGRAPHY

Amnesty International (AI). 2002–2008. *Amnesty International Report 2002–2008.* London: Amnesty International.

Amnesty International (AI). 2008. *2008 Annual Report for Kyrgyzstan.* London: Amnesty International.

Blank, Stephen. 2005. "Making Sense of the Shanghai Cooperation Organization's Astana Summit." *Central Asia–Caucasus Analyst,* July 27, 2005. www.cacianalyst.org/view_article.php?articleid= 3504 (accessed September 10, 2008).

Fumagalli, Matteo. 2008. "Uzbekistan Rejoins the CSTO: Are Russian-Uzbek Relations Heading toward Mutual Entrapment? *Central Asia–Caucasus Analyst,* September 18, 2008. www.cacianalyst.org/?q=node/4254 (accessed September 29, 2008).

Hiro, Dilip. 1999a. "Bomb Blasts in Tashkent." *Middle East International,* March 12, 1999, 16.

Hiro, Dilip. 1999b. "Failed Revolt." *Middle East International,* December 25, 1999, 19.

Human Rights Watch (HRW). 2008. *Human Rights Watch World Report 1993 to 2008.* New York: Human Rights Watch.

International Monetary Fund (IMF). 2004. *World Economic Outlook Database.* Washington, D.C.: IMF. April 2004. www.imf.org/external/pubs/ft/weo/2004/01/data/dbcselm.cfm?G=901 (accessed September 10, 2008).

Kazakhstan experienced significant economic growth in 2007. Unlike the period 2000–2004, when the oil industry was the main engine of growth thanks to continued foreign investment, its estimated GDP growth of 8.5 percent (ADB 2008d) was due only partly to its energy sector. In fact, its two non-oil sectors (construction and services), the principal economic stimuli since 2005, constituted the main contributors to that development (ibid.). However, the construction boom's role as the main single factor for this phenomenon was the result of heavy private borrowing from the Kazakh banks, which in turn had to borrow heavily from foreign banks. This pushed Kazakhstan's external debt to $90.9 billion in 2007 (ibid.). Because, reportedly, about 70 percent of Kazakh bank loans were directly or indirectly connected to the construction sector, a credit boom and rising real estate prices created the risk of a housing market bubble bursting (as happened in Japan during the 1990s and in the United States in 2008). Heavy intervention by the National Bank of Kazakhstan through injections of liquidity removed that possibility in 2007. However, the economic crisis revealed the unsustainability of the non-oil sectors as the engine of economic growth and showed that in reality, the oil industry was the main engine of growth and financial security, generating phenomenally large revenues for the Kazakh government to use to bail out the Kazakh banks. In late 2008, the forecast for Kazakhstan's GDP growth for the entire year was 5.0 percent, with a modest increase to 6.3 percent expected in 2009 (ibid.). These are much lower rates than in recent years and are below earlier expectations, the result of uncertainty about the Kazakh non-oil sector and oil prices' fluctuations between about $150 and $40 a barrel in 2008.

In the case of Kyrgyzstan, services, construction, and manufacturing were the engine of growth in 2007, securing a GDP growth of 8.2 percent (ADB 2008h). The service sector (mainly trade and tourism and its subsectors, especially communications) expanded by 12.4 percent, accounting for about two-thirds of GDP growth (ibid.). Responsible for about one-quarter of GDP growth, the industry sector (excluding gold) and construction grew by 12.5 percent and 20.2 percent, respectively, while the agriculture sector expanded at 1.5 percent (ibid.). Predictably, in the absence of official statistics in early 2009, Kyrgyzstan's economic growth for 2008 should be significantly less than 8 percent, to be repeated in 2009 for various reasons, including the country's political instability only four years after the Yellow (Tulip) Revolution of 2005, its expected weaker exports, and slower capital and remittance inflows and investment activity, because many of its trading partners are experiencing an economic decline.

Tajikistan experienced an economic growth rate of 7.8 percent in 2007 (ADB 2008g)—much lower than its average two-digit GDP growth rates of 2000–2004—as the result of electricity shortages, the high energy costs of its imported oil and gas, and the weak performance of an agriculture heavily focused on cotton. Light manufacturing and services advanced Tajikistan's economy in that year, based mainly on cotton and aluminum exports, both of which failed to grow significantly: that is, by only 4 percent and 1.5 percent, respectively. Rapid expansion in other sectors helped the Tajik economy grow significantly. Accordingly, the industrial sector nearly doubled its growth rate to 9.9 percent, the noncotton sectors of agriculture grew 6.5 percent, from 5.4 percent in 2006, and the service sectors—trade, construction, and finance—experienced 8.0 percent growth. In light of high oil and gas prices throughout 2008 and an expected continuation of this in 2009 (although with oil prices much lower on average than those of 2008), and the unlikely significant increase in cotton production and exports, Tajikistan is unlikely to have significantly better economic performance in 2008 than in 2007 and will unlikely experience such performance in 2009 unless it significantly increases its cotton production and exports, and fuel prices plummet drastically. Tajikistan's economy is expected to have expanded about 8 percent in 2008, according to data available in early 2009 (ibid.).

Turkmenistan's GDP growth in 2007 is estimated at about 10 percent (ADB 2008e), around 11 percent (IMF 2008), or nearly 20 percent (according to the Turkmen government), although in late 2008 the Asian Development Bank challenged the last figure as highly exaggerated (ADB 2008g). In 2007, Turkmenistan's main economic stimulus was the energy (gas and oil) sector, having experienced an estimated growth rate of 6.8 percent and an increase in gas exports that benefited from higher export prices even as the non-hydrocarbon sectors repeated their 2006 growth rate of 11.0 percent (ibid). Cotton, the dominant agricultural crop and a major export product, failed to meet the Turkmen government's targeted production level, but construction remained a major economic activity owing to government spending on public sector projects. Because the value of Turkmenistan's exports exceeded that of its imports, as in most years since 2000, that country registered a large surplus of $3.9 billion. Unlike the other main regional energy exporter (Kazakhstan), Turkmenistan does not suffer from a high foreign debt burden. Lacking any reliable economic statistics regarding 2008, in early 2009 there are grounds to suggest that it probably experienced a two-digit growth rate in 2008 and will likely have the same performance in 2009, in light of its growing oil and gas industry and the fact that its gas exports, in particular, are now also targeting the Chinese market.

Uzbekistan's economy grew by 9.5 percent in 2007 (ADB 2008c). It could actually perform in a more sustainable manner than other regional countries, because it is comparatively more diversified. The energy industry led Uzbekistan's economic growth in 2007 (10.1% growth rate), for which a significant hike in oil and gas prices was responsible. Benefiting from higher gas production, Uzbekistan boosted its gas export volumes by about 8 percent and secured a 40 percent increase in the export price. Industry and services were the major contributors to economic growth, expanding by 12.1 percent and 26.6 percent, respectively. Output of the auto industry climbed by 27 percent as a result of exports to Russia and other CIS countries. Uzbekistan's agriculture grew by 6.1 percent owing to the high world prices for cotton, rising grain harvests, and greater productivity springing from the privatization of agricultural cooperatives (ibid.). The Uzbek economy will likely grow significantly in 2009, in the range of 7 to 8 percent, for oil, gas, and cotton prices are expected to be high or at least higher than those in 2007, and the industrial sector, including the auto industry, will probably continue to grow. In the absence of supporting statistics in early 2009, Uzbekistan's economic performance in 2008 is estimated to be in the same range; many of the mentioned positive factors for 2009 were also true in 2008.

Political Constraints

Politics are a major internal factor slowing the Central Asian transition. The Soviet Union's fall changed the circumstances on which the totalitarian Soviet system was based. The new reality resulted in a less controlled and, only in this sense, a more democratic political system in the Central Asian countries. Their ruling elites, all of whom are ex-Soviet leaders turned nationalists, have a vested interest in preserving many aspects of the Soviet system, including a strong central government controlling all major aspects of life. Independence initiated a process of transition, but the Central Asian authoritarian regimes have been inappropriate vehicles for political, economic, and social reform, which require an ending of the transitional period and the building of fully functional and economically, politically, and socially viable countries. In addition to the other mentioned factors, those regimes have been a major cause of the failed transition, prolonging many transitional problems affecting human security, such as a prevailing income insecurity.

The Central Asian elites have two related reasons for opting for authoritarianism. Such a political system is well within their political thinking and experience as Soviet-trained elites. It is also needed to preserve the status quo and their power, because the breakdown of the Soviet system opened the way for the rise of dissent. In view of the growing dissatisfaction among the Central Asians caused by the political, economic, and social agonies of this seemingly never-ending transition, the realistic possibility of mass political movements challenging the elites' authority can only be prevented, delayed, or dealt with through suppression by strong authoritarian regimes. It is not a secret that although all the Central Asian leaders except the late Turkmen president Saparmurad Niyazov and his successor, Gurbanguly Berdimuhammedov, advocate democracy and the rule of law, they do not practice what they preach. Such practice would release forces of dissent, which practically no one could contain when the elites were unable to meet people's economic demands: a scenario proven by the Gorbachev political reforms, which facilitated the Soviet Union's fall. Hence, authoritarianism is both a reason for failed transition and a reaction to it. If it works properly, this type of regime ensures the continuity of the elites' rule in the post-Soviet era, when their authority could be challenged by dissatisfied people and their political leaders.

EXTERNAL FACTORS

External factors, of which two are major, have also contributed to the failed transition. As discussed earlier, the major Western economies (governments, the private sector, and such Western-dominated international institutions as the World Bank and the International Monetary Fund) have been reluctant to help the Central Asians financially, apart from major investments in their energy sectors, even as they have poured money into the former Communist states of Eastern Europe. Lack of adequate financial means has been a main—if not *the* main—factor responsible for the failed transition. For example, in 1997 the amount of assistance provided to Kazakhstan ($131 million), Kyrgyzstan ($240 million), Tajikistan ($101 million), Turkmenistan

($11 million), and Uzbekistan ($130 million) was significantly lower than that provided to Poland ($641 million), which was in a far better economic situation (UNDP 1999, 193–194). In 2003, the last year for which data exists, the same pattern prevailed. Hence, even as Poland received $1,191.5 million, the Central Asian countries received much less, despite their continued economic problems: Kazakhstan received $268.4 million, Kyrgyzstan $197.7 million, Tajikistan $144.1 million, Turkmenistan $27.2 million, and Uzbekistan $194.4 million (UNDP 2005, 281). In pursuit of their national interest, the Western countries in general and the U.S.-led coalition of countries in particular have indirectly damaged the transition by backing the Central Asian countries on their side, because of the preventive role played by authoritarianism in the transition process as mentioned before.

MAJOR EXPANDING SOCIAL AND ECONOMIC PROBLEMS AFFECTING HUMAN SECURITY

The failed transition in Central Asia has manifested itself in such various areas such as the social and the economic. Consequently, all the regional countries face many social and economic problems, although the extent varies from country to country. Thanks to the persistence of various factors, including those mentioned earlier, not only are such problems not disappearing, they have instead been deepening and expanding. In fact, 18 years after independence, they are now the main characteristics of the Central Asian transitional societies. These problems, which include poverty, unemployment, malnutrition, educational deficiencies, and drug abuse, will likely become permanent features should the current situation continue.

Poverty and Unemployment

Poverty has been a byproduct of the failed transition in Central Asia since independence. Unemployment, caused by the heavy loss of jobs as the result of the closure or subsequent low-level operation of state enterprises, has been a major contributor to poverty. Decreases in the income of the employed, significant increases in the prices of goods and services, and termination or scaling down of free or subsidized services have been other major contributors.

Many contradictory reports exist for unemployment rates. According to the United Nations Economic Commission for Europe (UNECE), the unemployment rates were very low in 2003, the latest year for which UNECE statistics are available: Kazakhstan had an unemployment rate of 1.8 percent, Kyrgyzstan 3 percent, Tajikistan 2.4 percent, Turkmenistan 3.6 percent, and Uzbekistan (in 2000, the only year for which the UNECE has statistics) 0.6 percent (UNECE 2005). However, ILO suggests much higher aggregate rates. Accordingly, the unemployment rate decreased in 2004 from "8.5 percent to 8.3 percent in Central and Eastern Europe and the CIS countries" (ILO 2005). The Asian Development Bank (ADB) also reports higher rates than UNECE does for some of the Central Asian countries in 2003 and 2004: Kazakhstan reported an 8.7 percent unemployment rate in 2003 (ADB 2004a, 2004b) and 8.4 percent in 2004 (ADB 2005).

A boy sits inside a cardboard box at a town dump in Bishkek, Kyrgyzstan in March 2005. Government corruption has fueled poverty in Kyrgyzstan, one of the poorest former Soviet republics, where unemployment is high. (Viktor Drachev/AFP/Getty Images)

Uzbekistan reported 3.1 percent officially or 6 percent unofficially in 2004 (ibid., 184). For 2006 and 2007, statistics are not available for all Central Asian countries. Those available indicate significant unemployment rates: Kazakhstan 7.2 percent (2006) and 6.6 percent (2007) (ADB 2008a), Kyrgyzstan 8.3 percent (2006) (ADB 2008b), and Tajikistan 2.3 percent (2006) and 2.6 percent (2007) (ADB 2008c).

However, although the improved economic environment has certainly reduced unemployment from the two-digit rates of the early 1990s, a decline in unemployment rates does not necessarily mean prosperity or even a reduction in poverty. For example, many employed Central Asians from less prosperous countries pay a high social price for their employment, for they must leave their families behind in search of employment in more prosperous regional countries (e.g., Kazakhstan). As reported by the ADB in 2004, based on a recent study by the International Organization for Migration, it is estimated that about 1 million Tajiks, who account for about 15 percent of the Tajik population, live in households where the "main source of income is derived from a family member working abroad" (ADB 2004). Despite lack of statistics, this percentage is almost certainly even higher today (early 2009), as the booming Russian construction industry that offers better-paid jobs than those available in most of Central Asia is attracting many Central Asians, including those who have some type of employment in their home countries.

It should also be stressed that unemployment rates based on government statistics may well be unreliable. According to the ADB, because the Turkmen government, for instance, officially guarantees employment to every citizen, official unemployment rates do not exist. There are only statistics on registered job seekers, the official number of which was 57,000 (2.6 percent of the labor force) in 2003; the number of unemployed seems to be much higher but is kept unpublished, owing to "substantial hidden unemployment and underreporting" (ibid.).

Reports on the rapid expansion of prostitution confirm that the unemployment rate should be high in Turkmenistan. According to Tajigul Begmedova, head of the Turkmen Helsinki Foundation (THF), "There is an unprecedented situation in Turkmenistan when [some] husbands, fathers and brothers push their wives, daughters and sisters into illegal ways, including prostitution, because they don't have a job and means to get by" (IRINnews.org, September 5, 2005).

Regardless of its cause, poverty in Central Asia has been a major problem affecting human security since 1991, reflecting the deep impact of transition on human security. The Central Asian governments are partly responsible for this phenomenon, apart from the economic constraints that limit their available resources to deal with poverty. However, to be fair, they have all sought to address it within their limits. Hence, compared to the 1990s, they have all made a significant progress in reducing at least the officially reported poverty because of their countries' better economic performance that has created employment and income, improved living standards (which fell sharply upon independence), and higher spending on social welfare and poverty reduction programs, assisted by international donors to some extent. In 1997, for example, 51 percent of Kyrgyz were poor (UN 2005f), but this percentage dropped to 39 percent in 2004 (ADB 2005, 174). Similarly, in 1996, 34.6 percent of Kazakhs were poor (ibid.), compared to 15 percent in 2004 (ADB 2005, 170). In 1999, the poor constituted

TABLE 10. Prevalence of Poverty among the Central Asian Peoples (Percentage of Population)

	Kazakhstan	Kyrgyzstan	Tajikistan	Turkmenistan	Uzbekistan
2003[a]	19.8	41.0	64.0	n/a	26.2
2004[a]	15.0	39.0	n/a	n/a	n/a
2000–2004[b]	56.7	72.5	84.7	79.4	16.9

Sources: [a]Asian Development Bank (ADB), 2005, "Kazakhstan," "Kyrgyzstan," "Tajikistan," "Turkmenistan," "Uzbekistan," Asian Development Outlook 2005, Manila: Asian Development Bank, 170, 171, 174, 182–184, www.adb.org/Documents/Books/ADO/2005/ ado2005-part2-ca.pdf (accessed September 10, 2008); [b]United Nations Development Programme (UNDP), 2008, *Human Development Report 2007/2008,* New York: UNDP, 242, 270–271, http://hdr.undp.org/en/media/HDR_20072008_EN_Complete.pdf (accessed October 4, 2008).

82 percent of Tajikistan's population, but only 64 percent in 2003 (ibid., 177). Statistics are unavailable for 2008 and for 2004–2007. However, as shown in Table 10, the most recent available statistics for the period 2000–2004 indicate a phenomenal expansion of poverty in all the Central Asian countries except Uzbekistan, for which, although the nation still has a serious poverty problem, statistics indicate an improvement.

For Turkmenistan, there are no official statistics on poverty, but it, too, should have a high percentage of poor, if only because its income inequality seems to be the worst in Central Asia, as suggested by Turkmenistan's National Institute of State Statistics in 2004 (ADB 2005, 182). Economic difficulties aside, a few major public service restructuring projects, resulting in major job losses for civil servants, have been a reason for poverty in a country where the state still dominates the economy in the absence of a strong private sector (ibid.). According to a 2005 report, the poverty rate could be as high as 44 percent, the reported percentage of Turkmen with a daily income of less than $2 (UNOCHA 2005b).

In all Central Asian countries, there is a particularly large gap between rural and urban areas in terms of poverty. In Kyrgyzstan, for example, three-fourths of the poor population lives in the rural areas (ADB 2005, 174). Hence, improving living standards in rural areas is a major challenge in Central Asia, including Kazakhstan (ibid., 170), the most prosperous regional country, having a booming energy industry.

Poverty is a blatant aspect of growing income inequality in Central Asia that is creating highly polarized countries, a recipe for social and political conflict and instability. The Central Asian countries are internally divided into two groups of the extremely rich and the poor or low-income, without the strong and growing middle class that is a necessity for social stability.

Malnutrition

Malnutrition is another byproduct of the failed transition in Central Asia. On the one hand, the sudden economic collapse in 1991 and the end of Moscow's transfers in cash and kind denied means to the Central Asian governments to continue many social

TABLE 11. Nutrition, Undernourished as Percentage of Total Population (FAO Estimates 1994 and 2001 and UNDP estimates 2002–2004)

	1994*	2001†	2002–2004
Kazakhstan	1	13	6
Kyrgyzstan	21	6	4
Tajikistan	21	61	56
Turkmenistan	13	9	7
Uzbekistan	8	26	25

*1993–1995 average. †2000–2002 average.
Sources: United Nations, 2008, "Commonwealth of Independent States: Nutrition, Undernourished As Percentage of Total Population (FAO Estimate)," New York: UN Statistics Division, Department of Economic and Social Affairs, http://unstats.un.org/unsd/mi/ mi_series_results.asp?rowID=566&fID=r15&cgID=172 (accessed September 8, 2008); United Nations Development Programme (UNDP), 2008, *Human Development Report 2007/2008,* New York: UNDP, 252–253, http://hdr.undp.org/en/media/HDR_20072008_EN_ Complete.pdf (accessed October 4, 2008).

welfare projects, including various food programs for children and generous subsidies for essential food items to make them affordable for all their citizens. On the other hand, a sudden sharp decrease in incomes and skyrocketing prices denied means to the Central Asians to compensate for their governments' inabilities to provide for their basic needs, including food. The result was the sudden expansion of malnutrition, which has continued to this date. Various factors, including economic improvements, have helped address this problem to varying extents. The available statistics (Tables 11 and 12) indicate the prevalence of this phenomenon in those countries in the 1990s, and show their achievements and failures in dealing with it.

TABLE 12. Nutrition, Undernourished, Number of People (FAO Estimates)

	1994*	2001†	2002–2004‡
Kazakhstan	171,273	200,907	840,000
Kyrgyzstan	929,868	287,885	204,000
Tajikistan	1,208,553	3,726,053	3,548,000
Turkmenistan	54,848	40,280	329,000
Uzbekistan	1,744,412	6,585,234	6,450,000

*1993–1995 average. †2000–2002 average. ‡Calculated by the author using Table 11's 2000–2004 statistics and Table 5's population statistics for 2003.
Source: United Nations, 2008, "Commonwealth of Independent States: Nutrition, Undernourished, Number of People (FAO Estimate)," New York: UN Statistics Division, Department of Economic and Social Affairs, http://unstats.un.org/unsd/mi/mi_series_results.asp?rowID=640&fID=r15&cgID=172 (accessed September 8, 2008).

TABLE 13. Net Primary Enrollment Rate (Percent)

	1990–1991[a]	2002–2003[a]	2005[b]
Kazakhstan	88	92	91
Kyrgyzstan	92	89	87
Tajikistan	77	94	97
Turkmenistan	n/a	n/a	n/a
Uzbekistan	78	n/a	n/a

Sources: [a]United Nations Development Programme (UNDP), 2005, *Human Development Report 2005,* New York: UNDP, 230, http://hdr.undp.org/reports/global/2005/pdf/HDR05_ HDI.pdf (accessed September 1, 2008); [b]United Nations Development Programme (UNDP), 2008, *Human Development Report 2007/2008,* New York: UNDP, 270–271, http://hdr.undp. org/en/media/HDR_20072008_EN_Complete.pdf (accessed October 4, 2008).

Educational Deficiencies

The educational system has also suffered from the transitional period. In part, this has been reflected in certain quantitative indicators, such as a decrease in the primary enrollment rate in Kyrgyzstan from 92 percent of eligible children in 1990–1991 to 87 percent in 2005 (UNDP 2005, 260). However, at least statistically, this has not been the case in two other Central Asian countries, Kazakhstan and Tajikistan, for which comparable statistics are available. Rather, they show clear progress in this regard (Table 13). Another set of comparable statistics covering the period 1998–2005 indicates noticeable fluctuations in enrollment rates in Kazakhstan and Tajikistan (Table 14). Compared to Table 13, its statistics suggest a significant increase in enrollment in Tajikistan. The enrollment rate of Uzbekistan, 101 percent for 2001, compared to 78 percent for 1990–1991 (Table 14), suggests a great leap forward.

TABLE 14. Education, Primary Completion Rate, Both Sexes (UNESCO)

	1998	1999	2000	2001	2005
Kazakhstan	91*	89*	90	92	114
Kyrgyzstan	98	97	96	97	97
Tajikistan	98	99	103	105	102
Turkmenistan	n/a	n/a	n/a	n/a	n/a
Uzbekistan	n/a	n/a	n/a	101*	97†

*UNESCO Institute for Statistics (UIS) estimate. †2004 data.
Sources: United Nations, 2008, "Commonwealth of Independent States: Education Primary Completion Rate, Both Sexes (UNESCO)," New York: UN Statistics Division, Department of Economic and Social Affairs, http://unstats.un.org/unsd/mi/mi_series_results.asp?rowID= 743&fID=r15&cgID=172 (accessed September 4, 2008); United Nations Common Database (UNCDB), 2008, "Primary Completion Rate, Both Sexes" (May 15), http://data.un. org/Data. aspx?q=Primary+Completion+Rate&d=MDG&f=seriesRowID%3a743 (accessed October 4, 2008).

The statistical nature of this positive phenomenon must be stressed, since enrollment is not equal to the actual attendance of students. In Tajikistan, for instance, where surveys have been conducted on school attendance, factors such as poverty and lack of proper facilities result in low school attendance (ADB 2005, 177).

Hence, the deficiencies of the educational system have been partly, perhaps more importantly, manifested in a decrease in the quality of education, for which various factors have been responsible. These include, as is the case in all other Central Asian sectors, limited resources available for proper operation of educational institutions, both in terms of essential nonhuman requirements (e.g., classrooms, electricity, fuel, educational material, computers) and human resources (adequate numbers of qualified and committed teaching staff). In Tajikistan, where income inequality is worse than in any other Central Asian country, according to a 2005 ADB report, inadequate funding for schools has resulted in a severe shortage of teachers; many have left their low-paid teaching positions for better-paid jobs (ibid.). Needless to say, this shortage has had a major negative impact on the quality of education Tajik students receive.

An issue of concern has been the re-emergence of gender discrimination in education, a reflection of this alarming phenomenon in the wider Central Asian society. It was observed as a surfacing phenomenon in the 1990s. Reportedly, some parents, but not educational authorities, showed a preference for male education while denying female children the same right. The absence of statistics on all Central Asian countries in this regard makes any generalization based on the available statistics inappropriate. However, a significant decline in primary-level enrollment of girls in Kyrgyzstan (from 92.2 percent of eligible children in 1990 to 84.4 percent in 2001) even as the rate of enrollment for eligible boys for the same years remained almost the same (92.5 percent and 91.7 percent, respectively), suggests gender preference for education as a likely factor (Tables 15 and 16). In the absence of comparable data

TABLE 15.   Education Enrollment Ratio, Primary Level, Girls (UNESCO)

	1990	1998	1999	2000	2001	2005
Kazakhstan	87.2*	83.5*	84.5*	86.6	89.0	90.0
Kyrgyzstan	92.2*	90.0†	88.7	88.3	88.4	86.0
Tajikistan	75.9*	94.3*	n/a	n/a	n/a	96.0
Turkmenistan	n/a	n/a	n/a	n/a	n/a	n/a
Uzbekistan	77.7*	n/a	n/a	n/a	n/a	n/a

*UNESCO Institute for Statistics (UIS) estimate. †National estimate.
Sources: United Nations, "Commonwealth of Independent States: Education Enrollment Ratio, Net, Primary Level, Girls (UNESCO)," New York: UN Statistics Division, Department of Economic and Social Affairs, http://unstats.un.org/unsd/mi/mi_series_results.asp?rowID= 634&fID=r15&cgID=172 (accessed September 4, 2008); United Nations Development Programme (UNDP), 2008, *Human Development Report 2007/2008*, New York: UNDP, 335–336, http://hdr.undp.org/en/media/HDR_20072008_EN_Complete.pdf (accessed October 4, 2008).

TABLE 16. Education Enrollment Ratio, Primary Level, Boys (UNESCO)

	1990	**1998**	**1999**	**2000**	**2001**	**2005**
Kazakhstan	88.0*	83.4*	84.1*	87.5	90.0	n/a
Kyrgyzstan	92.5*	92.0†	91.1	91.5	91.7	n/a
Tajikistan	77.5*	100.0*	n/a	n/a	n/a	n/a
Turkmenistan	80.3*	72.1	n/a	n/a	87.6*	n/a
Uzbekistan	78.7*	n/a	n/a	n/a	n/a	n/a

*UNESCO Institute for Statistics (UIS) estimate. †National estimate.
Sources: United Nations, "Commonwealth of Independent States: Education Enrollment Ratio, Net, Primary Level, Boys (UNESCO)," New York: UN Statistics Division, Department of Economic and Social Affairs, http://unstats.un.org/unsd/mi/mi_series_results.asp?rowID= 633&fID=r15&cgID=172 (accessed September 4, 2008); United Nations Development Programme (UNDP), 2008, *Human Development Report 2007/2008*, New York: UNDP, 335–336, http://hdr.undp.org/en/media/HDR_20072008_EN_Complete.pdf (accessed October 4, 2008).

for boys in 2005, an increase in enrollment of girls to 86 percent in 2005 cannot be interpreted positively or negatively.

Drug Abuse

Drug addiction has been increasing in Central Asia since 1991. Neighboring Afghanistan is the largest producer of opium, from which other narcotics—heroin and morphine—are extracted. That country also produces milder drugs, such as hashish. Estimates for 2004 suggest the production of 4,850 tons of opium, accounting for 87 percent of the world's production (UNODC 2005, 34). In August 2008, the United Nations Office on Drugs and Crimes (UNODC) estimated the 2008 production to be 7,700 tons (UNODC 2008, 1). Inability to secure borders with Afghanistan has enabled the international drug traffickers based in Afghanistan to flood Central Asian markets with inexpensive drugs on their way to Europe via the CIS countries. Various social and economic problems caused by the seemingly endless transition (dysfunctional families, poverty, unemployment, low-income, lack of opportunities, etc.) have created suitable ground for the rapid expansion of drug trafficking and drug addiction. Drug addiction is growing especially rapidly among the region's youth and women. As stated by the UNODC, drug use starts at "a very early age" (ibid.). Its rapid expansion among women is demonstrated in an estimate that suggests women account for about 30 percent of drug users in Dushanbe (Esfandiari 2004).

Accurate official statistics are unavailable on drug addiction, which is mainly addiction to heroin, the most common drug in Central Asia. According to James Callahan, the UNODC regional director, "the situation is continuing to deteriorate or get worse again because of the increasing traffic from Afghanistan" (ibid.). His organization estimates that drug addicts account for 1 percent of the Central Asian population (about 560,000, based on 2002 population statistics) and suggests a 17-fold increase in opiate abuse between 1990 and 2002 (Buckley 2005). Other estimates are close to this. A 2004 estimate, for example, suggests the number of addicts to be 100,000 in Kyrgyzstan, 55,000 in Tajikistan, and between 65,000 and 91,000 in Uzbekistan; a 2002 estimate suggests 186,000 for Kazakhstan (Esfandiari 2004). No statistics exist for Turkmenistan. However, it seems that country is following the regional trend, as suggested in 2005 by Tajigul Begmedova, head of the Turkmen Helsinki Foundation (THF). Accordingly, drug addiction is on the rise in Turkmenistan based on THF's recent informal survey of the residents of Ashghabad and other parts of that country (UNOCHA 2005a). As evident in the available statistics, and they are mainly conservative estimations, the number of drug addicts is on the rise. For instance, in January 2009, Tajikistan is estimated to have at least between 55,000 and 75,000 addicts (UNOCHA 2007).

Apart from obvious health hazard of drug addiction, the extensive use of morphine, the injectable version of heroin, has contributed to a rapid expansion of HIV/AIDS in Central Asia. Furthermore, this phenomenon has contributed to such social problems as expanding prostitution. In Tajikistan, for example, some female addicts become prostitutes to earn money to buy drugs, according to Murtazokul Khidirov, the director of RAN, an NGO helping drug addicts in Dushanbe (Esfandiari 2004).

There is no realistic hope for a significant decrease in Afghanistan's growing production of narcotics and the Afghan-based international drug trafficking, as indicated by UNODC's report of a 64 percent increase in opium cultivation in Afghanistan in 2004 from the 2003 level (UNIS 2004). The mentioned figure for 2008 reflects yet another major increase—63 percent compared to 2004. Against this background, the persistence of all types of social and economic ills in Central Asia suggests the continuity and expansion of drug trafficking and addiction in that region.

CONCLUSION

Despite some achievements, the Central Asian countries have basically failed to conclude their political, economic, and social transition 18 years after gaining independence. In early 2009, the Central Asians are suffering from the consequences of their failed economic transition, which in turn prevent their economic and social development and prosperity. In particular, economic and social difficulties have seriously damaged human security in Central Asia, affecting the majority of the Central Asians in a variety of forms, although its extent varies among countries. The resulting social problems negatively impact both the regional countries' economic development and—of course—political stability. In particular, the persistence of various social and economic difficulties is polarizing the Central Asian societies by dividing them between two extremes of wealth and severe poverty. Rooted in the poor performance of the Central Asian economies that characterizes their failed transition, expanding social discontent has contributed to political fragility—a recipe for disaster, for such fragility could lead to the rise and expansion of various types of instability in their respective countries.

Should the transitional failure continue, there are grounds to fear that such upheavals as the Yellow Revolution and the Andijan incident will become the rule, not the exception.

BIBLIOGRAPHY

Asian Development Bank (ADB). 2004a. "Tajikistan." *Asian Development Outlook 2004*. Manila: Asian Development Bank. www.adb.org/Documents/Books/ADO/2004/taj.asp (accessed September 12, 2008).

Asian Development Bank (ADB). 2004b. "Turkmenistan." *Asian Development Outlook 2004*. Manila: Asian Development Bank. www.adb.org/Documents/Books/ADO/2004/kaz.asp (accessed September 12, 2008).

Asian Development Bank (ADB). 2005. "Kazakhstan," "Kyrgyzstan," "Tajikistan," "Turkmenistan," "Uzbekistan." *Asian Development Outlook 2005*. Manila: Asian Development Bank. www.adb.org/Documents/Books/ADO/2005/ado2005-part2-ca.pdf (accessed September 10, 2008).

Asian Development Bank (ADB). 2008a. *Asian Development Bank & Kazakhstan*. Manila: Asian Development Bank. www.adb.org/Documents/Fact_Sheets/KAZ.pdf (accessed October 2, 2008).

Asian Development Bank (ADB). 2008b. *Asian Development Bank & Kyrgyzstan*. Manila: Asian Development Bank. www.adb.org/Documents/Fact_Sheets/KGZ.pdf (accessed October 2, 2008).

Asian Development Bank (ADB). 2008c. *Asian Development Bank & Tajikistan*. Manila: Asian Development Bank. www.adb.org/Documents/Fact_Sheets/TAJ.pdf (accessed October 2, 2008).

Asian Development Bank (ADB). 2008d. "Kazakhstan." *Asian Development Outlook 2008*. Manila: Asian Development Bank. www.adb.org/Documents/Books/ADO/2008/KAZ.asp (accessed October 1, 2008).

Asian Development Bank (ADB). 2008e. "Turkmenistan." *Asian Development Outlook 2008*. Manila: Asian Development Bank. www.adb.org/Documents/Books/ADO/2008/TKM.asp (accessed September 30, 2008).

Asian Development Bank (ADB). 2008f. "Uzbekistan." *Asian Development Outlook 2008*. Manila: Asian Development Bank. www.adb.org/Documents/Books/ADO/2008/UZB.asp (accessed September 30, 2008).

Asian Development Bank (ADB). 2008g. "Tajikistan." *Asian Development Outlook 2008*. Manila: Asian Development Bank. www.adb.org/Documents/Books/ADO/2008/TAJ.asp (accessed September 30, 2008).

Asian Development Bank (ADB). 2008h. "Kyrgyzstan." *Asian Development Outlook 2008*. Manila: Asian Development Bank. www.adb.org/Documents/Books/ADO/2008/KGZ.asp (accessed October 1, 2008).

Buckley, Sarah. 2005. "Central Asia's Deadly Cargo." *BBC News,* November 22, 2005. http://news.bbc.co.uk/2/hi/asia-pacific/4414922.stm (accessed September 27, 2008).

Esfandiari, Golnaz. 2004. "Central Asia: Drug Addiction Is on the Rise (Part 1)." *Radio Free Europe/Radio Liberty,* June 22, 2004. www.rferl.org/featuresarticle/2004/06/3eccd6d7-6600-4310-8656-6cfe150c5411.html (accessed September 25, 2008).

ILO. 2005. *Trends in Europe and Central Asia,* ILO/05/00, February 14, 2005, www.ilo.ru/news/200502/002.htm (accessed September 19, 2008)

International Monetary Fund (IMF). 2008. "GDP—Constant Prices, Annual Percent Change." *World Economic Outlook Database*. Washington, D.C.: IMF, April 2008. www.imf.org/external/pubs/ft/weo/2008/01/weodata/weoselgr.aspx (accessed October 1, 2008).

Johnson, Keith. 2008. "Oil Spike: Will a Financial Bailout Push Crude Back Up?" *The Wall Street Journal*, October 1, 2008. http://blogs.wsj.com/environmentalcapital/2008/10/01/oil-spike-will-a-financial-bailout-push-crude-back-up/ (accessed on October 2, 2008).

United Nations. 2005a. "Commonwealth of Independent States: Education Enrolment Ratio, Net, Primary Level, Boys (UNESCO)." New York: UN Statistics Division, Department of Economic and Social Affairs. http://unstats.un.org/unsd/mi/mi_series_results.asp?rowID=633&fID=r15&cgID=172 (accessed September 10, 2008).

United Nations. 2005b. "Commonwealth of Independent States: Education Enrolment Ratio, Net, Primary Level, Girls (UNESCO)." New York: UN Statistics Division, Department of Economic and Social Affairs. http://unstats.un.org/unsd/mi/mi_series_results.asp?rowID=634&fID=r15&cgID=172 (accessed September 10, 2008).

United Nations. 2005c. "Commonwealth of Independent States: Education Primary Completion Rate, Both Sexes (UNESCO)." New York: UN Statistics Division, Department of Economic and Social Affairs. http://unstats.un.org/unsd/mi/mi_series_results.asp?rowID=743&fID=r15&cgID=172 (accessed September 10, 2008).

United Nations. 2005d. "Commonwealth of Independent States: Nutrition, Undernourished as Percentage of Total Population (FAO Estimate)." New York: UN Statistics Division, Department of Economic and Social Affairs. http://unstats.un.org/unsd/mi/mi_series_results.asp?rowID=566&fID=r15&cgID=172 (accessed September 8, 2008).

United Nations. 2005e. "Commonwealth of Independent States: Nutrition, Undernourished, Number of People (FAO Estimate)." New York: Statistics Division, Department of Economic and Social Affairs. http://unstats.un.org/unsd/mi/mi_series_results.asp?rowID=640&fID= r15&cgID=172 (accessed September 8, 2008).

United Nations. 2005f. "Commonwealth of Independent States: Poverty, Percentage of Population below National Poverty Line, Total (WB)." New York: UN Statistics Division, Department of Economic and Social Affairs. http://unstats.un.org/unsd/mi/mi_series_results.asp?rowID=581&fID=r15&cgID=172 (accessed September 24, 2008).

United Nations Common Database (UNCDB). 2008. "Primary Completion Rate, Both Sexes." May 15, 2008. http://data.un.org/Data.aspx?q=Primary+Completion+Rate&d=MDG&f=seriesRowIDpercent3a743 (accessed October 4, 2008).

United Nations Development Programme (UNDP). 1999. *Human Development Report 1999*. New York: UNDP. http://download.at.kde.org/soc/undp/Backmatter2.pdf (accessed September 17, 2008).

United Nations Development Programme (UNDP). 2005. *Human Development Report 2005*. New York: UNDP. http://hdr.undp.org/reports/global/2005/pdf/HDR05_HDI.pdf (accessed September 17, 2008).

United Nations Development Programme (UNDP). 2008. *Human Development Report 2007/2008*. New York: UNDP, 270–271. http://hdr.undp.org/en/media/HDR_20072008_EN_Complete.pdf (accessed October 4, 2008).

United Nations Economic Commission for Europe (UNECE). 2005. "Unemployment Rates." *Trends in Europe and North America*. www.unece.org/stats/trends2005/profiles/Kazakhstan.pdf (accessed September 19, 2008).

United Nations Information Service (UNIS). 2004. "Record Opium Cultivation in Afghanistan Is a Threat to Central Asia and CIS Countries." UNIS/NAR/869, November 25, 2004. Vienna: United National Information Service. www.unis.unvienna.org/unis/pressrels/2004/unisnar869. html (accessed September 21, 2008).

United Nations Office for Coordination of Humanitarian Affairs (UNOCHA). 2005a. "Turkmenistan: Drug Addiction on the Rise." *IRIN*, August 2, 2005, www.irinnews.org/report. asp?ReportID=48406&SelectRegion=Asia&SelectCountry=TURKMENISTAN (accessed September 27, 2008).

Chapter 3

Elections in Azerbaijan and Georgia and Their Impact on Regional Security

The Caucasus has been the arena of rivalry for many regional and global powers over the last 3,000 years. Over time, many factors have been responsible for this, including the importance of the Caucasus as a land link between Asia and Europe, its shared borders with regional or global powers, its function as a buffer between rival regional powers, and, of course, its resources. In the first decade of the twenty-first century, a main cause of interest in the region—for major powers both regional and nonregional—is its proximity to Iran and Russia. Having differing strengths and claims to higher status in the international arena, these two nations are a source of concern for many states, including Western ones. To this should be added the strategic importance of the Caucasus in addressing part of the world's growing fuel requirements in the short and medium terms, owing to Azerbaijan's oil resources. Furthermore, the Caucasus offers a potential long-term transit route for Caspian oil and gas exports en route to international markets that bypasses Iran and Russia—a strong reason for interest, particularly on the part of the United States and some of its allies, such as the United Kingdom, all of whom have major investments in the Caspian region. Yet, the peaceful transition of the Caucasian states from their highly centralized, Soviet-inherited political and economic systems to democratic ones based on a type of free-enterprise economy can be achieved only in the context of a sustainable, long-term peace in the region. This prerequisite implies two interrelated conditions—stable regional states and the absence of inter- and intrastate wars—added to the availability of material means to create an economic basis for transition. Such conditions have been mainly absent in the Caucasus, in particular, in the two states of crucial importance for oil activities. Because of the unsettled conflicts in Georgia and those between Azerbaijan and Armenia, which dragged the region into war and instability in the early 1990s, the region bears the seeds of a new round of armed conflicts that could engulf all its constituent states. Against this background, it seems overly optimistic to hope that positive changes in the political systems of the Caucasus, especially Azerbaijan's and Georgia's—in particular, their recent so-called peaceful changing of the guard—have put them on the path toward stability while lessening the likelihood of armed conflict. The new governments have sought mainly to continue the political systems they inherited—a recipe for disaster in light of the widespread dissatisfaction with the overall situation among the Georgians and the Azeris. Against a background of unsettled territorial disputes between Armenia and Azerbaijan and active separatism in both Azerbaijan and Georgia, evidence suggests that if the current situation continues, the new administrations in Baku and Tbilisi, who came to power using democratic means (elections), will contribute to instability domestically and regionally in various forms, from civil unrest to intra- and interstate wars. Such wars will likely engulf the entire Caucasus in the foreseeable future, with the potential to involve the regional and non-regional powers having long-term interests in the region.

ELECTIONS IN AZERBAIJAN AND GEORGIA

The current Azeri and Georgian governments ascended to power through ostensibly democratic elections, Azerbaijan in 2003 and Georgia in 2004, that gave the appearance of legitimacy to what were essentially undemocratic transfers of power that merely appeared democratic. In both cases, despite differences in historical contexts, details, and forms, their two current leaders became heads of state in circumstances that are likely to undermine their countries' long-term stability by unintentionally sowing the seeds of internal and external conflict. The Georgian-Russian war of August 2008 serves as evidence for this proposition.

Azerbaijan's Political Situation

Azerbaijan gained independence in December 1991 when the Soviet Union disintegrated. The country inherited all the political, economic, social, and security problems of the last decade of the Soviet Union, including a devastating civil war over Azerbaijan's disputed Armenian-dominated region of Nagorno-Karabakh. Azerbaijan and Armenia fought each other until 1994, when a cease-fire ended the hostility without addressing its root causes. About 20 percent of Azerbaijan's land has since remained under the control of the Armenian separatists of Nagorno-Karabakh.

Between late 1991 and mid-1993, when the late President Haidar Aliyev ascended to power, two presidents headed Azerbaijan at a time when the country was experiencing numerous political, economic, social, and security problems caused by the sudden collapse of the Soviet Union and the devastating civil war. Aliyev's presidency and the war's end in 1994 helped normalize the situation.

Azerbaijan's political system has been dominated by Haidar Aliyev's family and friends, who have also controlled the country's economic life since 1993. Today, Haidar Aliyev's son, President Ilham Aliyev, governs Azerbaijan as the heir of his father, who passed away in December 2003.

Many political parties have operated in Azerbaijan since independence. The Azeri constitution provides for their peaceful political activities. However, in practice, the Azeri government has resorted to various means of limiting such activities in order to ensure the domination of the ruling elite.

on the widespread dissatisfaction among the Kyrgyz, the Georgians, and the Ukrainians to replace their elites with new elites fully loyal to Washington (Blank 2005). Because the environment in many CIS countries is so suitable for other "revolutions," this real or perceived U.S. policy is a looming threat to the elites' authority. What makes this scenario more convincing is the fact that in all three cases, security forces did not seriously intervene on behalf of the challenged ruling elites to prevent their downfall. Unsurprisingly, a spokesman for the Georgian Labor Party described the Rose Revolution in these terms: "What happened in Georgia was not a Rose Revolution but rather a coup involving transfer of power to heirs" (British Helsinki Human Rights Group 2004).

Against this background, real or perceived irregularities in the November 2003 Georgian parliamentary elections provoked demonstrations by the opposition parties. On November 22, the day of the opening session of the new Georgian parliament (illegitimate, in the eyes of the opposition), pro-opposition demonstrators led by Mikhail Saakashvili and holding roses in their hands—hence the revolution's name—seized the parliament building and interrupted President Shevardnadze's speech, forcing him to flee. Hampered by the refusal of the military forces to support him, Shevardnadze's efforts to control the situation by declaring a state of emergency and mobilizing the security forces failed. The next day, he met with the opposition leaders Saakashvili and Zurab Zhvania to discuss the situation, in a meeting arranged by the Russian foreign minister, Igor Ivanov. During this meeting, as a result of behind-the-scenes negotiations, President Shevardnadze resigned to avoid a civil war and thus paved the way for an early presidential election with (for all practical purposes) one single serious candidate, Mikhail Saakashvili, now hailed as the Rose Revolution's leader. There are suggestions of assistance provided by the U.S. government, including through American NGOs, to the opposition leader and the like-minded, and of a covert operation to ensure the inactivity of the security forces in defending their political master (Shevardnadze) to make his removal possible (GlobalSecurity.org 2003). The subsequent election of Saakashvili as president in the 2004 election, during which he was portrayed as a liberator fighting a corrupt political system, was not a surprise. By and large, the new Georgian government has been little different from the previous one, despite its anti-corruption and pro-democracy rhetoric and some superficial changes in the bureaucracy.

THE POST-ELECTION ERA IN GEORGIA AND AZERBAIJAN

Despite changes in appearances in the post-election era, Georgia and Azerbaijan are not qualitatively different today. This is particularly true in the case of Georgia, whose new leader claims legitimacy arising from a popular movement, the Rose Revolution. In the aftermath of elections in Azerbaijan and Georgia, the transition of power seemed successful on surface. However the new Georgian and Azeri governments are not building new, stable states, instead continuing the old ones in slightly different forms justified by new realities. Even though these two Caucasian countries are not currently experiencing massive internal unrest, although the April 2009 Georgian opposition's demonstrations in Tbilisi demanding President Saakashvili's resignation could potentially turn into a nation-wide movement, neither is on the track toward irreversible stability. In fact, the circumstances under which the changing of the guard took place in those countries contributed an additional factor to a situation already conducive to instability.

The Situation in Georgia

In Georgia, the pre-Saakashvili era was characterized by a high degree of corruption, which eroded the legitimacy of the entire Georgian political system. To that must be added the government's inability to address many other issues, including economic difficulties, rampant organized crime, and different secessionist movements. It is doubtful that the Saakashvili government has a sufficiently strong political will to fulfill its election promises. The new administration's promises to remedy all those ills at a time when it has neither the means nor the ability but only the same old political apparatus as always, have led, predictably, to disillusionment and a sudden decline in its popular support. The results of a public opinion poll released in April 2006 by the Georgian Opinion Research Business International indicated a sharp decline in Saakashvili's popularity (only 38 percent of Georgian voters would vote for him at the time of their asking), compared with the claimed backing of 98 percent of voters in the January 2004 election (Myers 2005). Another source suggested even less support for him in May 2005, reflected by an approval rating of only 25 percent (Jibladze 2005). Saakashvili's popularity continued to decline. Under undemocratic circumstances (discussed later in this section), his re-election in January 2008 showed his falling popularity when he won "about 52 percent of the vote," which was translated into "about 27 percent of the electorate"—a far cry from his having garnered "96 percent of the vote" in January 2004, in an election "with much higher turnout" (Fuller 2008). The free fall in popularity lasted until August 2008, when the majority of Georgians rallied around their government in a show of patriotism and hostility to Russia during the Georgian-Russian war of 2008. In its aftermath, President Saakashvili's popularity started to decline again, as Georgians facing the massive destruction of their country questioned the wisdom of their president's bid to restore Tbilisi's sovereignty over South Ossetia through military means, in addition to all their previous reasons for losing confidence in their government.

In particular, two major promises of President Saakashvili's merit elaboration for their clear negative impact on Georgia's stability. As for the promise of fighting corruption, the situation is not now qualitatively different from the Shevardnadze era, notwithstanding the highly publicized government commitment to eradicate the corruption engulfing the Georgian government and its bureaucracy. To that end, the removal of many pro-Shevardnadze people from top positions and promises for a serious plan for fighting corruption brought about hopes among the Georgians for a better future, reflected in the president's high approval rate in early 2004. But despite initial efforts to make fighting corruption a real project, the Georgian government has

DECLARATION OF INDEPENDENCE BY
ABKHAZIA AND SOUTH OSSETIA

One byproduct of the Georgian-Russian war of August 2008 was the declaration of independence by South Ossetia and Abkhazia. The two Georgian breakaway republics became practically, but not officially, independent as a result of two separate, devastating civil wars: South Ossetia's in 1992 and Abkhazia's in 1993. However, despite their practical independence, and their declaration of it in 1991 (South Ossetia) and 1992 (Abkhazia), they did not officially demand that other countries recognize them as independent countries until 2008. Nor did any regional or non-regional country officially recognize them as such. In the aftermath of the Georgian-Russian war, both declared independence and requested Russia's recognition of their independence. Against a background of enjoying the Russian military's support since the breakup of the Soviet Union, the military devastation of Georgia as a result of the Russian massive military reaction to the Georgian attack on Tskhinvali provided a suitable opportunity for the authorities of the two breakaway republics to make their independence official, knowing very well that Russian recognition would be forthcoming. In fact, Russian president Dmitri Medvedev tacitly promised it to them in his televised meeting with South Ossetian leader Eduard Kokoity and Abkhaz leader Sergei Bagapsh after the Georgian-Russian war, when he assured them of support for whatever decision they would take regarding their status. As the two breakaway republics officially requested, on August 25, 2008, the Russian parliament (Duma) unanimously demanded that Russian president Dmitri Medvedev recognize their independence, which he did the next day. Unsurprisingly, Georgia did not. Georgian president Mikhail Saakashvili promised to retake Abkhazia and South Ossetia and restore Tbilisi's sovereignty over them. Nor has any other country except Nicaragua recognized their independence, at least by early 2009. The Western allies of Georgia (EU and USA, and their organizations such as NATO) have all asked Russia to revise its decision in this regard. Revision is a highly unlikely scenario, notwithstanding that the EU-negotiated cease-fire agreement of September 8, 2008, included an article regarding the upholding of talks in October 2008 on the status of Abkhazia and South Ossetia. In spite of its acceptance of the agreement, Russia clearly stated that it would not withdraw its recognition of the republics' independence. Not only that, on September 17, 2008, Russian president Dmitri Medvedev signed treaties with South Ossetian leader Eduard Kokoity and Abkhaz leader Sergei Bagapsh that committed Moscow to defend their territories from any Georgian attack. Although the long-term status of Abkhazia and South Ossetia is far from clear in early 2009, it is certain that this issue will be a major source of tension and conflict, including military involvement, in Russia's relations with Georgia as well as Western countries — particularly the United States, the main military backer of Georgia.

President of Georgia Mikhail Sakhashvili during a visit to the European Community to confirm EU support for Georgia in April 2004. Sakhashvili was elected president in January 2004 by a claimed 98% margin. The election was the last stage in the process of changing guard, which many regional governments believed to be American-orchestrated. (European Commission/Breydel)

eventually changed course—although the rhetoric is still there, and some efforts have been under way to deal with the most blatant cases. In practice, fighting corruption has become mainly a means of uprooting the former president's power base while consolidating that of the new one. The country is still very corrupt, ranking among the most corrupt countries in the world. As reported by Transparency International, an NGO that produces a reliable annual report on corruption in all countries, in 2004, the first year of the new government, Georgia was ranked 130th of 158 nations in terms of the absence of corruption, scoring 2.2 on a 10-point scale, where 10 is "clean" (Transparency International 2005). Despite all the publicized efforts, this is only marginally better than the previous year, when President Shevardnadze was in power. In that year, according to the same source, Georgia ranked 133rd out of 145, scoring 2 on the 10-point scale (Transparency International 2004). Statistics on Georgia's rank and score for 2008 indicate a significant improvement, rising to 67th out of 180 and scoring 3.8 (Transparency International 2008). However this is not an impressive record for a government that came to power with a mandate to eradicate corruption.

Regarding human rights issues, the country still has major problems, as reported by reliable human rights organizations. For instance, Human Rights Watch's accounts for 2004 and 2005 suggest only limited improvements compared to the immediate past year, when Shevardnadze was in power. The source reports that the Georgian government's reform agenda in 2004 produced "mixed results" in the field of human rights (HRW 2005). Accordingly, although there was an improvement in religious freedom, torture, and ill-treatment in pretrial detention remained "widespread," and Chechen refugees became a target of state discrimination and abuse by Georgian security forces (ibid.). As reported by the same source, the situation remained more or less the same in 2005. Describing the Georgian government's human rights record since the Rose Revolution as "uneven," Human Rights Watch refers to that government's priorities of fighting corruption and securing territorial integrity to point out the "unchecked" continuity of human rights abuses in many areas "following patterns established under former governments" (HRW 2006b).

The human rights situation worsened in 2007, when the Saakashvili administration made a U-turn, resorting to the same suppressive practices criticized by the Georgian opposition under Saakashvili during his predecessor's time. The trigger was the expanding popular opposition to his government, reflected in opposition demonstrations in the streets of Tbilisi and the opposition news media's growing expression of dissent in 2007. The following account of the events in November 2007 by Human Rights Watch sheds light on this development.

> After several days of large-scale peaceful opposition protests in Tbilisi, the Georgian government initiated a violent crackdown on opposition protesters and instituted a nine-day state of emergency, saying that this was in response to a coup attempt. Riot police used excessive force to attack demonstrators, dispersing them with water cannons, large amounts of tear gas, and rubber bullets. Many policemen also beat individual protestors. According to official statistics, over 550 protestors and 34 police were hospitalized with injuries. President Saakashvili announced snap presidential elections for January 2008, which helped diffuse the immediate political crisis. (HRW 2008b, para. 2)

President Saakashvili was re-elected in January 2008 by resorting to undemocratic and suppressive measures. Using the Georgian security forces, he practically crippled the opposition by declaring an emergency situation through which he suppressed the opposition and denied them the means to challenge him in a meaningful manner during the election period. Like many other human rights organizations, Human Rights Watch documented this development.

On the evening of November 7 [2007] riot police raided the private Imedi television station, held the staff at gunpoint, destroyed archives, and smashed equipment. Both Imedi and another private station, Kavkasia, were taken off the air. The government then declared a state of emergency that lasted nine days, limiting freedom of assembly and banning all broadcast news programs except by the state-funded Georgian Public Broadcasting. The government lifted the state of emergency on November 16, but suspended Imedi's broadcasting license for three months.

The truncated pre-election period, the restrictions on assembly and media imposed during the state of emergency, and the absence of one of Georgia's key alternative media outlets all marred the pre-election campaign. (HRW 2008b, paras. 4, 5)

The suppression of opposition groups and individuals was not confined to Tbilisi. They were also targeted in other Georgian cities, including Zugdidi, where the police attacked protestors, "injuring at least two severely, as they were leaving a demonstration . . ." (ibid., para. 3). In Batumi, the police used "excessive force to disperse students gathering . . . to protest the previous day's violence in Tbilisi" (ibid.). Nor was suppressing the opposition limited to employing security forces in uniform. President Saakashvili also used security forces in civilian clothes to intimidate the opposition. There are reports of "unidentified attackers," believed to be plainclothes security personnel, assaulting "numerous opposition activists" before the November 7 demonstrations (ibid.).

Needless to say, the continuity of widespread although less blatant corruption and the expansion of human rights abuses are preparing the ground for popular discontent and thus social unrest and political instability, the outcome of the new government's domestic performance. However, the government's foreign policy has also paved the way for instability arising from tensions and conflict in Georgia's relations with its neighbor, Russia. The Georgian government's having sided with the United States in its regional ambitions has provoked a hostile reaction on the part of Moscow, negatively affecting the overall situation in Georgia. There is no question that Georgian-Russian relations have been deteriorating since Mikhail Saakashvili came to power. Continuing what President Shevardnadze began in 2001, Saakashvili has extended his country's military relations with the United States, which has military personnel in Georgia and access to a Georgian air base (used in its war in Iraq)—a major concern for Russia, especially since its own ties with Washington are gradually deteriorating.

Moreover, counting on unfailing U.S. support, the Saakashvili government has felt confident in risking tensions with Russia, notwithstanding their potential for major destabilizing conflicts. A noteworthy case was Tbilisi's gamble in May 2004 to remove Ajaria's warlord (Aslan Abashidze) from power, despite his enjoyment of Russian support for the purpose of expanding Georgian control over Ajaria, a Georgian region hosting a Russian military base, practically run by Abashidze as an independent state since Georgia's independence. Another noteworthy case was Georgia's bid to close the two remaining Russian military bases in its territory, serving as an indicator of Tbilisi's counting on American backing and also its readiness to face Russian hostility. Russia's hostility was a certainty in reaction to serious efforts to close down its bases, despite its official promises and agreements to that end, and despite the fact that it had begun to withdraw from its last base inside Georgia, excluding those in Abkhazia and South Ossetia, before August 2008. In that period, Moscow was concerned about being encircled by the U.S. military, which had been expanding its presence in Central Asia and the Caucasus since 2001. President Saakashvili clearly expressed his confidence in U.S. backing, and his intent to take advantage of it to close down those bases and to end Russia's influence in his country, in his address of April 19, 2005, to law students at Tbilisi State University. He stated, "This year, for the first time in 200 years, we [the Georgians] can resolve the issue of pulling the Russian troops out of Georgia and Georgia's de-occupation once and for all" (Eurasianet 2005). His statement reflected his government's ongoing negotiations with Moscow regarding the bases, which led to a subsequent agreement for their closure in 2008.

Apart from verbal attacks during the period 2004–2008, Moscow twice revealed its anger at the Georgian government, both times in 2006. Using its role as the major energy supplier to Tbilisi, Russia stopped supplying gas to Georgia, claiming inability as a result of an "accident" in the cold month of January. As this stoppage took place about a month after an intentional cutting of gas exports to Ukraine in December 2005, there was no doubt on the part of the Georgian government and those following the pace of events in Georgian-Russian relations that the event was a calculated move by Moscow. Although the stoppage ended in about a week—only when Iran started to supply gas to Georgia—the Russians used the event to reveal Georgia's weakness and their ability to punish Georgia at will, at least so long as it depends heavily on Russian gas. In a move resulting in major economic and financial consequences for Tbilisi, the Russians used their near-monopoly status to punish Georgia for the second time when they claimed health concerns and banned imports of Georgian wine in March 2006 (*Pravda* 2006). Wine exports to Russia were a major source of income for Georgia. In 2005, it exported to Russia $89 million worth of wine, accounting for 89 percent of its total wine exports (ibid.).

Facing the two Moscow-backed breakaway republics of Abkhazia and South Ossetia, since 2004 the Georgian government has hinted at regaining them by force, counting on U.S. support. In fact, President Saakashvili actually used the Georgian military to regain control of South Ossetia in August 2008, a miscalculated military bid that led to a highly destructive war with Russia, during which the Russian forces paralyzed the Georgian military and destroyed the bulk of Georgian military industry.

The Situation in Azerbaijan

The post-election era is no better in Azerbaijan in terms of political stability. The three major issues contributing to instability in that country—human rights abuses, rampant corruption, and territorial disputes with Armenia—have remained well in place, indicating no change for the better. The expanding opposition to President Aliyev, a reaction to the continuity of widespread corruption and human rights abuses and the manner in which he ascended to power, is surely a recipe for major social unrest and political instability, challenging the legitimacy and the survival of the Azeri regime. To this must be added the destabilizing effect of the unsettled dispute over Nagorno-Karabakh. This

THE LONG-TERM CONSEQUENCES OF THE GEORGIAN-RUSSIAN WAR

The August 2008 war between Georgia and Russia had major implications not only for the belligerents and the Caucasus but also for Russia's relations with the Western countries and their institutions. Undoubtedly, the war served as a catalyst severely damaging to the deteriorating Russian-Western relations, for in its aftermath, both sides accused each other of pursuing aggressive policies.

Accordingly, Russian authorities, including President Dmitri Medvedev and Foreign Minister Sergey Lavrov, accused Washington of instigating the war by building up the Georgian military, and by encouraging the Georgian government to launch the attack on South Ossetia on August 8, 2008. In particular, they characterized the attack as part of a U.S. policy to extend its influence in the ex-Soviet republics and encircle Russia. To a lesser extent, they also accused other Western countries and Israel of complicity by their arming of the Georgian military. Additionally, the Russian leaders considered the attack a consequence of NATO's eastward expansion to include the Caucasus by accepting Georgia's candidacy for future membership, an unacceptable scenario for Russia, which borders Georgia.

Russia's massive reaction to the Georgian attack on Tskhinvali prompted the angry reaction of the U.S. government and NATO, both of which described the Russian reaction as an act of aggression and a sign of rising Russian imperialism. NATO rejected the possibility of business as usual with Russia. That rejection met Russian president Medvedev's statement—"We do not need the illusion of partnership [with NATO]"—in his reference to NATO's hostile statements and its expansion to Russia's neighbors. Having canceled some cooperation with NATO, he declared Moscow's preparation to consider various scenarios, including "breaking off relations in full" with NATO.

The European Union (EU) failed to react as a bloc, with its members divided into two main camps: those who sided with Washington and those who refused to take a hostile stance toward Russia to avoid further worsening of EU-Russia relations. As a result, the EU members agreed only to facilitate a cease-fire and to send humanitarian aid to Georgia.

Certain Western actions further worsened Russian-Western relations after the war, including American vice president Dick Cheney's promise of Washington's backing for Georgia's NATO membership in late August, the mid-September session in Tbilisi of NATO's highest organ (North Atlantic Council), and the inaugural session of the NATO-Georgia commission. Such actions also include the use of military aircraft and naval vessels by the U.S. to deliver humanitarian aid to Georgia, a clear sign of their military support for Georgia, and the dispatch to the Black Sea by their allies (e.g., the United Kingdom, Germany, Spain, and Poland) of sufficient naval vessels to outnumber those of Russia.

Although a degree of improvement in Russian-Western relations is conceivable because of practical considerations, such as the importance to both sides of Russian oil and gas exports to the EU countries, the extent of their conflict of interest, as evident in the case of Georgia, will likely ensure further deterioration of those relations in the foreseeable future.

failure has kept about a million Azeris refugees in their own country for over a decade and a half, increasing their frustration with their dismal situation and thus their opposition to the status quo. Allowing their homes to remain under Armenian control is paving the way for another round of civil war.

Because of their impact on Azerbaijan's stability, three issues demand elaboration. The Azeri government has remained highly corrupt. As is the case in just about all the CIS countries, there are many reports of rampant corruption in Azerbaijan, including in its government (the security forces not excepted) as well as its private sector. One of the reliable sources writing extensively on this issue is the previously mentioned anti-corruption NGO, Transparency International. According to its annual report for 2004,

Ilham Aliyev followed in his father's footsteps as president of Azerbaijan in 2003. The presidential election was marred by reportedly widespread Soviet-style fraud and intimidation. (European Commission/Berlaymont)

the *Corruption Perception Index 2004,* covering the first three months of President Ilham Aliyev's term and the last nine months of his father's, Azerbaijan's corruption was "acute," on a par with a few other countries scoring less than 2 (1.9 for Azerbaijan) on a scale where 10 equals "clean" (Transparency International 2004). The publication reports that 14 oil exporting countries, including Azerbaijan, have extremely low scores. In these countries, the government's role in contracting in the oil sector results in corruption involving "western oil executives, middlemen and local officials" (ibid.). Based on the level of corruption in countries as presented in the *Corruption Perception Index 2004*, Azerbaijan ranked 140th of 145 (ibid). In the same NGO's most recent report, the *Corruption Perception Index 2008,* Azerbaijan ranks 158th of 180. In contrast to a "clean" score of 10, Azerbaijan scored 1.9, unchanged from 2004—demonstrating the depth of corruption in that country (Transparency International 2008).

Human rights abuses are still a major problem in Azerbaijan. Certain new realities have necessitated some limited improvements that have nonetheless not changed the overall poor human rights situation. For example, Azerbaijan's membership in the European Council has forced it to decrease the number of its political prisoners, but this has not ended that phenomenon once and for all (HRW 2006a). Nor has it changed the Azeri government's intolerance of political opposition and suppression of its opponents under various pretexts. Against a background of popular dissatisfaction with the Azeri elite dominated by the Aliyev family and friends, the orchestrated transfer of power from Haidar Aliyev to his son and all its necessary undemocratic actions, followed by the massive suppression of all opposition groups, further weakened the popular support and legitimacy of the Azeri political system. These actions have certainly contributed to expanding political dissent in a society already having many political, economic, and social reasons for unrest. Evidence for this conclusion may be seen in the extensive coverage by human rights organizations of human rights abuses targeting political opponents of the Azeri regime. In its 2006 report, Human Rights Watch, for instance, refers to such widespread human rights abuses in Azerbaijan as torture, police abuse, and excessive use of force by Azeri security forces (HRW 2006a). The report also refers to the "long-standing record" of Azerbaijan's government in pressuring opposition political parties and civil society groups (ibid.). Citing repression, harassment, and imprisonment of opposition party members, it elaborates on various government efforts to influence the 2005 parliamentary elections in its favor, including the intensification of a repressive environment surrounding those elections, turning them into anything but free and fair (ibid.). In 2008, evidence suggested continuity of the poor human rights situation. In its *World Report 2008,* Human Rights Watch summarizes Azerbaijan's human rights situation in 2007 as follows:

> The government continues to use defamation and other criminal charges to intimidate independent and opposition journalists, some of whom have also been assaulted by unknown men. Media freedoms rapidly deteriorated in 2007, with at least ten journalists imprisoned. High-profile government officials, businessmen, and opposition politicians remain in custody, and politically-motivated arrests and trials, torture in police custody, and conditions of detention remain unresolved

problems. Less than a year ahead of major presidential elections in Azerbaijan, the ground is set for an unfair presidential campaign. (HRW 2008a, para. 1)

Against this background, Azerbaijan's October 2008 presidential election could only be undemocratic, a secured and unchallenging election for President Ilham Aliyev. In fact, he easily won the election, among other factors, as many opposition parties boycotted it on the ground of the absence of the required conditions for a free and fair election.

Not only has the Ilham Aliyev government been unsuccessful in the domestic realm, it has failed to deal with its territorial conflict with the Armenians. After about six years of open conflict, a cease-fire in 1994 ended the devastating war over Nagorno-Karabakh without addressing its root causes. The cease-fire agreement—not a peace treaty—stopped the armed hostility and left about 20 percent of Azeri territory under Karabakhi Armenian control backed by Armenia. In addition to the tragic memories of the war and its high human cost, the occupation of Azeri land and its subsequent displacement of about 1 million Azeris as internal refugees have created grounds in Azerbaijan for the resumption of hostility.

The territorial dispute between Azerbaijan and Armenia over Nagorno-Karabakh has been not only a major source of tension in the bilateral relations of the two Caucasian neighbors, but also a major source of instability in the Caucasus. For different reasons, the status quo is unacceptable for both sides, particularly Azerbaijan, which has lost a significant part of its territory and has about 1 million internally displaced people. For Baku, to accept the status quo is to accept occupation, which undermines its territorial integrity. For the Karabakhi Armenians in control of the Azeri territory, an inability to receive international recognition for their self-declared state or to unify it with Armenia has been a source of frustration. Both sides are prepared to resort to war out of sheer frustration. Given the incompatibility of the two parties' positions, the territorial dispute over Nagorno-Karabakh has continued. Unless one side changes its position radically—something unlikely to happen in the foreseeable future—there is no prospect of a peace treaty settling the dispute once and for all.

If the current situation continues, the outbreak of another round of war is a strong possibility. The failure of peaceful means, including negotiations and international mediations, to settle the conflict in a mutually acceptable manner will leave the resort to arms as the only option. Such a war will not be in the best interests of the Azeris or the Armenians, and nor will it serve the interests of the Caucasus, which has had more than its fair share of conflict and war since the Soviet Union's collapse.

However, fear exists that the Azeri government, under pressure from the Azeri refugees and facing growing internal opposition and eroding legitimacy, could indeed resort to war. The government could try to use war as a means to temporarily address its threatening political fragility by provoking Azeri nationalism in a patriotic war. Such a war would surely destabilize the entire region, not just the belligerent parties, for it has great potential to involve certain regional (Iran, Turkey and Russia) and non-regional (the United States, and possibly the European Union) powers in some form.

CONCLUSION

The new pro-West ruling elites of Georgia and Azerbaijan have basically failed to remove the basis of instability by addressing their peoples' main sources of dissatisfaction, or at least by moving toward that end. They have also failed to resolve their territorial issues. The result is a fragile situation that could burst into popular discontent and also the resumption of civil war, for the separatists in both countries are also frustrated.

Within this context, elections as a means of creating legitimate and stable governments to help stabilize the countries, and of preparing grounds for addressing regional destabilizing conflicts, have contributed to the opposite in the Caucasus. Held under questionable (Azerbaijan) and extraordinary (Georgia) circumstances, the elections in Azerbaijan (2003) and Georgia (2004), perceived as signs of peaceful political transition at very sensitive junctures in their contemporary history, laid the foundation of future political instability in the form of intra- and interstate conflicts, an unintended objective of their organizers.

BIBLIOGRAPHY

Amnesty International. 2004a. "Azerbaijan." *Amnesty International Report 2004*. Amnesty International. http://web.amnesty.org/report2004/aze-summary-eng (accessed September 15, 2008).

Amnesty International. 2004b. *Azerbaijan: Political Opposition Leaders Must Receive Fair Trial*. May 4, 2004. AI Index: EUR 55/001/2004 (Public), News Service No. 113. London: Amnesty International. http://web.amnesty.org/library/Index/ENGEUR550012004?open&of=ENG-AZE (accessed September 15, 2008).

Amnesty International. 2004c. *Concerns in Europe and Central Asia: July to December 2003*. May 1, 2004. AI Index: EUR 01/001/2004. London: Amnesty International. http://web.amnesty.org/library/Index/ENGEUR010012004?open&of=ENG-AZE (accessed September 14, 2008).

Blank, Stephen. 2005. "Making Sense of the Shanghai Cooperation Organization's Astana Summit." *Central Asia–Caucasus Analyst*, July 27, 2005. www.cacianalyst.org/view_article.php?articleid=3504 (accessed September 14, 2008).

British Helsinki Human Rights Group. 2004. *Executive Summary: Presidential Election 4th January–Developments Following the Rose Revolution*. www.bhhrg.org/CountryReport.asp?ReportID=219&CountryID=10 (accessed September 18, 2008).

Eurasianet. 2005. "RFE/RL: Georgian President Anticipates Decision on Closure of Russian Bases This Year." *Georgia Daily Digest*. April 20, 2005. www.eurasianet.org/resource/georgia/hypermail/200504/0037.shtml (accessed on August 31, 2008).

Fuller, Elizabeth. 2008. "Despite Apparent Reelection, Saakashvili's Popularity Not High." *Council on Foreign Relations*, January 7, 2008. www.cfr.org/publication/15185/ (accessed October 2, 2008).

GlobalSecurity.org. 2003. *Military: Georgia Train and Equip Program* (GTEP). www.globalsecurity.org/military/ops/gtep.htm (accessed September 18, 2008).

Human Rights Watch (HRW). 2004a. *Azerbaijan: Government Launches Post-Election Crackdown*. New York: Human Rights Watch. January 23, 2004. http://hrw.org/english/docs/2004/01/23/azerba6992.htm (accessed September 21, 2008).

Human Rights Watch (HRW). 2004b. "Azerbaijan: Opposition Leaders Sentenced after Flawed Trial." New York: Human Rights Watch. October 27, 2004. http://hrw.org/english/docs/2004/10/26/azerba9565.htm (accessed September 21, 2008).

Human Rights Watch (HRW). 2004c. "Post-Election Violence." *Crushing Dissent: Repression, Violence and Azerbaijan's Elections.* New York: Human Rights Watch. January 1, 2004. http://hrw.org/reports/2004/azerbaijan0104/6.htm#_Toc61754935 (accessed September 12, 2008).

Human Rights Watch (HRW). 2005. "Georgia." *Human Rights Watch World Report 2005.* New York: Human Rights Watch. www.hrw.org/english/docs/2005/01/13/georgi9903.htm (accessed September 27, 2008).

Human Rights Watch (HRW). 2006a. "Azerbaijan." *Human Rights Watch World Report 2006.* New York: Human Rights Watch. http://hrw.org/english/docs/2006/01/18/azerba12226.htm (accessed September 18, 2008).

Human Rights Watch (HRW). 2006b. "Georgia." *Human Rights Watch World Report 2006.* New York: Human Rights Watch. http://hrw.org/english/docs/2006/01/18/georgi12229.htm (accessed September 27, 2008).

Human Rights Watch (HRW). 2008a. "Azerbaijan." *Human Rights Watch World Report 2008.* New York: Human Rights Watch. http://hrw.org/englishwr2k8/docs/2008/01/31/azerba17742.htm (accessed October 3, 2008).

Human Rights Watch (HRW). 2008b. "Georgia." *Human Rights Watch World Report 2008.* New York: Human Rights Watch. http://hrw.org/englishwr2k8/docs/2008/01/31/georgi17743.htm (accessed October 3, 2008).

Jibladze, Kakha. 2005. "Georgia: The Honeymoon Is Over." *Central Asia and Caucasus Analyst* (Baltimore), May 4, 2005. www.cacianalyst.org/view_article.php?articleid=3285 (accessed September 27, 2008).

Myers, Joel. 2005. "Saakashvili on the Ropes?" *Central Asia and Caucasus Analyst* (Baltimore), May 4, 2005. www.cacianalyst.org/view_article.php?articleid=3279 (accessed September 27, 2008).

Pravda. 2006. "Grapes of Wrath: Russian Wine Ban for Georgia, Moldova." April 7, 2006. http://english.pravda.ru/news/world/78917-0/ (accessed September 12, 2008).

Rasulzade, Zaur. 2004. "Seven Opposition Leaders Convicted." *Caucasian Knot*, October 22, 2004. http://eng.kavkaz.memo.ru/news/?srch_section1=engnews&srch_section2=azerb_repressii (accessed September 20, 2008).

Transparency International. 2004. *Corruption Perception Index 2004.* October 20, 2004. London: Transparency International. http://ww1.transparency.org/pressreleases_archive/2004/2004.10.20.cpi.en.html (accessed September 15, 2008).

Transparency International. 2005. *Corruption Perception Index 2005.* October 18, 2005. London: Transparency International. http://ww1.transparency.org/cpi/2005/cpi2005_infocus.html (accessed September 15, 2008).

Transparency International. 2008. *Corruption Perception Index 2008.* September 23, 2008. London: Transparency International. www.icgg.org/downloads/CPI_2008.xls (accessed October 3, 2008).

U.S. Department of State. 2004. "Azerbaijan." *Country Reports on Human Rights Practices–2003.* February 25, 2004. Bureau of Democracy, Human Rights, and Labor. Washington, D.C.: U.S. Department of State. www.state.gov/g/drl/rls/hrrpt/2003/27826.htm (accessed September 21, 2008).

U.S. Department of State. 2006. *Background Note: Azerbaijan.* Washington, D.C.: U.S. Department of State. www.state.gov/r/pa/ei/bgn/2909.htm (accessed September 21, 2008).

THE GEORGIAN-RUSSIAN WAR OF AUGUST 2008

The Georgian government's bid in August 2008 to restore its sovereignty over the breakaway republic of South Ossetia rapidly developed into a devastating war between Georgia and Russia. On August 8, the Georgian military attacked the South Ossetian capital of Tskhinvali and initially made advances. However, in a day, the Russian military's intervention in South Ossetia's favor reversed the process quickly. Not only did the Russian troops repel the Georgian forces from South Ossetia, they launched a major land, naval, and aerial operation inside Georgia to punish the Georgian government. Many Georgian military facilities and industries were destroyed during the course of this operation. The Russian military also advanced inside Georgia to occupy the Georgian territories in the proximity of Abkhazia and South Ossetia, in addition to other parts of the country, including the Black Sea port of Poti and the city of Gori. Meanwhile, the Abkhaz military, enjoying Russian support, pushed the Georgian forces back from the only part of the breakaway republic of Abkhazia under Georgian control, the Khodori Gorge. Officially, the war ended on August 12, when Tbilisi and Moscow agreed to a European Union (EU) cease-fire negotiated by EU rotational president being French president, Nicholas Sarkozy. However, practically it continued at lesser intensity at least for another week during which both Georgia and Russia accused each other of violating the cease-fire.

Reportedly, the cease-fire agreement provided for the total withdrawal of the Russian troops from Georgia and the two breakaway republics but allowed a small Russian peacekeeping contingent to remain in each republic. Yet, Russia's failure to withdraw prompted a new round of negotiation between President Sarkozy and his Russian and Georgian counterparts, leading to another agreement on September 8, 2008. Accordingly, Russia would withdraw its forces from Georgia within a month while leaving military units larger than merely peacekeeping ones in Abkhazia and South Ossetia (a 4,000-strong unit in each) to deter any future Georgian attack on them. However, Russia clearly subjected its full withdrawal to Georgia's signing a nonaggression pact with Abkhazia and South Ossetia, while stressing as "irreversible" its August 2008 recognition of Abkhazia's and South Ossetia's declared independence and its military support for them. Regardless of whether or not Russia's full withdrawal from Georgia could take place in the near future, the depth of hostility between Moscow and Tbilisi and their blatant conflicting interests suggest major upheavals in Georgian-Russian relations, including possible armed conflicts of various scales and scopes in the foreseeable future.

effectively stopping oil and gas exports for an unpredictable period. In fact, although British Petroleum (BP) denied any damage to its pipelines passing through Georgia during the August conflict, it accepted the closure of its major pipelines for unspecified reasons (Fineren 2008). These include the closure of the Western Route Export Pipeline (WREP), which transports crude oil from Baku to the Georgian Black Sea port of Supsa, and the stoppage of gas pumping from Azerbaijan's Shah Deniz field into the South Caucasus pipeline connecting Azerbaijan to Turkey via Tbilisi. BP attributed the closure of its main oil pipeline, the Baku-Tbilisi-Ceyhan, which links Azerbaijan to Turkey via Georgia, to "a fire."

In the best of times, exporting through the Caucasus is not an ideal choice, and even less so these days, in the wake of the Georgian-Russian war. Yet, because U.S. opposition to the Iranian route is especially strong today (2009), the Caucasus is the only remaining option to total dependency on Russia. Yet, large and long-term exports via the Caucasus require the construction of a very expensive and difficult-to-maintain undersea oil pipeline to connect Central Asia and the Caucasus, which are separated by the Caspian Sea.

Any land pipeline would have to pass through either Russia or Iran, each of which borders two regions in the north and the south, respectively. Even though an onshore pipeline is out of the question for the aforementioned reasons, there is no serious plan for a (predictably) very expensive offshore pipeline—a very controversial project because of prospects of its obvious environmental damage to the already highly damaged environment of the Caspian Sea. To this should be added the fierce opposition of Iran and Russia to such a pipeline, not just because of the predictable environmental hazards but also because it would undermine their national interests, depriving them of oil and gas exports through their countries.

Currently, Central Asian oil exports via the Caucasus are limited to small oil tankers operating between the two regions. However, the United States, whose oil companies dominate the Caspian oil industry, has been trying to convince the Central Asians to increase their exports via the Caucasus. Washington's already-discussed objective is to bypass Iran and Russia by offering the Caspian oil exporters an alternative export route.

PIPELINE PROJECTS: POLITICAL AND ECONOMIC SIGNIFICANCE

The potential of the Caucasus as a transit route has justified the construction of pipelines through it. Chief among these in terms of both political and economic significance is the Baku-Tbilisi-Ceyhan oil pipeline (BTC). Capable of handling 1 million barrels of oil per day, the controversial $3.7-billion pipeline project, the idea for which emerged in the 1990s, finally became a reality on May 25, 2005, when its construction was completed (hydrocarbons-technology.com 2006). Operational on July 13, 2006, the 1,768-kilometer pipeline connects Azerbaijan's oil fields to Turkey's Mediterranean port of Ceyhan via Georgia, connecting the two countries by land.

The BTC is a blatant example of the policy of bypassing Iran and Russia for Caspian oil exports. In particular, the U.S.-backed pipeline project is meant to eliminate Iran as a logical export route for neighboring Azerbaijan and to weaken its presence in Azerbaijan's oil industry, as a means (among others) of eventually excluding Iran from the strategically important Caucasus. Among other purposes, U.S. pressure

A crude oil jetty of the Baku-Tbilisi-Ceyhan pipeline in Yumurtalik, Turkey. Provided its operation is not interrupted by sabotage, as it has been in the past, the pipeline can transport one million barrels of oil a day from Azerbaijan's Caspian capital of Baku via Georgia to Turkey's Mediterranean oil terminal in Ceyhan. (Yoray Liberman/Getty Images)

on the Central Asian oil exporters to use the BTC for their oil exports also aims at denying Iran economic and political gains in Central Asia by making its territory available to the Central Asians as an export route. It is no surprise that the BTC is a potential source of dispute for Iran in its relations with Azerbaijan, Georgia, and Turkey, through which the pipeline passes.

For the aforementioned reasons, the BTC is currently the most important pipeline of the Caucasus. Of course, there are a few other, shorter pipelines either existing or under construction in that region. Many of them are primarily meant to facilitate Azerbaijan's exports, such as the Baku-Supsa pipeline and the Baku-Novorossiysk pipeline, which connect Azerbaijan's oil fields to the Georgian and Russian Black Sea ports, respectively. However, certain factors provide for the construction of other pipelines of significance, including the following.

Pipeline to Armenia

Armenia and Georgia's lack of major fossil energy resources forces them to rely on large energy imports. For example, Georgia imports 9 million cubic meters of gas per day from Russia. This makes the Caucasus a point of attraction for regional energy exporters, especially gas exporters, because of the various difficulties the two countries have experienced in securing Russian gas. This situation has practically started a quiet competition between Iran and Russia over supplying these Caucasian states, providing them with revenues but also with political influence. Within this context, Russia's loss of market enables Iran, which has abundant oil and gas resources, to fill the gap as a neighboring state with friendly ties to both Georgia and Armenia. Moreover, the geographical location of the Caucasus as a land link between Asia and Europe offers Iran an opportunity to use the region for energy exports to Europe via pipeline, a way to end its current reliance on Turkey for any such project in the future. Because conflicts and wars in the Caucasus can remove such opportunities altogether, Iran has a large stake in the region's stability. Among many other factors, including Iran's friendly relations with Georgia despite the latter's pro-American orientation, and its concerns about Russia's resurgence, notwithstanding their current friendly relations, concern about long-term instability in the Caucasus motivated Iran not to side with Russia in its August 2008 war with Georgia. Iranian foreign affairs minister Manouchehr Mottaki's visit to Tbilisi after the war, when Moscow was seeking Georgia's isolation, manifested Iran's stakes in the stability of the Caucasus (IRNA 2008).

Certain pipeline projects in the Caucasus have the potential to become major. These include the Iran-Armenia pipeline supplying Armenia with Iranian gas. The 142-kilometer pipeline, of which 42 kilometers are laid in Armenia, was inaugurated in March 2007 (IRNA 2007). Through the pipeline connecting the Iranian gas export infrastructure near the Iranian city of Tabriz to the Iranian-Armenian border and thence to Armenia, Iran supplied its neighbor with as much as 1.1 billion cubic meters of natural gas in the pipeline's first year. However, the pipeline is now capable of handling more than twice as much, enabling Iran to export at least 36 billion cubic meters of gas to Armenia over a 20-year period. Thanks to completion of its second phase in September 2008, Armenia will annually receive between 2.3 and 2.5 billion cubic meters of Iranian gas from 2009 onward (UPI.com 2008).

The $220-million project addresses Armenia's heavy dependence on Russia for its gas imports by means of a neighbor friendly to Armenia. This is especially important for Yerevan in 2009, for it is fully aware of the tension-prone Georgian-Russian relations that have existed since 1991. In particular, in the post–Georgian-Russian war era, Georgia's hostile ties with Russia, which will probably last for a long time, make it unwise for Armenia to depend on Russian gas supplies only available via Georgia bordering both Russia and Armenia. Gas is provided through the Iran-Armenia pipeline on terms favorable to Armenia, as Yerevan pays for it with electricity generated by the fifth unit of the Armenian Hirazdan power station, which is constructed and fully financed by Iran (Peimani 2004).

Moreover, the pipeline can be connected through a short link to Georgia and can even be extended to Ukraine via Russia or the Black Sea, a project in which both Tbilisi and Kiev have expressed interest, to rid themselves from heavy reliance on Russia for piped gas. Washington's opposition aside, the Georgians and the Ukrainians must be very much interested in the project now, as the Georgian-Russian war of 2008 and deteriorating Russian-Ukrainian relations make Iran a very plausible energy supplier for both nations.

political, and security reasons. Such exports would change their status from that of net gas importers to include that of transit hosts as well and would generate long-term annual revenues in transit fees for them. In turn, those revenues would help finance their imports from Iran, and the construction, operation, and eventual expansion and modernization of the gas export infrastructure, including the required pipelines, would create long-term employment opportunities and additional income. Being on the gas export transit route would also give Iran and Ukraine stakes in their security and stability. Connecting the Iranian-Ukrainian pipeline to Central and Western Europe in the future would also create stakes for the EU in their security while providing more income for Armenia and Georgia as well as Ukraine. Because the Georgian-Russian war of August 2008 made the EU wary about its heavy dependency on Russia as a gas and oil supplier and made it especially urgent to find alternative suppliers (something heralded by British prime minister Gordon Brown), the EU should be interested in Iranian gas exports to Europe via Ukraine, despite its troubled relations with Iran. However, an improvement in these relations will be a prerequisite for such exports to become a reality.

In light of the growing hostility between Iran and the United States, the U.S. effort to deny Iran any major economic gain in its foreign relations, and Kiev's recent political shift towards the United States, it is a little too early to speculate on the implementation in the near future of the Iranian-Ukrainian gas pipeline.

Other Significant Pipelines

In the Caucasus, another major project is a gas pipeline connecting Azerbaijan to Turkey via Georgia (442 km in Azerbaijan and 248 km in Georgia). The South Caucasus Pipeline (SCP), also known as the Shah Deniz Pipeline, links Azerbaijan's Caspian gas field of Shah Deniz to Turkey's gas pipeline network near its border with Georgia to initially supply customers in Azerbaijan, Georgia, and Turkey (Kildrummy 2006). Because of the limited capacity of Turkey for additional imported gas—resulting from its lower-than-expected economic growth (and thus demand for gas), coupled with its overcommitment to gas suppliers, including Iran, Russia, Algeria, Turkmenistan, and Azerbaijan—Turkey is expected to eventually function mainly as an export route for Azeri gas. The $1 billion pipeline, construction of which began in the fourth quarter of 2004, became operational in July 2007 (Peimani 2007, 14). Constructed in the same corridor as the BTC, the SCP is capable of carrying up to 7 billion cubic meters of gas each year, with the possibility of doubling its capacity in the future. However, many technical problems have so far resulted in numerous closures.

OBSTACLES TO CAUCASIAN PROSPECTS

As discussed earlier, the region has the potential to benefit from oil as an exporter and a transit route, but that hinges on a major prerequisite: durable peace and security to ensure continued oil exportation from and through the Caucasus. However, the region and all its constituent states contain sources of inter- and intrastate instability that could spill over to neighboring powers or drag them into armed conflicts in one form or another, serving only to expand them.

The Resurgence and Expansion of Civil War

Armenia, Azerbaijan, and Georgia experienced major armed conflicts upon independence. In Georgia, the rise of the two breakaway republics of South Ossetia and Abkhazia instigated bloody civil wars that ended in their practical, but not official, independence, as cease-fire agreements ended the conflicts in 1992 and 1993, respectively. Armenia and Azerbaijan found themselves on hostile terms as a dispute over independence from Azerbaijan of the Armenian-dominated Nagorno-Karabakh region (backed by Armenia) that had begun in the Soviet era (1988) escalated into a civil war after independence. Another cease-fire agreement ended the conflict in 1994, leaving 20 percent of Azeri territory under the control of Nagorno-Karabakh's Armenian separatists. Owing to a prevalent sense of dissatisfaction with the status quo on both sides of the conflicts in all three Caucasian countries, instability could well engulf the region. The fact that their armed conflicts have been ended by cease-fire agreements, and not peace treaties addressing root causes, has been alarming. Such unsettled conflicts could lead—and if the current situation continues, likely will lead—to another round of civil wars.

In particular, this is true for the unresolved territorial dispute between Armenia and Azerbaijan over Nagorno-Karabakh. The frustration of both sides could lead to the resumption of civil war, pitting the Azeris against the Karabakhi Armenians and escalating into a war between Armenia and Azerbaijan, both of which share borders with Iran. The Iranians could not be indifferent to such a war, for many reasons, including their ethnic ties with both countries and the possible expansion of the war to Iranian territory adjacent to those countries. Moreover, even in the absence of such expansion, this scenario would create serious challenges to Iran's border security, including an expected flow of arms into Iran. The inflow of war refugees would also be a source of concern for the Iranians, for its financial costs as well as the security implications of the predictable smuggling of weapons and drugs into Iran from the belligerent countries and its possible radicalizing impact on the Iranians.

Furthermore, a new round of intra- and interstate wars in the Caucasus, whether they involved Azerbaijan and Georgia or engaged the Georgian government and its breakaway republics of Abkhazia and South Ossetia, could—and likely would—involve other regional powers (Russia and Turkey) and a nonregional power (the United States). Against a background of growing dissatisfaction among the regional peoples with their ruling governments, intra- and interstate wars could therefore engulf the entire Caucasus, where a variety of unresolved ethnic and territorial issues have prepared grounds for such expansion—as has the existence of Azeris, Armenians, and Georgians as minorities in their non-native regional countries. Because Iran could not remain impartial in a military conflict along its borders or near the regions that border it, Iran, too, would become involved, quite possibly

Energy Information Administration. 2005a. *Country Analysis Brief: Azerbaijan.* Washington, D.C.: Energy Information Administration. June 2005. www.eia.doe.gov/emeu/cabs/azerbjan.html (accessed September 15, 2008).

Energy Information Administration. 2005b. *Country Analysis Brief: Kazakhstan.* Washington, D.C.: Energy Information Administration. July 2005. www.eia.doe.gov/emeu/cabs/kazak.html (accessed August 30, 2008).

Energy Information Administration. 2006a. *Country Analysis Brief: Caspian Sea–Oil.* Washington, D.C.: Energy Information Administration. www.eia.doe.gov/emeu/cabs/Caspian/Oil.html (accessed August 30, 2008).

Energy Information Administration. 2006b. *Country Analysis Brief: Iran–Oil.* January 2006. www.eia.doe.gov/emeu/cabs/Iran/Oil.html (accessed August 30, 2008).

Energy Information Administration. 2007. *Country Analysis Brief: Caspian Sea.* Washington, D.C.: Energy Information Administration. January 2007. www.eia.doe.gov/cabs/Caspian/Full.html (accessed August 30, 2008).

Eurasianet. 2005. "RFE/RL: Georgian President Anticipates Decision on Closure of Russian Bases This Year." *Georgia Daily Digest.* April 20, 2005. www.eurasianet.org/resource/georgia/ hypermail/200504/0037.shtml (accessed on August 31, 2008).

Eurasianet. 2007. "Georgia Shows Interest in Iran-Armenia Gas Pipeline." *Energy Bulletin.* May 2007. www.cere.gr/upload/ENERGY%20BULLETIN-may%202007.pdf (accessed October 1, 2008).

Fineren, Daniel. 2008. "Conflict Stems Georgia Oil, Gas Pipeline Flows." Reuters. August 12, 2008. http://uk.reuters.com/article/gc07/idUKLC53581720080812 (accessed September 10, 2008).

hydrocarbons-technology.com. 2006. "Baku-Tbilisi-Ceyhan (BTC) Caspian Pipeline." www.hydrocarbons-technology.com/projects/bp/ (accessed August 25, 2008).

Islamic Republic News Agency (IRNA). 2007. "Iran-Armenia Gas Pipeline Inaugurated." March 19, 2007. http://www2.orna.ir/en/news/view/line18/0703190191144210.htm (accessed October 3, 2008).

Kildrummy Technologies Ltd. 2006. *The South Caucasus Pipeline (SCP).* www.kildrummy.com/ about/casestudy.asp?csid=2 (accessed May 3, 2008).

Mossavar-Rahmani, Bijan. 2000. "The Challenge of the U.S. Caspian Sea Oil Policy." *Motaellat-e Asyaie Markazi va Ghafghaz* [Central Asia and the Caucasus Review] 28 (Winter): 45–60. Quoted in Peimani, Hooman. 2001. *The Caspian Pipeline Dilemma: Political Games and Economic Losses.* Westport, CT: Praeger.

Islamic Republic News Agency (IRNA). 2008. "Mottaki: Tehran Closely Following Up Caucasus Events." September 17, 2008. http://www1.irna.ir/en/news/view/line-17/0809172789195647.htm (accessed October 3, 2008).

Parsons, Robert. 2006. "Caucasus: Georgia, Armenia Consider Options after Russia Pipeline Explosions." *Radio Free Europe/Radio Liberty (RFE/RL),* February 1, 2006. www.referl.org/ featuresarticle/2006/02/d2074170-d820-4948-812e-69551d17c950.html (accessed April 29, 2008).

Peimani, Hooman. 2003. "Light at the End of Baku-Asghabad Tunnel?" *Central Asia-Caucasus Analyst.* July 16, 2003. www.cacianalyst.org/view_article.php?articleid=1571 (accessed May 8, 2008).

Peimani, Hooman. 2004. "The Iran-Armenia Pipeline: Finally Coming to Life." *Central Asia–Caucasus Analyst.* September 22, 2004. www.cacianalyst.org/issues/20040922Analyst.pdf (accessed May 10, 2008).

Peimani, Hooman. 2005. "Georgia and Ukraine: Buying Iranian Gas?" *Central Asia–Caucasus Analyst.* April 6, 2005. www.cacianalyst.org/view_article.php?articleid=3197 (accessed May 7, 2008).

Peimani, Hooman. 2007. "A Global Update." *World Pipelines* 7, no. 12 (December 2007), 12–19.

Shchedrov, Oleg, and Yuri Kulikov. "Russia and Ukraine to Meet for Gas Talks." Reuters, January 15, 2009. http://uk.news.yahoo.com/22/20090115/tpl-uk-russia-ukraine-gas-02bfc7e_9.html (accessed January 28, 2009).

UPI.com. September 12, 2008. "Work on Iran-Armenia pipeline concludes." www.upi.com/Energy_Resources/2008/09/12/Work_on_Iran-Armenia_pipeline_concludes/UPI-57451221254449/ (accessed January 28, 2009).

Upstreamonline.com. 2007. "Russian Flows via Belarus Halted." January 8, 2007. www.upstreamonline.com/live/europe/article125800.ece (accessed September 9, 2008).

Chapter 5

Major Trends of Significance to Long-Term Stability in Central Asia

The five Central Asian countries (Kazakhstan, Kyrgyzstan, Tajikistan, Turkmenistan, and Uzbekistan) gained independence in 1991 after about two centuries of rule by Moscow under the Russian tsars and the Soviet leaders. Gaining and losing in terms of strength and popularity, and expanding and contracting geographically, anti-Russian, nationalist, and independence movements characterized a good number of years of this period. In the first two decades of the Soviet era, the Soviet Red Army brutally crushed such movements, which, at a high price, brought about seven decades of peace and stability for Central Asia, ending when the demise of the Soviet Union opened the gates to the rise of destabilizing factors. Despite this reality, not all the Central Asian states have experienced major destabilizing conflicts, armed or otherwise, internally or externally caused. So far, Tajikistan has experienced a five-year civil war (1992–1997), ended by a peace treaty that has largely held, and Kyrgyzstan has survived the Yellow Revolution (2005). Uzbekistan has encountered limited armed struggle, with potential for expansion, waged by the extremist Islamic Movement of Uzbekistan (IMU). Tajikistan and Kyrgyzstan have also suffered, to an extent, from conflict with the IMU, which has been fought in the Ferghana Valley, a region shared by Uzbekistan, Tajikistan, and Kyrgyzstan. However, despite the absence of significant armed conflict or even destabilizing forces in Kazakhstan and Turkmenistan, and the overall limited nature of instability and conflict in Central Asia's recent past, evidence suggest that the future may be turbulent and unstable. This is because in spite of their differences in terms of area, population, mineral and energy resources, and degree of achievement in addressing their numerous Soviet-inherited problems since independence, the prevailing trend has been a negative one in the political, economic, and social spheres of all the Central Asian countries. After the establishment of authoritarian regimes, their ruling elites have been unable to address most of the numerous and ever-increasing problems. If the current negative trend continues, Central Asia will likely head toward long-term tension and instability affecting not only peace and security in the region but also its social, political, and economic development. In turn, this will only ensure a fragile social and political environment conducive to instability.

RECENT ALARMING SIGNS

The signs of this bleak future have been particularly evident since the beginning of the twenty-first century. In addition to the unsettled political, economic, and social issues that ignited the destructive Tajik civil war (being capable of fomenting another round of civil war, not necessarily with the same actors on the opposition side), certain recent major incidents have left no doubt about the feasibility of this scenario in the foreseeable future. Two blatant cases of this nature took place in 2005: Kyrgyzstan's Yellow Revolution in March, and the May armed conflict in Uzbekistan's Andijan region.

The Yellow (Tulip) Revolution

Kyrgyzstan's February 27, 2005, parliamentary elections were far from free and fair, according to Kyrgyz opposition groups. Led by President Askar Akayev, who was known to head a corrupt and undemocratic regime, the Kyrgyz government ignored the allegations of fraud only to provoke protests, including demonstrations, that led to the government's practical loss of control of most parts of southern Kyrgyzstan (Telekova 2005). Despite its efforts, the Kyrgyz government failed to end the protests, which expanded to the capital, Bishkek, and continued in March. On March 24, a group of demonstrators estimated at about 20,000 demanded the resignation of President Akayev and marched toward and subsequently captured the Kyrgyz presidential palace, the White House (Kobonbaev 2005). The president had left about half an hour earlier along with many other senior politicians, but the rest of his staff were beaten by the angry crowd, which was afterward addressed by Kurmanbek Bakiev, one of the opposition leaders. He heralded the end of the Akayev era and declared that the people were in charge of the government (ibid.). Known as the Yellow Revolution because the opposition supporters chose yellow as their identifying color, this event did not bring about a radical change and was mainly limited to a change of ruling figures. The limited efforts made by the security forces to prevent the protestors from advancing and capturing the White House, and the resulting ease of the capture, raised questions about the revolution's true nature. This reality lent credence to rumors that security forces had collaborated with the opposition leaders, including Bakiev, who were mainly former high-ranking officials of the Akayev administration. The new government has yet to embark on a program to address the root causes of the revolution: rampant corruption within the ruling elite and government institutions, major economic problems, poverty, inequality, and human rights abuses. The recurrence of mass street protests in 2006 in Kyrgyzstan, including in Bishkek, and their continuity in 2007, 2008, and early 2009, indicate growing popular dissatisfaction with the unfulfilled promises and the county's political and social fragility, preparing the ground for future instability (HRW 2006–2008).

The Andijan Incident

On May 13, 2005, certain disputed anti-government activities led to a massive crackdown in Andijan, a city in Uzbekistan's part of the Ferghana Valley. The incident left about 200 "terrorists" (according to the Uzbek government) or hundreds of "people" (according to opposition/human rights sources) dead. Yet, it is certain that the arrest and trial of respected local businessmen created a defiant mood among the people. On May 13, both popular protests of disputed extent and antigovernment violent activities occurred in Andijan, including the attack and seizure of the government building and the prison, the killing of government security personnel, and hostage-taking by antigovernment individuals of unknown political affiliation. Reportedly, they set free hundreds of prisoners. However, although the Uzbek government described the incident as a well-calculated "terrorist operation" to destabilize the Ferghana Valley, during which scores of Uzbek security forces and people were attacked, disarmed, wounded, and killed and "terrorists" were released from a captured prison, opposition and human rights groups reported the "massacre" by the security forces of "unarmed protestors" demonstrating against the government (HRW 2006b). However, the latter also do acknowledge that some unknown armed opposition activists committed violence against government property and security forces (ibid.). The Uzbek government reserves the term *terrorist* for members of two banned extremist groups, the Islamic Movement of Uzbekistan (IMU) and Hizb ut-Tahrir (Liberation Party). The real nature and extent of the Andijan incident are a matter of disagreement, and both the Uzbek

A local man in Andijan's central square gestures next to the bodies of victims from clashes between Uzbek government forces and "terrorists" (as described by the Uzbek government) or "local protesters" (the term used by Western sources) on May 14, 2005. (Denis Sinyakov/AFP/Getty Images)

government and the human rights/opposition groups may have exaggerated their accounts. Yet, it is noteworthy that a scholarly account suggests that the incident was initiated by "armed, trained insurgents, some of them came from outside Uzbekistan" and that the death toll was closer to the Uzbek government's estimate (Akiner 2005, 10). Stressing the purely political nature of the event, this source views it as the "opening phase of a coup d'etat, on the lines of the Kyrgyz model" (ibid.).

The Uzbek government immediately restored order to Andijan. However, the seeds of conflict are still there. Poverty and unemployment provide grounds for the rise of popular dissatisfaction in various forms, which could lead to mass movements. Harsh suppression of the incident against a background of 18 years of authoritarianism tolerating no sign of dissent have created a fragile social situation on which extremist groups, including armed ones, could capitalize. Hence, riots and armed conflicts such as the Andijan incident are distinct possibilities. The decade-long armed opposition of the IMU, despite its severe suppression and current limited activities, substantiates this claim.

Implications for Central Asia

The Yellow Revolution of Kyrgyzstan revealed the fragility of the Central Asian states and their vulnerability to the sudden rise and expansion of popular opposition. The latter has made all the Central Asian regimes concerned about the possibility of a duplication of the Kyrgyz "revolution" in their countries, and consequently all have sought to prevent it by further consolidating their authoritarian regimes. Ironically, the same concern is shared by the "revolutionary" Kyrgyz government, whose grip on power is very weak because of the rapid erosion of its popular base, a result of its demonstrated inability to embark on a program to deal with the root causes of the Yellow Revolution.

The Andijan incident alarmed not only the Uzbek government but other Central Asian governments as well. The situation is ripe in their countries for the rise of possibly violent opposition. In particular, sudden armed anti-government activities are distinct possibilities in just about all of them, especially Kyrgyzstan, Tajikistan, and Uzbekistan. The three states have armed groups in their shared Ferghana Valley and have experienced periods of armed conflict in the valley; Tajikistan also suffered from a five-year-long civil war in the 1990s that engulfed the entire country. Reported and assessed differently by the Uzbek government and others, the Uzbek government's bloody suppression of those involved in the Andijan incident, during which hundreds were allegedly killed and hundreds arrested, prompted criticism for use of excessive force not only by human rights organizations but by the U.S. government and the European Union (EU). The EU demanded a foreign-led inquiry, a demand rejected immediately by the Uzbek government. The Uzbek government has hinted at U.S. involvement as a force behind the incident, an allegation rejected by Washington. Regardless of the real role of the American government, the Uzbek authorities, rightly or wrongly, blame Washington. Hence they requested the closure of the U.S. air base in Uzbekistan within six months; this was completed in November 2005 (VOA 2005). The alleged U.S. role through U.S. NGOs has since resulted in Washington's weakening political influence in Central Asia, as evidenced by the regional countries' expanding relations with Russia, China, and Iran.

OTHER SOURCES OF CONFLICT

Widespread corruption and undemocratic rule are not the only contributing factors to armed conflicts and instability. To such factors should be added many ethnic grievances (e.g., between the Tajiks and Uzbeks in Tajikistan; among the Kyrgyz, the Uzbeks, and the Tajiks in Kyrgyzstan), territorial and border disagreements (such as between Tajikistan and Uzbekistan), and disputes over division of the water of the main regional rivers, the Amu Darya and the Syr Darya, among the five regional countries. These factors will likely create a suitable ground for new conflicts and territorial disputes in violent forms, apart from the extensive U.S. military presence in Central Asia, with its potential to provoke popular opposition. For a number of reasons, many of these could escalate to civil wars and interstate wars. Among other factors, the ethnic makeup of Central Asia—that is, the existence of large ethnic minorities in each country with ties to their kin in a neighboring state where they form the majority—and the persistence of many sources of conflict between the regional states (e.g., between Uzbekistan and Tajikistan) will pave the way for their further escalation to the level of regional wars despite the intention of their initiators.

MAJOR REGIONAL TRENDS OF SIGNIFICANCE FOR PEACE AND STABILITY

Certain trends in Central Asia will have a significant impact on its security and stability in the foreseeable future. Should the current situation continue, they will contribute to conflict and instability in the region, affecting all the regional countries in one form or another. The major trends discussed in the following sections are political, economic, social, and security-related.

Political Trends

The end of the Soviet regime and the creation of independent states in Central Asia created expectations for a transition from the Soviet totalitarian regime to a democratic political system, both inside Central Asia among its peoples, and outside the region. However, 18 years after independence, it is quite clear that all five Central Asian governments have opted for an undemocratic style of statecraft. At the time of independence, none of them aimed at democratizing their societies—which would have required, among other things, the democratization of the political system—although there were differences among them in terms of their tolerance of political dissent. In a comparative sense, Kazakhstan and Kyrgyzstan were more democratic and tolerant than the other Central Asian countries. Despite initial differences and the existence of differences even today, all the Central Asian countries, without exception,

KYRGYZSTAN: ANOTHER REVOLUTION IN THE PIPE

The Yellow (Tulip) Revolution of March 2005 ended the era of President Askar Akayev but failed to address the root causes of popular dissatisfaction. The administration of his successor, President Kurmanbek Bakiev, not only has done little to change the unacceptable situation for the majority of the Kyrgyz, it has actually replicated the same method of government as its predecessor's, characterized by extensive corruption, lack of transparency, human rights abuses by security forces, and repression of opposition parties and individuals. The massive anti-government demonstrations in major Kyrgyz cities in 2004 and 2005 that eventually led to the change of power on March 24, 2005, subsided for only a few months. The disillusionment of the Kyrgyz with the new government gave rise to another round of anti-government demonstrations in mid-2005. Such activities have since continued to engulf the major urban areas. In particular, their expansion in 2006 indicated the Kyrgyz people's diminishing tolerance of the new government and their movement toward ending the "revolutionary" government incapable of fulfilling their demands. Various types of expression of opposition to the Kyrgyz government, including mass demonstrations, continued in different Kyrgyz cities, including the capital city of Bishkek, in 2007, 2008, and early 2009. Unless the Kyrgyz government changes its course, there is little doubt that another "revolution" will occur, destabilizing Kyrgyzstan and possibly sending shock waves through its neighboring states, whose populations are more or less equally dissatisfied but currently quiet.

are heading toward consolidation of their authoritarian rule. This also includes the new administration in Kyrgyzstan, which came to power in March 2005 when Kyrgyz president Askar Akayev was forced to leave for Russia upon the outbreak of the Yellow Revolution. Despite claims to the contrary, evidence does not suggest that the new administration led by President Kurmanbek Bakiev is pursuing a type of governance qualitatively different from that of his predecessor. He presides over the same political and bureaucratic systems inherited from his predecessor while showing no serious interest in addressing their shortcomings and corruption. Consequently, all the regional countries and their ruling elites, despite their differences, are consolidating their authoritarian regimes. Predictably, this policy will lead to further expansion of human rights abuses and alienation of their peoples, apart from its negative impact on the economic development of their countries resulting from the perpetuation of mainly corrupt and inefficient Central Asian bureaucracies. Against a background of dismal economic growth and rampant poverty, and in the absence of any major effort to change this reality, their societies are moving in the direction of polarization along political, economic, and social lines to pit a growing economically and politically dissatisfied people in every Central Asian country against an authoritarian regime with a shrinking social base. This is a recipe for instability, conflict, and violence that can only negatively affect the human security of the Central Asians by causing economic, political, and social situations to worsen. Hence inequality,

region. For instance, in Tajikistan, a dose of heroin costs only $1.45 (ibid.), the result of its mass production in Afghanistan despite the presence of more than 50,000 NATO-led troops.

In addition to the availability and affordability of drugs for low-income Central Asians, various social and economic problems caused by the seemingly endless transition (dysfunctional families, poverty, unemployment, low income, lack of opportunities, etc.) have created a suitable ground for a rapid expansion of drug addiction. Drug addiction is growing especially rapidly among the region's youth and women. As stated by the UNODC, drug use starts at "very early age" (UNODC 2005, 34). Based on the most recent available statistics in 2008, its rapid expansion among women is demonstrated in an estimate suggesting that women account for about 30 percent of the drug users in Dushanbe in 2004 (Esfandiari 2004).

Reliable official statistics on drug addition are simply nonexistent. However, unofficial reports suggest an increasing number of addicts who are mainly addicted to heroin, owing to Afghanistan's status as the world's largest producer of opium and its derivate, heroin (ibid.). According to the UNODC, 1 percent of Central Asians were drug addicts in 2005, or about 560,000 people (Buckley 2005). The same authority suggests a phenomenal seventeen-fold increase in opium addiction between 1990 and 2002 (ibid.) As evident in the available statistics, which are mainly conservative estimates, the number of drug addicts is on the rise. For instance, in June 2007, Tajikistan is estimated to have had between 55,000 and 75,000 addicts (UNOCHA 2007).

Finally, deepening social polarization will likely encourage large-scale immigration of economically unsecured people to better-off Central Asian countries (e.g., Kazakhstan) or to other CIS countries (e.g., Russia). Apart from its negative long-term economic impact on their respective societies, such a scenario will weaken family structure, especially when only one or both parents immigrate, whether legally or illegally. The result will be various social, mental, and physical problems for children and single parents.

Security-Related Trends

Despite their social and political fragility, the five countries of Central Asia do not face major security challenges. At least for the time being, none of them is confronting major immediate internal or external threats undermining its security and stability. Nevertheless, without exception, the seeds of conflict, whether internal or external, exist in all of them—but the main threat is internal. This is a predictable outcome of the social polarization of these countries, which has rendered the majority of the population dissatisfied with the status quo. Large dissatisfied populations could and likely will challenge the authority of their respective regimes in the form of spontaneous or organized nonviolent and violent activities. In the absence of guaranteed free expression of dissent, frustration with the status quo will push at least part of the population to violence. Furthermore, harsh suppression of popular manifestations of dissent (strikes, demonstrations, meetings, etc.) on any scale, a highly likely scenario in light of the post-independence experience, will also make a growing number of people consider violence an acceptable means. Currently, the weaknesses of political opposition groups in the Central Asian countries, and their practical absence in the case of Turkmenistan, will leave any such event without leadership, guaranteeing their probable failure when opposing organized regimes. However the ripe situation could well lead to a sudden expansion of currently weak groups, especially in countries like Tajikistan and Uzbekistan, where illegal opposition groups have a degree of organization as well as popular backing.

A major conceivable threat is the sudden expansion of extremism, a distinct possibility in both Tajikistan and Uzbekistan, which are home to groups subscribing to Islamic fundamentalism. Yet, this is a significantly less likely threat for other Central Asian states for the time being. Central Asian countries are vulnerable to extremist ideologies and political groups capitalizing on the economic deprivation and thus the social alienation of people. A large and growing dissatisfied population offers a ripe ground for recruitment by such groups. The existence of these groups in Tajikistan (e.g., Hizb ut-Tahrir) and Uzbekistan (e.g., the Islamic Movement of Uzbekistan) makes their rapid expansion a clear possibility in the future, at least in parts of those countries (e.g., the Ferghana Valley). As a reaction to the totalitarian regime of Turkmenistan having retained its totalitarian nature, by and large, to this date (2009) despite the death of President Saparmurad Niyazov in 2006, a breakdown in that regime for whatever reason could lead not only to the rise of various political groups and ideologies but also to a rapid expansion of extremist ones. Because of this, internal conflicts, including armed ones, are a possibility for Central Asia.

Apart from intrastate conflicts, interstate conflict is also a possibility—although to a much lesser extent—because of the existence of territorial claims, for example, between the three countries sharing the Ferghana Valley. Moreover, Tajikistan's claim to Samarkand and Bukhara, although not actively pursued, could become a source of tension in the future if Tashkent-Dushanbe relations deteriorate, a distinct possibility in view of their post-independence history. Tajikistan and Uzbekistan have been suspicious about each other and since the 1990s each has accused the other of intervention in its internal affairs, including the backing of secessionist groups. The existence of large minorities in all Central Asians states also provides ground for separatist and irredentist movements in certain parts of Central Asia, such as in Tajikistan's City of Khojand, populated mainly by ethnic Uzbeks. Kyrgyzstan and Uzbekistan's suspicion of each other, and accusations that each is courting anti-government groups of the other side or tolerating drug trafficking, also create grounds for tension and conflict between these two countries.

LIKELIHOOD OF CONFLICT AND INSTABILITY IN CENTRAL ASIA

If the current situation continues, internal and external factors will likely foment conflicts that will affect the regional countries to a varying extent. Apart from affecting the Central Asian countries, conflict and instability will also have major implications for a number of regional (Iran, China, Turkey, and Russia) and nonregional (the United States) powers with long-term interests in Central Asia, most of which share borders with it. Predictably, these countries could not remain idle should major instability in any regional country threaten their short- or long-term political and economic interests or affect their national security—a clear problem for neighboring Iran, China, and Russia. Hence, depending on the case, each or all of them could be dragged, willy-nilly, into a regional conflict whose form, scale, and scope would be determined by various factors, including the significance of threat to their interests, the specific nature of their relations with affected states, the means available to them, and the suitability of the regional and international moods for their engagement, added to the degree of consensus in their respective countries for such engagement.

Nevertheless, instability is not an inevitable scenario for Central Asia. On the contrary, serious efforts by the Central Asian governments (backed by foreign states having interests in Central Asia) dealing with various problems (ranging from eradication to alleviation) could significantly decrease the likelihood of the destabilizing threats mentioned above, especially the internal ones. In particular, the economic problems affecting just about everyone in the region in some form are the single most important issue, which, could and should be dealt with. This issue has pushed the Central Asians toward low incomes and poverty since they gained independence.

Apart from working within regional organizations to end interstate disputes and thus to avoid their escalation to major conflicts, serious efforts to conduct major, long-overdue political, economic, and social reforms can and will help avoid various intra- and interstate conflicts. At minimum, in the short run, such efforts could decrease the likelihood or scale of conflicts, should they occur, by decreasing the social ground for their emergence and expansion. In the absence of comprehensive development projects, using the limited available resources, the focus should be on improving the economic situation and enabling the Central Asians to increase their means for coping with difficulties when their governments cannot address them all. In this case, by ensuring job creation on a steady and significant basis and by increasing average incomes to reduce the number of unemployed, underemployed, or poorly paid people, the social basis of any major mass movement, and thus of internal conflicts, will be reduced. This is a necessity for economic development at a time when Central Asia as a whole requires, in the best-case scenario, a decade or two of steady, double-digit economic growth to end its transition. Otherwise, transition as an agonizing process will likely become an institutionalized economic, political, and social system.

In the absence of this kind of effort to deal with internal and external threats, or in the event of the failure of such efforts, and thus continuation of the current trend, interstate or intrastate conflicts (depending on the specifics of each Central Asian country) will likely be the norm, potentially in all the Central Asian countries. In particular, in view of the growing dissatisfaction among the Central Asians, intrastate conflicts ranging from the peaceful, popular expression of dissent to violent activities at various scales and scopes will be a sure bet. This will also be the case even in Kyrgyzstan, despite its recent experience of a revolution, as evident in the reemergence of popular demonstrations throughout the country in 2006 that have lasted to this day (early 2009).

IMPLICATIONS OF INSTABILITY AND CONFLICT FOR THE CENTRAL ASIANS

Intra- and interstate conflicts affect the Central Asians in different ways, as evident in the Tajik civil war of the 1990s and Uzbekistan's Andijan incident of May 2005. In both cases, the vulnerable social groups tolerated the brunt of the conflict. Regardless of their specific details, the instability caused by interstate and intrastate conflicts, whether armed or unarmed, always damages economies by creating uncertainly, fear for the future, and an unsafe, insecure environment that discourages economic activities and investment. Instability also encourages an outflow of resources: mainly the humans (especially skilled workers) and capital necessary for the operation of their societies.

This situation has the (predictable) result of reducing employment opportunities, lowering wages and thus income—apart from the economic consequences of damage to private and public assets, with additional negative impact on the economic capabilities and prosperity of individuals and their respective governments. For a complete picture, add inevitable increases in security spending by governments facing conflicts and instability. Needless to say, security spending swallows a large and growing chunk of a country's budget in the event of an armed conflict, whether it is civil or interstate in nature. The result is a decrease in spending in other fields. If history is any indication, the first and foremost victims of such decreases are programs and services

Children forage for food in a garbage dump in the Leninski District of Tajikistan. The former Soviet republic was ravaged by five years of civil war. (Chuck Nacke/Time Life Pictures/Getty Images)

Esfandiari, Golnaz. 2004. "Central Asia: Drug Addiction Is on the Rise (Part 1)." *Radio Free Europe/Radio Liberty,* June 22, 2004. www.rferl.org/featuresarticle/2004/06/3eccd6d7-6600 -4310-8656-6cfe150c5411.html (accessed August 27, 2008).

Human Rights Watch (HRW). 2006a. "Kyrgyzstan." *Human Rights Watch World Report 2006.* New York: Human Rights Watch.

Human Rights Watch (HRW). 2006b. "Uzbekistan." *Human Rights Watch World Report 2006.* New York: Human Rights Watch. http://hrw.org/english/docs/2006/01/18/uzbeki12288.htm (accessed May 14, 2008).

Human Rights Watch (HRW). 2007. "Kyrgyzstan." *Human Rights Watch World Report 2007.* New York: Human Rights Watch.

Human Rights Watch (HRW). 2008. "Kyrgyzstan." *Human Rights Watch World Report 2008.* New York: Human Rights Watch.

International Monetary Fund (IMF). 2005. *World Economic Outlook Database.* www.imf.org/ external/pubs/ft/weo/2004/01/data/dbcselm.cfm?G=901 (accessed April 20, 2008).

International Monetary Fund (IMF). 2008. *World Economic Outlook Database.* April 2008. Washington, D.C.: IMF. www.imf.org/external/pubs/ft/weo/2008/01/weodata/weoselgr.aspx (accessed October 1, 2008).

Kobonbaev, Maks. 2005. "Costs and Benefits of the 'Kyrgyz Revolution'." *Central Asia–Caucasus Analyst,* April 6, 2005. www.cacianalyst.org/view_article.php?articleid=3194 (accessed September 6, 2008).

Telekova, Aya. 2005. "Kyrgyz Government's Control Slips, Creating Dangers and Opportunities." *Central Asia–Caucasus Analyst,* March 23, 2005. www.cacianalyst.org/view_article.php ?articleid=3158 (accessed September 6, 2008).

United Nations Office for the Coordination of Humanitarian Affairs (UNOCHA). 2005. "Turkmenistan: Drug Addiction on the Rise." *IRIN,* August 2, 2005. www.irinnews.org/report .asp?ReportID=48406&SelectRegion=Asia&SelectCountry=TURKMENISTAN (accessed September 28, 2008).

United Nations Office for the Coordination of Humanitarian Affairs (UNOCHA). 2006. "Kyrgyzstan: Reform Demonstrations Planned for Weekend." *IRIN,* April 26, 2006. www.irinnews.org/report .asp?ReportID=52976&SelectRegion=Asia&SelectCountry=KYRGYZSTAN (accessed August 11, 2008).

United Nations Office for the Coordination of Humanitarian Affairs (UNOCHA). 2007. "Tajikistan: Afghan Narcotics Fuel Drug Addiction." *IRIN,* June 26, 2007. www.irinnews.org/report.aspx ?ReportID=72937 (accessed September 29, 2008).

United Nations Office on Drugs and Crimes (UNODC). 2005. *World Drug Report 2005.* Vienna: UNODC. www.unodc.org/pdf/WDR_2005/volume_1_chap1_dynamics.pdf (accessed August 21, 2008).

United Nations Office on Drugs and Crimes (UNODC). 2008. *Afghanistan: Opium Survey 2008.* Vienna: UNODC. August 2008. www.unodc.org/documents/data-and-analysis/ExSum25August -standard.pdf (accessed October 2, 2008).

Voice of America (VOA). 2005. "America Evacuated Its Air Base in Uzbekistan." *VOA News in Persian,* November 21, 2005.

Part 2

COUNTRY PROFILES
AND CHRONOLOGIES

Section I

Central Asia

authorities of the ethnic Uzbeks living near the Turkmen-Uzbek border; both sides amass troops along the border.

In December, a bomb attributed to the IMU explodes in Bishkek, leaving 7 people dead and more than 50 injured.

2003   In January, clashes take place between Kyrgyz security forces and armed groups along the Kyrgyz-Tajik border (Tajikistan's Vorukh enclave and Kyrgyzstan's region of Batkan).

In February, 11 Islamic militants of Tajikistan are sentenced to death and dozens are given lengthy jail sentences for murder and kidnapping during and after the civil war of the 1990s.

In April, Turkmen president Saparmurad Niyazov visits Moscow and signs an agreement with Russian Gazprom that provides for Russia to buy 60 billion cubic meters of Turkmen gas annually. Russian president Vladimir Putin visits Tajikistan and announces plans to boost Russia's military presence.

In May, an explosion in a gas station in Kyrgyzstan's city of Osh, attributed to the IMU, leaves one dead.

In June, a referendum is held, allowing Tajik president Imomali Rahmonov to run for another two consecutive seven-year terms when his current term ends in 2006.

In July, the Central Asian Cooperation Organization (CACO) summit is held in Almaty, Kazakhstan. Kazakhstan takes the CACO chair. The heads of the CACO member states create a number of consortia within the CACO to deal with water, energy, food, and communications.

In August, the Shanghai Cooperation Organization (SCO) members, excluding Uzbekistan, hold their first joint anti-terror military exercises in Kazakhstan and China.

In September, in Beijing, the SCO members ratify the Program of Multilateral Trade and Economic Cooperation. The CSTO Treaty of Chisinau takes effect.

In October, Russia formally opens an air force base in the town of Kant near Bishkek, Kyrgyzstan.

In December, Mahmadruzi Iskandarov, the leader of Tajikistan's opposition Democratic Party, is arrested in Moscow at the request of the Tajik prosecutor's office. Tajik authorities seek his extradition for his alleged involvement in terrorism, arms offenses, and corruption. His supporters say the move is politically motivated.

2004   In February, the parliament of Kazakhstan ratifies the Treaty on the Establishment of the Central Asian Cooperation Organization (CACO), the first Central Asian parliament to do so.

In March, at least 47 people are killed in shootings and bombings in Turkmenistan. The Turkmen authorities blame unspecified Islamic extremists. In Turkmenistan, 15,000 public health workers, including medical workers, are dismissed.

In June, Mongolia becomes the first formal SCO observer.

In July, suicide bombers target the U.S. and Israeli embassies in Tashkent; a third blast hits Uzbekistan's general prosecutor's office.

In October, Russia inaugurates a military base near Dushanbe, Tajikistan. Russia joins the CACO.

In November, restrictions on trading practices spark civil disorder in Turkmenistan's city of Kokand. The Turkmen and Uzbek presidents (Saparmurad Niyazov and Islam Karimov) sign a friendship declaration.

2005   In January, a car blows up near a government building in Dushanbe, killing at least one person; it is blamed on Islamic extremists. Fire breaks out at the Ministry of Security.

In February, the parliamentary elections in Kyrgyzstan provoke waves of protest, as many independent and opposition candidates are barred from running.

In March, protests over alleged widespread irregularities following the second round of Kyrgyz parliamentary elections lead to the Yellow Revolution (Tulip Revolution) as protestors occupy many government buildings in Bishkek. President Askar Akayev escapes to Moscow, and the election's results are annulled. Kurmanbek Bakiev forms a new government. Many stores in Bishkek are looted during the Tulip Revolution. The CSTO conducts military exercises in Central Asia.

In May, an armed uprising in Uzbekistan's city of Andijan results in armed clashes between Uzbek security forces and armed opposition/unarmed protestors. Many people are killed and arrested, and hundreds of Uzbeks flee to Kyrgyzstan. The United States and EU's demands for an international investigation damage their bilateral relations with Uzbekistan. The Uzbek government accuses the U.S. government of involvement in the Andijan incident and demands the closure of the U.S. air base in Uzbekistan (Karshi-Khanabad) in six months. Uzbekistan withdraws from GUUAM, which is renamed GUAM. Turkmen deputy prime minister Elly Kurbanmuradov, who is in charge of the energy sector, is dismissed and subsequently given a 25-year jail sentence for a series of charges, including corruption.

In June, Russian border guards complete their withdrawal from the Tajik-Afghan borders, handing the task over to the Tajik forces.

In July, the SCO leaders demand that the U.S. government present a timetable for withdrawing its forces from Central Asia. In the July 2005 summit in Shanghai, India, Iran, and Pakistan achieve formal SCO observer status. Rejep Saparov is dismissed as the head of Turkmenistan's presidential administration and sentenced to 20 years in jail for corruption.

In August, the upper house of the Uzbek parliament votes to evict U.S. forces from the air base at Karshi-Khanabad. Turkmenistan

Chapter 6

Kazakhstan

GENERAL STATISTICS

Area	2,724,888 km²
Population	15,340,533 (2008 est.)
Population Density	6 inhabitants per km² (1999 census)
Major Cities	Almaty (former capital)
	Aqtöbe
	Astana (new capital)
	Karaganda
	Pavlodar
	Shymkent
	Taraz
	Ust-Kamenogorsk
Gross Domestic Product	$161.2 billion (2007 est.)
Total Active Armed Forces	About 60,000
Annual Military Expenditure	$222 million (2007 est.)
Military Service	Compulsory military service for men 18 years of age, with a two-year conscripted service obligation (2004).

International Organization	CIS (1992)
Membership	CSTO/CST (1992)
	ECO (1992)
	NATO Partnership for Peace (1994)
	OSCE (1992)
	SCO/Shanghai Five (1996)
	UN (1992)

HISTORY OF KAZAKHSTAN

A Caspian littoral state, Kazakhstan is Central Asia's largest and potentially richest country. Like all other Central Asian states, it emerged as an independent state when the Soviet Union collapsed in December 1991. It borders Russia, Turkmenistan, Uzbekistan, Kyrgyzstan, China, and the Caspian Sea. Although Kazakhstan is a young state that emerged only during the Soviet era, the Kazakhs have lived in Central Asia for centuries.

Kazakhstan's history is marked by long periods of internal armed conflict. The first evidence of human civilization in Kazakhstan is that of nomads, traced back to the first millennium BC; the Turkic nomads appeared several centuries later. Over time, Kazakhstan's rich, vast steppes have attracted many large and small empires, including those led by Attila, Genghis Khan, and Timur, that conquered and ruled it completely or partially in the case of the Mongols, for a few centuries.

In their westward migration, the Turkic tribes of Inner Asia entered Central Asia, including Kazakhstan, and Turkified the Kazakh land over the next few hundred years, ending by the sixth century (Menges 1989, 84; Abolhassan Shirazi 1991, 90). By that time, the steppe (nomadic) part of central Asia (what is now Kazakhstan, Kyrgyzstan, and parts of Turkmenistan) was completely Turkified (Bregel 1991, 54). The Turkic nomads of what is today Kazakhstan did not form a cohesive people having a firm and unified political system. Rather, they formed rival groups of tribes affiliated with mini-states or *khanates,* whose territories in the sixth century included parts of present-day Kazakhstan, Uzbekistan, and Tajikistan (Abolhassan Shirazi 1991, 65, 83, 109). As a loose confederation of nomads, the khanates lasted until the eighth century (ibid., 109). Later, three major Turkic dynasties emerged, the most significant of which created the Seljuk (Seljuq) Dynasty in the eleventh century. The Turkmen Seljuk tribes conquered almost the entire region, but they lost their territories in Central Asia and Iran to another Turkic dynasty (Khawrazmshahian) in the twelfth century (ibid., 66). The Mongols' conquest of Central Asia in the thirteenth century completed the Turkification of its settled part—that is, the rest of Central Asia, excluding today's Tajik-dominated areas (ibid., 83), since most of the nomads brought to the region by the Mongols were Turkic peoples (Bregel 1991, 60). Between the sixth century and the fifteenth century, when the Kazakhs emerged as a distinct ethnic group, their ancestors remained divided mainly into many large and small tribes affiliated with one or another of the rival khanates, which almost constantly fought with each other. Their territories, being consisted of parts of present-day Kazakhstan, Kyrgyzstan, Turkmenistan, and Uzbekistan, were in a constant process of expansion and contraction because of their wars. The Mongols' domination of Central Asia did not end the division and hostility among these tribes, for the Mongols were not able to control the entire region directly; in many cases, the tribal structure was left almost intact. Moreover, Genghis Khan's death in 1227 led to the division of his empire among his descendants. Consequently, most of present-day Kazakhstan became part of the territory ruled by his son Chagatai, but its western part and most of its northern part were included in another empire, the Golden Horde, established by Genghis Khan's grandson, Batu Khan.

By the end of the fifteenth century, the Kazakhs had emerged as a distinctive group, created (according to some scholars) by the intermingling of Mongol and Turkic peoples. In the early sixteenth century, the Kazakh tribes united to form a great nomadic empire under the warlord Kasim Khan. This empire soon fell apart as a result of infighting, leading to the emergence of three major Kazakh groupings: the Great Horde (Ulu Zhuz) in the southeast portion of present-day Kazakhstan, the Middle Horde (Orta Zhuz) in the central steppe region, and the Little Horde (Kishi Zhuz) between the Aral Sea and the Ural River in the west. Each horde consisted of a number of tribes collectively ruled by a khan. For a short while (1538 to 1580), Khan Haq Nazar united the Kazakh hordes, but by the seventeenth century the Kazakhs were again fragmented. The invasion of certain Mongol tribes (Oirots), including Dzungars, united the Kazakhs for a short while in the 1680s, but by 1720 the Dzungar invasions had exhausted the Kazakhs. This situation facilitated Russia's expansion into their land, which had started earlier when the Kazakh tribe sought Russia's protection against the invaders.

The Turkic tribes living in the vast Kazakh steppes fought with each other constantly, for they lacked one single, strong state to unite them all. Yet they contributed to the development of trade routes, including the famous Silk Road connecting China to Europe via Central Asia, Iran, the Caucasus, and Turkey. Although initially pagan, the Turkic tribes gradually converted to Islam during a few-century-long process that began in the eleventh century. The Kazakhs as a distinct ethnic group and a people with their current characteristics emerged only in the late fifteenth century, when the first Kazakh states were formed, each ruled by a khan. For the next four centuries, the Kazakhs failed to end their constant tribal wars and establish a Kazakh state; in the nineteenth century, Russia annexed their land.

The Kazakh land was the first area of Central Asia to come under Russian rule through war and diplomacy. Russia's incorporation of Central Asia took a long time and concluded in the 1880s, but the Kazakh land and its tribe became part of Russia in 1848, when Russia dismantled the remnants of the three Mongol hordes. At that time, the Russian immigrants began settling there in large numbers, after about three centuries of gradual migration in relatively small numbers to grab land and help their government rule the newly conquered territory. The Russian era helped advance the Kazakh land to some extent by introducing industry and large-scale agriculture. However, the Russians did not try to change it drastically, for various reasons—including their fear of a popular backlash leading to armed conflict that would weaken Russian rule.

Kazakhstan, like other present-day Central Asian countries, was a component of the multi-ethnic khanates (Central Asian states) before their incorporation into the Russian Empire in the nineteenth century. These khanates did not correspond to the current five Central Asian states in terms of number, name, size, population, or ethnic makeup. Before their annexation by the Russian Empire, the khanates were in conflict with each other, with the remnants of the Mongol Empire, with other Central Asian khanates based in southern Central Asia (e.g., Samarkand, Bukhara, and Khiva), and with the regional powers (Iran and Russia). These conflicts ended when the Russians conquered and subsequently annexed the entire Central Asia.

Unsuccessful anti-Russian movements emerged throughout Central Asia in the nineteenth century as a reaction to Russian rule. The major anti-Russian uprising took place in 1916 in the form of an ethnic conflict between the Kazakhs and the Russian settlers over land and water, which the Russian tsarist military suppressed brutally, forcing about 300,000 Kazakhs to flee into the mountains and to China.

The Bolshevik Revolution of 1917 replaced the tsarist regime with a Communist one interested in keeping Kazakhstan and the rest of Central Asia under its rule. In the midst of World War I and in the first two decades of the Soviet era in the early twentieth century (1916–1933), anti-Russian, anti-Soviet, and independence movements emerged in Kazakhstan and the rest of Central Asia, all of which the Soviet regime suppressed (d'Encausse 1989a, 1989b). The Kazakhs experienced a short period of independence and self-government as they established the Alash Autonomy (December 1917 to August 1920), a Kazakh autonomous state comprising a territory more or less corresponding to the current Kazakhstan. It was run by a government known as Alash Orda. As it consolidated its power and defeated the White (tsarist) forces, the Soviet government disbanded the Alash Autonomy and renamed its territory the Kyrgyz Autonomous Soviet Socialist Republic, which was subsequently changed to the Kazakh ASSR in 1925 and to the Kazakh SSR in 1936.

As with all the Central Asian countries, Kazakhstan's current borders are the result of the artificial division of Central Asia by the Soviet government without regard to the region's historical realities. The Soviet government divided and redivided Central Asia to create five so-called ethnically based republics, including Kazakhstan, whose borders did not correspond to the pre-Soviet era's boundaries of the Central Asian khanates. Thus, Kazakhstan ended up with large non-Kazakh ethnic groups in addition to a very large Slavic population that immigrated to Kazakhstan over a few centuries. This ethnic makeup, in which the Kazakhs were not the majority, did not develop into major ethnic conflicts challenging the Kazakh authorities in the Soviet era. Nor did Kazakhstan give birth to large-scale political conflicts able to damage the stability of the Soviet Union, except in one incident in the last years of the Soviet era. Accordingly, Secretary General Mikhail Gorbachev's attempts to curb corruption within the Communist Party of Kazakhstan led to the removal of its Kazakh first secretary, Dinmukhamed Kunayev, in December 1986, and his replacement by an ethnic Russian, Gennady Kolbin, who had no work experience in Kazakhstan. The replacement provoked Kazakh nationalism, which developed into violent mass protests of mainly young Kazakhs in Almaty, known as the Jeltoksan Riot. According to various reports, the Soviet security forces killed three, seven, or several people, wounded hundreds, and detained hundreds more. Allegedly, Kunayev had a role in organizing the street protests, which failed to remove Kolbin from the position. Only in June 1989 was he replaced with Nursultan Nazarbayev, a Kazakh.

As part of the Soviet Union, Kazakhstan's history of conflict with other nations is the same as the well-known hostilities the USSR experienced in its relations with the

Nursultan Nazarbayev shortly after his election as the first president of independent Kazakhstan in December 1991. (Georges de Keerle/Sygma/Corbis)

non-Communist bloc, having no direct bearing on the Kazakhs per se. However, as a Soviet republic bordering China along with Kyrgyzstan and Tajikistan, Kazakhstan directly experienced the territorial conflict between the USSR and China prompted by a schism in the Communist bloc over its leadership. Accordingly, the Sino-Soviet hostility reached a dangerous level in the 1960s, when it was translated into border disputes. The two neighbors engaged in skirmishes along their long borders, which now form the borders of China with Russia, Kazakhstan, Kyrgyzstan, and Tajikistan. The unsettled border disputes remained a potential source of conflict in Sino-Soviet relations throughout the Soviet era.

Following the regional trend, Kazakhstan did not experience major mass political activities in the last years of the Soviet Union, unlike many other Soviet republics. As the Soviet government's control was apparently disappearing, in October 1990 Kazakhstan declared its sovereignty, but not its independence, within the USSR. Yet, as the aborted August 1991 communist coup paved the way for the dissolution of the Soviet Union, Kazakhstan declared independence in December 16, 1991. Nursultan Nazarbayev won the first popular election in this same month to become Kazakhstan's first president.

Compared to other central Asian countries, Kazakhstan's political system was more tolerant of dissent and more democratic in the first decade of its independence, mainly because of the absence of any major source of internal conflict in the form of radical or extremist political groups and movements. Such tolerance was also needed partly to keep the multiethnic country together. Because ethnic minorities accounted for about 60 percent of the country, and the ethnic Kazakhs were clearly in the minority, efforts to establish an authoritarian system of government would probably have contributed to social unrest and secessionist groups or movements, especially because ethnic Russians accounted for 40 percent of the population and were concentrated mainly in the north of Kazakhstan, bordering Russia. That geographical reality would have made their separation from Kazakhstan and unification with Russia technically possible. Toward the end of the first decade of independence, the Kazakh government followed the regional trend, opting for an authoritarian system of government reflected in its growing intolerance of political dissent and its crackdown on opposition groups showing potential for growth. Although it is still more democratic than Tajikistan, Turkmenistan, and Uzbekistan, the Kazakh government is surely consolidating its expanding authoritarian system of government. Having been in power since 1989 and president since 1991, Nursultan Nazarbayev, whose family dominates Kazakh economic life, is a clear manifestation of this trend, as evidenced by the Kazakhstan parliament's passage of a law in June 2000 that tacitly but officially made Nazarbayev president for life by granting him lifetime powers and privileges, including access to future presidents, immunity from criminal prosecution, and influence over domestic and foreign policy (Hogan 2000).

Internal Conflicts since Independence

Unlike most of its Central Asian counterparts, Kazakhstan has not experienced major internal conflicts during its post-independence era. Its opposition political groups have not resorted to violence to promote their objectives, nor have they developed into major organizations with a significant enough social basis to challenge the authority of the Kazakh political system. Extremist groups of enough significance or having enough potential for growth have simply not yet emerged in Kazakhstan. Aside from the absence of organized, popular, anti-government political movements, the country has not witnessed the rise of spontaneous mass movements capable of weakening the pillars of the Kazakh state. It has enjoyed internal peace and stability, notwithstanding the existence of many opposition groups and a pervasive sense of dissatisfaction with a post-independence era marked by numerous economic and social problems, lower living standards, and rampant corruption—a reality throughout the Central Asian region.

External Conflicts since Independence

Kazakhstan has not experienced major conflicts with foreign states. However, it has had significant tensions and difficulties with its southern neighbor, Uzbekistan, with a potential for escalation. Border disputes have been the major source of tension, a common problem all over Central Asia owing to the Soviet Union's artificial division of the region into five states without regard to historical and ethnic realities. This division planted the seeds of multiple territorial claims and thus armed conflicts over disputed territories. On many occasions, the Kazakhs and the Uzbeks have sent troops to change the border lines in certain districts disputed since independence, although such incidents have not escalated to major crises or military conflicts. Border disputes with Uzbekistan officially ended when the two sides signed a border agreement in Astana on September 9, 2002 (Yermukanov 2004). However, this has remained, and will likely remain, a source of interstate tensions, since the agreement has not practically addressed the issue, leaving many sources of territorial conflict in place. For example, it has left many passport-holding citizens of the two countries on the wrong side of the common border, dividing ethnically homogenous villages between the two countries and creating ethnic enclaves in each country with social attachments to the neighboring state. Consequently, many Kazakhs and Uzbeks are dissatisfied with the official settlement, which is viewed as a sign of disgrace and unwarranted concessions. Moreover, border demarcation to turn the agreement into a reality has yet to be completed in early 2009, Astana and Tashkent having agreed to begin this effort only recently (2005). It is no surprise that many small-scale armed clashes have occurred between the countries' border guards, as well as shots being fired at civilians crossing the common border. Border disputes have been a major source of conflict between Astana and Tashkent, but none has yet developed into a major armed conflict.

Disagreements on how to deal with the Aral Sea's environmental disasters (Spoor 1998, 409–435) have been another source of tension in Kazakh-Uzbek relations. Large-scale cotton production in the Soviet era resulted in the rapid depletion of the waters of the Aral Sea, which is located partly in Kazakhstan and partly in Uzbekistan. This type of agriculture created the Aral Sea environmental disaster: its shrinkage to about one-third of its original size, the salinization of arable land, and soil exhaustion arising from the heavy use of chemical fertilizer to turn Central Asia into the USSR's

Abandoned ship near the Kazakh city of Aral sits on sand that was once part of the Aral Sea. (P. Christopher Staecker)

largest exporter of cotton (a major source of hard currency for the Soviet government). Cotton production has remained a dominant economic activity in Turkmenistan, Uzbekistan, and Tajikistan and a major cultivated crop in Kazakhstan and Kyrgyzstan since their independence. This explains the perpetuation and expansion of the environmental disaster, as all the Central Asian countries except Kyrgyzstan use the main water resources (rivers) of the Aral Sea for their cotton production, activity that has sharply reduced the Aral Sea's water level.

The environmental disaster has affected about 3 million people living around the Aral Sea in Kazakhstan and Uzbekistan, damaging their health and nutrition and also increasing poverty and unemployment by limiting economic activities. The two countries have not yet agreed on a sustainable common policy for stopping the disastrous process and starting its restoration. Nor have they agreed on an environmentally sustainable plan for using their common water resources to avoid conflicts over water, a rare and valuable commodity in both countries. Kazakhstan's unilateral policy has become a source of tension in Kazakh-Uzbek relations. Thus, because what is left of the Aral Sea is now divided into two lakes, the Kazakh government has sought to focus on saving the northern lake (located in Kazakhstan) while doing basically nothing about the southern part (which is shared with Uzbekistan and used in cooperation with that country) (Christou 2007). Of the two main sources of water for the lake (Amu Darya and Syr Darya rivers), only the

Syr Darya, passing through Kazakhstan, reaches the lake. Kazakhstan's decision will simply result in the gradual disappearance of the southern lake, located in Uzbekistan. This will surely be the case if current Kazakh policy continues and if Uzbekistan does not modernize its irrigation system to let the Amu Darya flow into the Aral Sea again.

Although Kazakhstan's sources of tension and potential conflicts still exist, for the most part, the Kazakhs have successfully resolved the source of potential armed conflicts with China: the Sino-Soviet border disputes. Accordingly, Kazakhstan, along with all other CIS countries sharing a border with China, settled their Soviet-inherited source of tensions, crises, and conflicts (including armed ones) in the 1990s through negotiations and compromises. The latter finally led to bilateral and multilateral agreements to finalize borders between China and its four new neighbors. Toward that end, Russia, Kazakhstan, Kyrgyzstan, and Tajikistan formed a joint commission on the border regime between their countries and China in September 1992 (*KRWE* 1992). Negotiations within the context of the Shanghai Cooperation Organization (SCO) (known as the Shanghai Five in the 1990s) also contributed to settling the major border disputes between China and the mentioned states, including Kazakhstan.

MAJOR PEOPLES AND NATIONS IN KAZAKHSTAN'S HISTORY

The Turkic Tribes

The appearance of the Kazakhs as a Turkic people in the northern part of Central Asia is the result of a process that began about 1,400 years ago. Kazakhstan's indigenous populations are mainly Turkic, whereas the main inhabitants of the region prior to its Turkification were non-Turkic, including different Iranian peoples living all over Central Asia (Bregel 1991, 54). The ethnic link between the Turkic Central Asians, including the Kazakhs, and Turkey can be traced back to the migration of Central Asian Turkic tribes in the eleventh and twelfth centuries (Sarli 1994, 75–76; Saray 1994, 47–48). The Turkmen Oghuz tribe led by Seljuk (Seljuq or Seljug) founded the Seljuk Dynasty (1041–1118). In their westward migration, the Seljuks conquered and ruled Central Asia and the territories between that region and the Mediterranean Sea. Despite their Central Asian origin, they gradually lost interest in Central Asian affairs in the course of their migration. Over time, their power in Iran and Central Asia vanished, and the Seljuks finally settled in Asia Minor. Their offspring established the Ottoman Empire in 1290 (Fuller 1991, 194; Saray 1994, 48). In the aftermath of World War I, after losing many territories, the Ottoman Empire became Turkey.

Kazakhstan's bilateral relations with Iran and Turkey have been tension-free, friendly, and growing. However, the latter's political influence in and economic ties with Astana are currently limited, for neither country has the financial means to meet the extensive need for developing the Kazakh fossil energy industry. Both are involved in mainly small and medium-scale industrial, construction, and commercial projects. Kazakhstan and Iran have also been conducting oil swap deals since the 1990s. To a limited extent, they have helped Kazakhstan reduce its heavy reliance on Russia for oil exports by offering an alternative export route. Washington's opposition to Iran's engagement in the Caspian oil industry has limited this activity. Swap deals amounted to 70,000 barrels per day (bpd) in 2007 (Energy Information Administration 2007). Apart from bilateral relations, Kazakhstan's joining the Economic Cooperation Organization in March 1992 created another forum for cooperation between the Kazakhs and the Iranians and the Turks, which has lasted to this day (2009).

Russia

The Russians' contact with Central Asia started in the sixteenth century. The Cossacks, arriving from Russia, began to settle along the Ural River, acting as pioneers for the subsequent purposeful migration of Russians to Kazakh land that started in the eighteenth century. Russia's success therefore remained negligible until the second half of the eighteenth century, when the Russians penetrated the Kazakh steppes and began to control that area through various means, both military and nonmilitary. As part of a new wave of invasion of the Kazakh land by Mongol tribes, the Dzungar invasion enabled the Russians to further expand their control, as many Kazakh khans appealed to Russia for protection and military supplies. The subjugation of the remnants of the Mongol hordes expanded Russian influence in the Kazakh steppes; the Little Horde signed an oath of allegiance in 1731, followed by the Middle Horde in 1740 and the Great Horde in 1742. Russia's growing influence weakened that of the Kazakh khans and limited the economic opportunities for the Kazakhs, resulting in their revolts, especially in the 1790s, which the Russian military suppressed.

Emerging as a power, Russia's massive expansion into the Kazakh territories began in the early nineteenth century. The tsarist government finally decided to turn its practical control of the Kazakh territories into official control by ending Kazakh autonomy, dismantling the Middle Horde (1822), the Little Horde (1824), and the Great Horde (1848) and annexing their lands for the Russian Empire. In short, through sheer force and diplomacy, by 1850 Russia had conquered the Kazakh land (Allworth 1989, 47–53; Takmil-Homayoon 1993, 21–47; d'Encausse 1989c).

The Russian annexation of current Kazakhstan changed Kazakhstan's ethnic and linguistic composition by introducing ethnic Russians and the Russian language. The Bolshevik Revolution had a great impact on all of Central Asia and therefore on Kazakhstan's social makeup, for the Soviet regime enthusiastically implemented a policy to change Kazakhstan's ethnic and linguistic structure to ensure its docility to Moscow. This divide-and-conquer policy was translated into ethnic engineering and Russification to replace the Central Asians' culture and history with an artificial sense of belonging to distinct ethnic and linguistic groups (Shykh-Attar 1992, 17–21). The creation of a Soviet people in place of many nationalities—that is, a Russian-speaking people loyal to Moscow—was the final goal of this policy.

The policy of ethnic engineering aimed to create "ethnically based" republics. After several divisions and redivisions of the region, Moscow finally created five such republics, each named after one specific "dominant" ethnic group. The planners delib- erately drew borders in such a way that monoethnic regions were divided among dif- ferent republics, leaving large numbers of ethnic minorities in each republic. This policy was completed by the imposition of a "national language" on each republic in place of the three main languages of the region's pre-Soviet era. Persian was the administrative and cultural language of most Central Asians, Arabic was their religious language, and Joghatai Turkic the Turkic people's oral and literary language. To change this linguistic makeup, various measures were used, including giving importance to four Turkic local languages at the expense of Joghatai Turkic, and the gradual imposition of the Cyrillic alphabet on all Central Asians, who had previously used Persian script. Hence, the ethnic engineering policy actually planted the seeds of ethnic conflict by creating grounds for ethnic and linguistic discrimination and terri- torial claims, a current problem.

The Soviet Russification scheme, with its clear impact on current Central Asia and its future, consisted of several policies. Many peoples of European origin, including Ukrainians and Volga Germans, but most of all Russians, were settled in Central Asia to change its ethnic structure, and mainly to occupy sensitive positions (Atta'ie 1993, 158). As a result, the Kazakhs were a minority in their own land, where 40 percent of the population were Slavs—chiefly Russian—when Kazakhstan gained independence in 1991. The Soviet regime also attracted and educated young Central Asians, including Kazakhs, to create regional Russified elites. The Russification scheme also targeted the indigenous languages to ensure a preeminent status for Russian, the "supraethnic language," as the means of communication for all Soviet citizens. The adopted Cyrillic alphabets facilitated the Russification of the regional languages.

Undoubtedly, the Russians have been the major influence in the recent history of the Kazakhs, as they have been for other Central Asian countries, having had a long- term impact on all of Central Asia in the social, economic, political, military/security, and environmental spheres. Russian rule turned the Central Asian nomads, who pri- marily inhabited in present-day Kazakhstan, Kyrgyzstan, and parts of Turkmenistan, into settled, urbanized peoples, while expanding literacy. On a much smaller scale than had been done in Russia's Slavic regions, and in an uneven manner that favored Kazakhstan and Uzbekistan, the Russians introduced industries to the region and created a significant industrial basis for those countries, including heavy and military industries. On the negative side, the Russians developed Central Asia as the hinterland for their country's European segment, resulting in Central Asia's limited industrial- ization and its mainly cotton-based agriculture and economy. The region became unable to feed itself and thus grew to be highly dependent on large-scale imports from the rest of the USSR while it also faced the Aral Sea environmental disaster. Furthermore, the artificial division of the region into five republics left many large ethnic minorities in every republic and provided grounds for ethnic and territorial disputes in the post-Soviet era. The Central Asians will suffer from the results of these policies for a long time.

Formed under Russian rule, the Russian community of Kazakhstan will guarantee a degree of presence and influence for Russia in that country for some time to come. That community, concentrated mainly along the Kazakh-Russian border to make unification with Russia a feasible scenario, accounts for about 40 percent of the population. Forming the region's largest Russian community, its members include many highly educated people. Apart from the preeminence of the Russian language throughout Central Asia, other factors that act to secure Russia's continued influence in Kazakhstan include economic, industrial, and military/security ties (those inherited from the Soviet era as well as those made since 1991). They also include Russia's long border with Kazakhstan, and the membership of Moscow and Astana in the Shanghai Cooperation Organization (SCO) and the Collective Security Treaty Organization (CSTO). Despite Kazakhstan's close ties with the United States and other Western countries, Astana has kept good relations with Russia. Kazakhstan exports the bulk of its oil, the engine of its economic growth and prosperity, via the Russian pipelines.

The United States

Although newcomers, the Americans have become an important nation in Kazakhstan. The Kazakhs opened up to the United States upon independence while maintaining ties with Russia. As with other Central Asian countries, relations with Washington help Astana balance Moscow by avoiding heavy reliance on Russia, and thus secure Kazakhstan's independence. Astana also views Washington as a necessary economic partner in the development of its significant fossil energy resources (mainly oil), on

U.S. Secretary of Defense Donald H. Rumsfeld (middle) and Minister of Defense Gen. Mukhtar Altynbayev leave the Ministry of Defense in Astana, Kazakhstan, after their meeting and press conference on February 25, 2004. Rumsfeld was meeting with local civilian and military leaders while visiting troops deployed in Southwest Asia. (U.S. Department of Defense)

from Uzbekistan across Kazakhstan into the Aral Sea. Because the Syr Darya is used heavily for cotton cultivation, Uzbekistan's probable increases in the use of its water will likely prompt a conflict between the two neighbors, especially when the Uzbeks have depleted the other main regional river, the Amu Darya, to the extent that it no longer reaches the Aral Sea (one of the chief reasons for the Aral Sea's ongoing shrinkage). Unless the two sides—and, for that matter, other countries of the region—agree on a workable plan for using rivers that flow through, start, or end in their countries, a major conflict between and among the Central Asian countries, especially Kazakhstan and Uzbekistan, is a distinct possibility.

Relations with China and Russia

Kazakhstan's relations with Russia and China will likely remain close and will expand, owing to their common security interests as neighbors, their concern about Washington's plans for their region, and the necessity for cooperation created by their various economic, technological, and ethnic ties. Currently, their bilateral relations lack major unresolved issues with potential for developing into armed conflict, although potential sources of conflict do exist.

Astana has addressed, at least on paper, its territorial disputes with China and Russia, leaving no strong reason for either side to resort to arms to settle disputes. However, the demarcation of their borders has yet to be completed and could lead to disagreement over the effects of demarcation on nationals living in the border areas.

Moreover, conflict between Kazakhstan and China over use of the water from the Ili River, which flows from China into Kazakhstan's Lake Balkash, could also be a possibility, given China's increasing water consumption by its growing population and industries, and the lake's struggle with environmental problems. Although unlikely, conflict between Astana and Beijing could also arise from Kazakhstan's offer—directly, or indirectly through its nationals of Uyghur ethnicity—of assistance to the Uyghur separatist movement in China's Sinkiang Province bordering Kazakhstan. That movement has been a concern for Beijing, especially since Kazakhstan's independence.

More likely potential sources of conflict include the growing Kazakh-U.S. military relations. In particular, a long-term U.S. military presence in Kazakhstan and its expansion would probably be a serious source of conflict in Astana's relations with Beijing and Moscow. By the same token, Kazakhstan's expanding cooperation with NATO and, if at all possible, its future membership in that organization would certainly be another major instigator for such a scenario. In both cases, the growing disagreement between Washington and Moscow and Beijing, which seems likely to continue and expand in the foreseeable future, will make the Chinese and the Russians especially sensitive to any U.S. or NATO military presence in their proximity, including in Kazakhstan. This is a sure bet, especially in the case of Russia, in the aftermath of the Georgian-Russian war of August 2008: the Russians blame Washington for the Georgian attack on Tskhinvali, view Washington as the instigator of the war, and categorically oppose NATO membership for Georgia, something now backed by Washington.

Finally, a potential source of conflict in Kazakh-Russian relations could be Kazakhstan's exportation of oil to international markets. Currently, much of the exported Kazakh oil flows through the Russian pipelines, with the exception of a small amount that is transferred through Azerbaijan and its neighboring Georgia in small oil tankers that cross the Caspian Sea to Azerbaijan, added to some oil exports to China via Kazakh-Chinese pipelines. If it becomes a reality, a proposed pipeline under the Caspian Sea, meant to bypass Russia by connecting Kazakhstan's oil terminals to the Baku-Tbilisi-Ceyhan pipeline (see the country profile of Azerbaijan) could seriously threaten Kazakh-Russian relations.

CHINA'S ENERGY REQUIREMENTS AND EMERGING CONFLICT OF INTEREST

China's growing need for imported fuel for its rapidly expanding economy is making it a major player in the Central Asian fossil energy industry, in which Russia and the United States both seek to secure the lion's share. Since 2005, China has expanded its involvement—particularly in the Kazakh and Turkmen oil and gas industry—in various forms, such as by the purchase of operating energy companies, pipeline construction, and oil and gas import contracts. A number of noteworthy instances have taken place since:

In October 2005, the Chinese acquired Petro Kazakhstan, a major Canadian-owned oil company operating in Kazakhstan, with the commitment to expand its operation—a $4.2 billion acquisition.

In May 2006, Kazakhstan began exporting oil to China through the Atasu-Alashankou pipeline, which was completed in November 2005. At 962 kilometers long, the $700 million pipeline will provide China with 20 million tons of oil once it reaches its maximum capacity.

In April 2006, China and Turkmenistan agreed in principle on the construction of a gas pipeline through which Ashgabat will annually supply China with 30 billion cubic meters of gas for 30 years. To that end, in July 2007 China signed an agreement for a pipeline project with Turkmenistan that would allow China to produce gas on the southern bank of the Amu Darya River, which would be pumped to China via a pipeline to be built by 2009.

In Tashkent, in April 2007, China (CNPC), and Uzbekistan (Uzbekneftegas) signed an agreement to build a 530-kilometer Uzbekistan-China gas pipeline with an annual capacity of 30 billion cubic meters.

Against a background of constant growth of Chinese interest in the Central Asian energy industry, these projects, if they become reality, will further increase Beijing's engagement in that industry. Because both the United States and Russia are eager to expand their own shares of the industry, the continuation of this trend will likely create tensions in the bilateral relations of China with Russia and the United States while damaging Moscow's relations with such rival Central Asian energy exporters as Turkmenistan—for Moscow is also aiming at establishing itself as the largest energy supplier to China.

Yet, given the growing economic, political, and security ties between Kazakhstan and its two large, nuclear neighbors, the likelihood is very small that such issues will escalate into major crises and armed confrontation in the near future. Additionally, the existence of a large ethnic Russian community in Kazakhstan will make the Kazakhs further inclined to tension-free relations with Russia.

Relations with the United States

Washington has been a major economic partner of Astana owing to the extensive engagement of American oil companies in Kazakhstan. Political and military cooperation between the two have also expanded, especially since 2001. In view of the importance of oil exports for both sides—and, in particular, the importance of American investment and technology to the development of the Kazakh oil resources—the two sides have every reason to avoid conflict and confrontation. However, potential sources of conflict do exist, with the possibility of escalation in the foreseeable future. Concern about U.S.-backed color revolutions promoted by American NGOs has been shared by all Central Asian governments, including that of Kazakhstan, since the Georgian Rose Revolution in 2003. Hence, efforts on the part of the U.S. government to question the legitimacy of the Kazakh government by challenging its undemocratic record, demanding reforms to address its human rights shortcomings, or backing, in some form, NGOs advocating democratic reforms would likely damage Kazakh-American relations as a prelude to major political conflict. As detailed in the country profile of Uzbekistan in this book, sudden deterioration of relations of the Central Asian states with Washington is a clear possibility. Once the closest regional ally of Washington, Tashkent has become the most vocal opponent of Washington over its alleged involvement in the aforementioned Andijan incident in 2005 and its alleged efforts to provoke a color revolution.

Difficulties that all NGOs, foreign and local, face throughout Central Asia, including in Kazakhstan, especially since that incident, reflect Kazakhstan's growing concern about a possible U.S.-backed color revolution. The consolidation of the SCO, in which Kazakhstan is a member, and its unanimous demand in 2005 for a U.S. military withdrawal from Central Asia, including Kazakhstan, clearly indicate a growing concern among Kazakh leaders about U.S. objectives in their country and a growing interest in expanding relations with China and Russia.

Conflicts over the Caspian Sea's Legal Regime

Disputes over the legal regime for the division of the Caspian Sea among its five littoral states (Iran, Russia, Azerbaijan, Kazakhstan, and Turkmenistan) have been a source of tension and conflict in the Caspian region since the Soviet Union's fall. The inability of the littoral states to agree on a legal regime has created uncertainty about the ownership of many Caspian offshore oil fields and prevented their development, while creating a situation ripe for tension and hostility between and among the littoral states. Until 1999, Iran and Russia opposed dividing the Caspian Sea into national zones, in favor of dividing it based on the condominium principle. Eager to develop their offshore oil and gas fields to address their deep financial problems, the other three states insisted on the Caspian's division into unequal national zones. Russia joined them in 1999 when it found large offshore oil reserves close to its Caspian coastline. Lacking the support of other Caspian states, Iran has accepted in principle the division of the Caspian seabed into equal national zones, a position backed only by Turkmenistan, although it still favors a condominium arrangement. Russia has sought to address the issue through bilateral agreements with its neighbors. It signed agreements with Azerbaijan in September 2002 and with Kazakhstan in May 2002, which solved most, but not all, territorial disputes. After all, it has addressed only the division of the seabed, leaving many other issues unresolved. For Kazakhstan, border disputes in the Caspian Sea have been settled as a result of the mentioned bilateral agreement with Russia, but methods for sharing the Caspian water with other littoral states and dividing the seabed with neighboring Turkmenistan and Azerbaijan are still unsettled. Additionally, not all the littoral states have agreed on the legality of the mentioned bilateral agreements, and nor is there any indication that they will in the near future. As discussed in their respective country profiles in this book, the tension between Turkmenistan and Azerbaijan and between Iran and Azerbaijan over the ownership of certain disputed offshore oil fields, coupled with the threat of an arms race and the use of force early in this decade, indicate that the absence of a legal regime acceptable to all the Caspian littoral states will likely create conflicts. These could well escalate to armed conflict because of the high stakes all these countries have in developing the offshore oil fields. The continued absence of such a regime could drag Kazakhstan into a conflict at least with its immediate neighbor, Turkmenistan.

BIBLIOGRAPHY

Abolhassan Shirazi, Habibollah. 1991. *The Nations of Central Asia.* Tehran: The Institute for Political and International Studies.

Allworth, Edward. 1989. "Encounter." In *Central Asia: 120 Years of Russian Rule,* edited by Edward Allworth, 1–59. Durham, NC: Duke University Press.

Atta'ie, Farhad. 1993. "A Retrospective Glance at the History and the Current Situation of the Central Asian Republics." *The Journal of Central Asia and Caucasus Review* 1, no. 3 (Winter), 151–164.

Blank, Stephen. 2005. "Making Sense of the Shanghai Cooperation Organization's Astana Summit." *Central Asia–Caucasus Analyst,* July 27, 2005. www.cacianalyst.org/view_article.php?articleid=3504 (accessed August 10, 2008).

Bregel, Yuri. 1991. "Turko-Mongol Influences in Central Asia." In *Turko-Persia in Historical Perspective,* edited by Robert L. Canfield, 53–77. Cambridge: Cambridge University Press.

Christou, Alana. 2007. "The Aral Sea." http://aquaticpath.epi.ufl.edu/waterbiology/studentprojects/AralSea-Alana.pdf (accessed October 6, 2008).

D'Encausse, Hélène Carrère. 1989a. "Civil War and New Governments." In *Central Asia: 120 Years of Russian Rule,* edited by Edward Allworth, 224–253. Durham, NC: Duke University Press.

D'Encausse, Hélène Carrère. 1989b. "The Fall of the Czarist Empire." In *Central Asia: 120 Years of Russian Rule,* edited by Edward Allworth, 207–223. Durham, NC: Duke University Press.

modernity to Kyrgyzstan, the Russian era did not bring progress and prosperity. On the contrary, the Russians' exploitation of its resources, their imposition of forced labor, and their heavy taxation provoked hatred and hostility among the Kyrgyz. Apart from many small-scale anti-Russian fights, the unbearable situation led to a rebellion in the summer of 1916 as other Central Asians also resorted to arms. The bloody conflict left about 2,000 Slavic settlers and many more Kyrgyz dead. Russia's brutal reaction generated fear among the Kyrgyz, one-third of whom fled to China (Abolhassan Shirazi 1991, 101–108).

The Bolshevik Revolution ended the tsarist rule in Kyrgyzstan, but it did not bring independence for the Kyrgyz. The Soviet regime had extended its control to Kyrgyzstan by 1919, at which time Kyrgyzstan was renamed the Kara-Kyrgyz Autonomous Region. The Kyrgyz were referred to as Kara-Kirghiz until the mid-1920s to distinguish them from the Kazakhs, known at the time as Kirghiz. The Kara-Kyrgyz Autonomous Region was renamed the Kyrgyz Autonomous Republic in 1926, only to be renamed the Kyrgyz Soviet Socialist Republic in 1936.

In the Soviet era, Kyrgyzstan faced no major internal conflicts until its last years. In September 1990, a bloody ethnic conflict left hundreds dead and wounded as ethnic Kyrgyz and ethnic Uzbeks fought over scarce land near the Kyrgyz city of Osh. The Kyrgyz Republic government's efforts to settle ethnic Kyrgyz in the region traditionally dominated by the Uzbeks had prompted this armed conflict, which it ended by declaring a state of emergency and using force.

During the Soviet era, the Soviet Union's conflicts with other nations with a bearing on the Kyrgyz were confined to the Sino-Soviet border disputes in the 1960s, which affected the Central Asian Soviet republics bordering China, including Kyrgyzstan. Relations between the Soviet Union and China deteriorated over ideological and political disagreements in the late 1950s, only to provoke a split in the communist bloc, turning these two countries into hostile rival states. Their conflicts escalated to armed border disputes in the 1960s that had the potential for escalation to war between the two nuclear states. Skirmishes took place along the parts of their long joint borders that correspond today to the borders shared by Russia, Kazakhstan, Kyrgyzstan, and Tajikistan with China. The two sides managed to contain their hostilities to avoid an all-out war, although their border disputes remained unsettled until the fall of the Soviet Union. Such disputes kept a potential source of conflict in Moscow's relations with Beijing that the Kyrgyz inherited at the time of their independence in 1991.

The reforms of the Gorbachev era did not pave the way for the rise of mass pro-democracy or anti-Soviet movements in Kyrgyzstan. In fact, the process of Kyrgyzstan's independence was actually controlled by the Kyrgyz Soviet elite. In December 1990, the Kyrgyz Supreme Soviet voted to change the republic's name to the Republic of Kyrgyzstan. In February 1991, the name of its capital city, Frunze, was changed to Bishkek, its prerevolutionary name. In the aftermath of the aborted Communist coup of August 1991—the leaders of which sought to remove the reform-minded Kyrgyz president—Askar Akayev, both Akayev and his vice president (German Kuznetsov) resigned from the Communist Party of the Soviet Union. On August 31, 1991, the Kyrgyz Supreme Soviet voted to declare independence from the

Soviet Union. The following October, Askar Akayev was elected the first president of independent Kyrgyzstan.

MAJOR PEOPLES AND NATIONS IN KYRGYZSTAN'S HISTORY

The Iranians and the Turkic Tribes

The ethnic structure of Central Asia has changed drastically as a result of the developments of the last 1,400 years. As a result, the region whose native population consisted of Iranian peoples has become mainly Turkic (Bregel 1991, 54). Present-day Kyrgyzstan, like the rest of Central Asia (excluding Tajikistan) began to be Turkified when the Turkic tribes of Inner Asia arrived (Menges 1989, 84; Abolhassan Shirazi 1991, 90). This development resulted in the Turkification of the steppe (nomadic) part of Central Asia (currently Kazakhstan, Kyrgyzstan, and parts of Turkmenistan) by the sixth century (Bregel 1991, 54). In their bid to expand their empire, the Mongols' occupation of Central Asia in the thirteenth century, which lasted until the early sixteenth century in Kyrgyzstan, accelerated the Turkification of the rest of the region, namely its settled part, with the exception of the Tajik-dominated areas (Abolhassan Shirazi 1991, 83). This was because Turkic peoples constituted most of the Mongol army (Bregel 1991, 60).

The Kyrgyz and other Turkic Central Asians trace their ethnic ties to Turkey to the westward migration of the Central Asian Turkic tribes in the eleventh and twelfth centuries (Sarli 1994, 75–76; Saray 1994, 47–48). Chief among them was the Turkmen Oghuz tribe, led by Seljuk (Seljuq or Seljug), the founder of the Seljuk Dynasty (1041–1118). During the course of their migration, the Seljuks conquered and ruled Central Asia and the territories between that region and the Mediterranean Sea. However, their ties with Central Asia did not last long, notwithstanding their Central Asian roots. Preoccupation with ruling their vast territories outside Central Asia on the one hand, and their disappearing power in Iran and Central Asia on the other, helped them lose interest in Central Asia. The Seljuks finally settled in Asia Minor. Their offspring founded the Ottoman Empire in 1290 (Fuller 1991, 194; Saray 1994, 48). That vast empire shrunk to what is now Turkey as a result of massive territorial losses during World War I. In short, the historical links between the Central Asians and Iran and Turkey have helped the latter establish political, economic, social, and cultural ties with Kyrgyzstan since 1991. In the case of Turkey, its ethnic link with the Kyrgyz constitutes another positive factor in this regard.

Iran and Turkey have enjoyed friendly, tension-free relations with Kyrgyzstan since its independence. Compared to their experience with Kazakhstan, they have been more successful, especially in the economic field, including trade and investment in mainly small and medium-scale industrial, construction, and commercial enterprises for which the Kyrgyz lack adequate resources. They have also had limited military/security cooperation with the Kyrgyz. Turkey has provided the Kyrgyz with some military training. In 1993, Iran and Kyrgyzstan concluded a security accord

(*Izvestiia* 1993). In both cases, low-level military/security cooperation has continued to this date (2009). In addition to their bilateral relations, both Ankara and Tehran have extended political and economic relations with Bishkek within the framework of the Economic Cooperation Organization (ECO).

Russia

Russia's contact with Central Asia's nomadic part can be traced back to the sixteenth century. However, this contact was mainly limited to ties with the Kazakh tribes and their forced or voluntary integration into Russia's sphere of influence, until the mid-nineteenth century. In a significant and purposeful manner, Russia's contact with the Kyrgyz began in the second half of the nineteenth century, when the Kyrgyz tribes under the Khanate of Kokand repeatedly failed to defeat their Uzbek enemies. Out of frustration, the tribes appealed to Russia for protection, paving the way for Russia's 1876 war with that khanate and the occupation and eventual annexation of Kyrgyzstan (Allworth 1989, 47–53; Takmil-Homayoon 1993, 21–47; d'Encausse, 1989c, 151–171).

This development had a major effect on the ethnic makeup and the language of the Kyrgyz, owing to the migration of ethnic Russians and the introduction of the Russian language. To exploit the resources of the Kyrgyz, the Russians began various projects that to a limited extent advanced the Kyrgyz land, including the construction of schools, houses, mines, and roads. Yet, they did not change it drastically, and they left the majority of the Kyrgyz illiterate and poor, although they did help the publication of Kyrgyz literature to some extent.

However, drastic changes occurred in the aftermath of the Bolshevik Revolution as the Soviet regime implemented a systematic policy to change the ethnic and linguistic structure of the entire Central Asia, including Kyrgyzstan, as a means of guaranteeing the region's submission to Moscow. The policy had two major components: ethnic engineering and Russification. Its objective was to impose an artificial sense of belonging to distinct ethnic and linguistic groups in place of the Central Asians' culture and history (Shykh-Attar 1992, 17–21). The final goal of the Soviet decision-makers was to create a Russian-speaking people loyal to Moscow, a so-called Soviet people to replace all nationalities.

In pursuit of the policy of ethnic engineering, Moscow created five "ethnically based" republics, each to be named after one "dominant" ethnic group. This goal was achieved over about three decades, during which the region was divided several times, finally reaching its current form only to foster ethnic and inter- and intrastate conflicts. This is the result of the Soviet regime's intentional division of monoethnic regions among different Central Asian republics in such ways as to leave large communities of ethnic minorities in each of them. The Soviet planners also imposed a "national language" on each republic to change the pre-Soviet linguistic structure of the region, although the administrative and cultural language of most Central Asians was Persian. Their religious language was Arabic, and the Turkic Central Asians' oral and literary language was Joghatai Turkic. Certain measures were implemented to change the regional linguistic structure, including the gradual replacing of the Persian script used by all Central Asians with the Cyrillic alphabet, and the weakening of Joghatai Turkic by promoting four Turkic local languages, each for a Turkic republic. In practice, the ethnic engineering policy prepared the ground for future ethnic conflicts to contribute to the outbreak of civil as well as interstate wars, planting as it did the seeds of ethnic and linguistic discrimination and territorial claims. This is a serious problem in Central Asia today.

The Soviet government's Russification program affected the Kyrgyz and other Central Asians in ways that are still felt today, and will be felt for the foreseeable future. In a bid to change the regional ethnic structure, Moscow settled many Soviets of European origin in Central Asia, mostly Russians as well as Ukrainians and Volga Germans, who were appointed to sensitive positions (Atta'ie 1993, 158). Furthermore, the Russians created a Russified local elite in every Central Asian republic by attracting and training young Central Asians. A major component of the Russification scheme was to use the weakening of the indigenous languages to ensure preeminent status for the Russian language as a "supraethnic language" to be used for the communication of all Soviet citizens. Closely attached to this, and in order to facilitate the Russification of the Central Asian languages, the Soviet government imposed the Cyrillic alphabet on all its Central Asian republics, not only for writing Russian but also for writing their respective local languages.

There is no question that the Russians have been the major people in the recent history of the Kyrgyz and other Central Asians. They have had a long-term impact on the regional peoples in many spheres, including social, economic, political, military/security, and environmental. Russian rule turned the Central Asian nomadic tribes of current Kazakhstan, Kyrgyzstan, and parts of Turkmenistan into largely settled, urbanized peoples. The Russians also expanded education and science, resulting in the elimination of illiteracy in Central Asia, while introducing industries to the region. Of course, their industrialization plan for the region was discriminatory, favoring Kazakhstan and Uzbekistan. It produced their strong industrial basis and heavy and military industries although the level of industrialization of the five Soviet republics, including those countries, was but a fraction of the Slavic parts of the Soviet Union. In consequence, Kyrgyzstan was mainly a single-product (cotton), agrarian country with a limited degree of industrialization, at the time of independence unable even to feed its population.

In the post-Soviet era, certain factors have secured Russia's continued ties with Kyrgyzstan in the foreseeable future. One is Kyrgyzstan's Russian community, formed over a century and ensuring, among other factors, influence for Russia in Kyrgyzstan. Predominantly but not exclusively concentrated in Bishkek, this community now accounts for about 22 percent of the Kyrgyz population, many of whom are highly educated, the result of the Soviet policy to secure the domination of the ethnic Russians in Central Asia. Another factor is the Russian language's preeminence in Kyrgyzstan, which will last for a long time. Yet another factor is the extensive ties inherited from the Soviet era and made since the Soviet Union's fall in the economic, industrial, and military/security fields. Inaugurated in October 2003, Russia's air force base in Bishkek has strengthened Russia's military presence and political influence in Kyrgyzstan. Finally, Russia and Kyrgyzstan are both members of the Shanghai Cooperation Organization (SCO) and the Collective Security Treaty Organization (CSTO), providing grounds for expanding military/security ties and cooperation.

consolidate its independence, to end its heavy reliance on Russia because of Soviet-inherited ties, and to broaden its political, economic, and military/security horizon.

For the same reasons and also to ensure peace along its long borders with China, Kyrgyzstan also terminated hostile relations with China. Rising as a superpower, China also wanted to secure friendly and predictable relations with the newly independent Central Asian countries. Within this favorable context, Kyrgyzstan and China settled their border disputes in the 1990s through bilateral and multilateral agreements to finalize borders between China and its four new neighbors, namely Russia, Kazakhstan, Kyrgyzstan, and Tajikistan. The four states established a joint commission on the border regime between their countries and China in September 1992 (KRWE 1992). That provided a workable framework for all of them in their negotiations with China. Furthermore, they used the Shanghai Cooperation Organization (SCO), known in the 1990s as the Shanghai Five, of which all four, with China, were members, to end their disagreements over the common borders with China—a declared objective of the Shanghai Five.

Although the Kyrgyz have been successful in settling their border disputes with China, they have yet to resolve their territorial disputes with their neighboring Central Asians. In fact, the latter have been a source of tension in Kyrgyzstan's ties with Tajikistan and Uzbekistan. The three countries have territorial claims upon each other regarding the divided Ferghana Valley that leave many ethnic Kyrgyz, Tajiks,

Kyrgyz border guard watches over a refugee camp just outside the Kyrgyz village of Barash on the Uzbek-Kyrgyz border on May 23, 2005. Kyrgyzstan sheltered many Uzbek citizens who fled across the border from the embattled city of Andijan. (Vyacheslav Oseledko/AFP/Getty Images)

and Uzbeks in the wrong countries. For example, Uzbekistan has territorial claims to Tajikistan's city of Kokand and part of Kyrgyzstan's Osh Province. Sensitivity to that province on both sides of the Kyrgyz-Uzbek border could well instigate a violent ethnic conflict with a potential for escalation to an armed conflict between the two neighbors, as became evident in the Soviet era. Against a background of scarcity of land, the Kyrgyz government–supported settlement of ethnic Kyrgyz in that province, the original inhabitants of which were Uzbeks, sparked a bloody ethnic conflict in 1990 that left at least 320 dead (Ratter 1993, 197). Many ethnic Uzbeks from the then Soviet Republic of Uzbekistan tried to cross the border from the Province of Andijan to help their brethren, but the Uzbek authorities stopped them (ibid.). There is no guarantee that the latter will have a strong incentive to do so in a similar incident in the future, in view of the cold Uzbek-Kyrgyz relations. Tajikistan and Kyrgyzstan also disagree about their borders in the Ferghana Valley, and thus about the ownership of border territories and enclaves of their ethnic brethren in each other's territories.

Although none of them has resorted to the use of its military to settle the borders in its favor once and for all, the three countries have experienced limited border skirmishes or use of force to change the borders since independence. In particular, many exchanges of fire between the two sides have taken place on the border between Kyrgyzstan and Uzbekistan. Additionally, many other factors have contributed to the small-scale use of arms along their common borders. These include illegal border crossing by border troops and nationals as well as mutual firing on each other's territories to attack drug traffickers and IMU fighters who cross their borders to evade the security forces of one of the three neighboring countries. A major case recently reported includes a skirmish in May 2005 between Uzbek government forces and a large group of "Uzbek militants" (i.e., IMU fighters) trying to cross into Kyrgyzstan (Oliver 2005). In particular, the issue of dealing with the armed traffickers and the IMU has been a source of tension in the relations between Bishkek and Tashkent; both sides accuse each other of failure to deal with the problem.

The May 2005 armed incident in Uzbekistan's Andijan created tension in Kyrgyz-Uzbek relations. In reaction to the Uzbek security forces' iron-fisted approach to the armed groups involved in the incident, many Uzbeks fled the City of Andijan to neighboring Kyrgyzstan, where its government sheltered hundreds of them. This angered the Uzbek government, which considered at least some of the escapees potential terrorists involved in the incident. However, the two sides have since moved ahead and increased their security cooperation in the form of joint operations on both sides of their borders against the armed groups, including the IMU (Kimmage 2006).

THE OUTLOOK FOR FUTURE CONFLICTS

Kyrgyzstan is one of the Central Asian states that will likely experience a turbulent future should the current situation continue. At least in the foreseeable future, its main source of conflict will be domestic, as the country is far from stable politically and socially.

Internal Sources of Conflict

In the post-Akayev era, the new administration of President Kurmanbek Bakiev has not made any significant step toward addressing the political, economic, and social factors that prepared the ground for the Yellow (Tulip) Revolution. By and large, that "revolution" resulted only in removing President Akayev from the political scene and ending his family's domination of the country while leaving his corrupt administration in place. The new president and his team, the majority of whom are the political figures of the Akayev era, have simply failed to embark on a plan to address the grievances and thus the roots of popular discontent of the post-independence era. Consequently, the social, political, and economic grounds for popular dissent are still well in place, making the country prone to instability. There is no wonder that mass anti-government demonstrations reemerged in the major cities, particularly in Bishkek in 2006, less than a year after the Yellow Revolution, and have continued to this date (early 2009). The Kyrgyz political system evidently suffers from a lack of legitimacy and sustainable popular backing, despite its having come to power through a "revolution." In the absence of any major effort to address the causes of popular dissatisfaction and instability, major political upheavals, including events along the line of the 2005 revolution, are to be expected in the foreseeable future.

Supporters of Kyrgyzstan's Tulip Revolution hold a poster that reads "People Are for Justice" as they protest the newly elected Zhogorku Kenesh (parliament) in the capital, Bishkek, on March 30, 2005. (Viktor Drachev/AFP/Getty Images)

External Sources of Conflict

Territorial disputes between Kyrgyzstan and its neighbors Tajikistan and Uzbekistan are possible but not inevitable in the foreseeable future. Such disputes could ignite crises in Bishkek's bilateral relations with Dushanbe and Tashkent, especially in the case of ethnic movements or uprisings in the Ferghana Valley, with the predictable effect of stimulating nationalism among the peoples of the three countries in support of their ethnic kin. Such crises could well lead to armed confrontations among Kyrgyzstan and Tajikistan and Uzbekistan, intentionally or unintentionally.

In the case of Kyrgyz-Uzbek relations, certain factors could also lead to conflicts with a potential for escalation to armed ones. A repetition of the May 2005 Andijan incident in Uzbekistan and the Kyrgyz government's sheltering Uzbek refugees could provoke an Uzbek military border crossing in pursuit of such refugees, which would likely meet a Kyrgyz military response. Among other factors, the overall state of the two countries' bilateral relations would determine the scale and scope of such response and the possibility of its development into a major armed conflict. Furthermore, disagreements between the two neighbors over their dealings with armed groups operating along their common borders—including the IMU, like-minded groups, and the armed international drug traffickers—could well exacerbate tensions and conflicts.

BIBLIOGRAPHY

Abolhassan Shirazi, Habibollah. *The Nations of Central Asia*. Tehran: The Institute for Political and International Studies, 1991.

Allworth, Edward. "Encounter." In *Central Asia: 120 Years of Russian Rule,* edited by Edward Allworth, 1–59. Durham, NC: Duke University Press, 1989.

Anderson, John. *Kyrgyzstan: Central Asia's Island of Democracy?* London: Taylor & Francis, 1999.

Atta'ie, Farhad. 1993. "A Retrospective Glance at the History and the Current Situation of the Central Asian Republics." *The Journal of Central Asia and Caucasus Review* 1, no. 3 (Winter), 151–164.

Blank, Stephen. 2005. "Making Sense of the Shanghai Cooperation Organization's Astana Summit." *Central Asia–Caucasus Analyst*, July 27, 2005. www.cacianalyst.org/view_article.php?articleid=3504 (accessed May 10, 2008).

Bregel, Yuri. 1991. "Turko-Mongol Influences in Central Asia." In *Turko-Persia in Historical Perspective*, edited by Robert L. Canfield, 53–77. Cambridge: Cambridge University Press.

Buckley, Sarah. 2005. "Central Asia's Deadly Cargo." *BBC News*, November 22, 2005. http://news.bbc.co.uk/2/hi/asia-pacific/4414922.stm (accessed July 10, 2008).

D'Encausse, Hélène Carrère. 1989a. "Civil War and New Governments." In *Central Asia: 120 Years of Russian Rule,* edited by Edward Allworth, 224–253. Durham, NC: Duke University Press.

D'Encausse, Hélène Carrère. 1989b. "The Fall of the Czarist Empire." In *Central Asia: 120 Years of Russian Rule,* edited by Edward Allworth, 207–223. Durham, NC: Duke University Press.

D'Encausse, Hélène Carrère. 1989c. "Organizing and Colonizing the Conquered Territories." In *Central Asia: 120 Years of Russian Rule,* edited by Edward Allworth, 151–171. Durham, NC: Duke University Press.

Fuller, Graham E. 1991. *The "Center of the Universe": The Geopolitics of Iran.* Boulder, CO: Westview Press.

Human Rights Watch. 2004. *Creating Enemies of the State: Religious Persecution in Uzbekistan.* March 29, 2004. New York: Human Rights Watch.

Human Rights Watch. 2006. "Kyrgyzstan." *Human Rights Watch World Report 2006.* New York: Human Rights Watch.

Human Rights Watch. 2007. "Kyrgyzstan." *Human Rights Watch World Report 2007.* New York: Human Rights Watch.

Human Rights Watch. 2008. "Kyrgyzstan." *Human Rights Watch World Report 2008.* New York: Human Rights Watch.

Izvestiia. 1993. June 24, 1993, 3. In *Commonwealth of Independent States and the Middle East (CISME)* 18, no. 6 (June 1993), 9.

Keesing's Record of World Events (KRWE). 1992. "CIS: Other CIS Agreements." *KRWE* 38, no. 9 (September 1992), 39106.

Kimmage, Danile. 2006. "Analysis: Extremist Threats, and Doubts, in Kyrgyzstan, Tajikistan." Radio Free Europe/Radio Liberty (RFE/RL), July 24, 2006. www.rferl.org/featuresarticle/2006/07/212f8957-a0bf-4963-aacb-0efe6fbf28a5.html (accessed August 1, 2008).

Kommersant. 2007. "Gendarme of Eurasia." October 8, 2007. www.kommersant.com/p812422/CIS_CSTO_Russia_Lebedev/ (accessed September 30, 2008).

Marat, Erica. 2006a. "Bishkek Becomes Scene of Continuous Anti-Government Demonstrations." *Eurasia Daily Report* 3, no. 109 (June 6). www.jamestown.org/edm/article.php?article_id=2371154 (accessed July 30, 2008).

Marat, Erica. 2006b. *The Tulip Revolution: Kyrgyzstan One Year After.* New York: The Jamestown Foundation.

Menges, Karl H. 1989. "People, Languages, and Migrations." In *Central Asia: 120 Years of Russian Rule,* edited by Edward Allworth, 60–91. Durham, NC: Duke University Press.

Oliver, Mark, and Agencies. 2005. "'700 dead' in Uzbek Violence." *The Guardian,* May 16, 2005. www.guardian.co.uk/international/story/0,1485270,00.html (accessed August 15, 2008).

Peimani, Hooman. 2000. "Drug-Trafficking in the Fergana Valley and Instability in Central Asia." *The Times of Central Asia* (Bishkek), November 2, 2000, 4–5.

Peimani, Hooman. 2002. *Failed Transition, Bleak Future?: War and Instability in Central Asia and the Caucasus.* Westport, CT: Praeger.

Ratter, Igor. 1993. "Will Central Asia Explode?" *The Journal of Central Asia and Caucasus Review* 2, no.1 (Summer), 195–204.

RIA Novosti. 2008. "Kyrgyzstan Will Demand US Close the Base Eventually." February 20, 2008. http://en.rian.ru/world/20080220/99718840.html (accessed October 9, 2008).

Saray, Mehmet. 1994. "Political, Economic [a]nd Cultural Relations between Turkey [a]nd Central Asian Republics." *Eurasian Studies* 2 (Summer), 47–52.

Sarli, Araz Mohammad. 1994. "The Emergence and Collapse of Turkmen States." *The Journal of Central Asia and Caucasus Review* 2, no. 3 (Winter), 71–82.

Shykh-Attar, Ali-Reza. 1992. *The Roots of Political Behavior in Central Asia and the Caucasus.* Tehran: Centre of Central Asian and Caucasian Research in the Institute for Political and International Studies.

Takmil-Homayoon, Nasser. 1993. "A Glance at Asia: Understanding Central Asia." *The Journal of Central Asia and Caucasus Review* 1, no. 3 (Winter), 21–47.

United Nations Development Programme (UNDP). 2005a. "Demographic Trends." *Human Development Report 2005,* 232–235. New York: UNDP.

United Nations Development Programme (UNDP). 2005b. "Survival: Progress and Setbacks." *Human Development Report 2005,* 250–253. New York: UNDP.

United Nations Office for Coordination of Humanitarian Affairs (UNOCHA). 2007. "Tajikistan: Afghan Narcotics Fuel Drug Addiction." *IRIN*, June 26, 2007. www.irinnews.org/report.aspx? ReportID=72937 (accessed September 29, 2008).

United Nations Office on Drugs and Crimes (UNODC). 2005. *World Drug Report 2005*. Vienna: UNODC. www.unodc.org/pdf/WDR_2005/volume_1_chap1_dynamics.pdf (accessed August 21, 2008).

United Nations Office on Drugs and Crimes (UNODC). 2008. *Afghanistan: Opium Survey 2008*. August 2008. Vienna: UNODC. www.unodc.org/documents/data-and-analysis/ExSum25August-standard.pdf (accessed October 2, 2008).

Weitz, Richard. 2004. "Storm Clouds over Central Asia: Revival of the Islamic Movement of Uzbekistan (IMU)?" *Studies in Conflict and Terrorism* 27, 465–490.

Chapter 8

Tajikistan

GENERAL STATISTICS

Area

143,099 km²

Population

7,215,700

Population Density

50 inhabitants per km²

Major Cities

Dushanbe (capital)
Khojand

Gross Domestic Product

$4.8 billion (2008 est.)

Annual Military Expenditure

3.9% of GDP (2005 est.)

Military Service

Compulsory military service for men
18 years of age, with a two-year conscripted
service obligation (2007).

*International Organization
Membership*

CIS (1993)
CST/CSTO (1992)
ECO (1992)
OSCE (1992)
SCO/Shanghai Five (1996)
UN (1992)

HISTORY OF TAJIKISTAN

Tajikistan ranks along with its neighbor Kyrgyzstan as one of the smallest and poorest Central Asian countries. This small but mountainous Central Asian state was host to human settlements as early as 3000 BC. The Tajiks, descendants of Iranian peoples whose presence in the area was first recorded around 500 BC, were members of the ancient kingdom of Bactria and part of the Achaemenid Persian empire before its defeat by the armies of Alexander the Macedonian. Unlike their nomadic, Turkic-speaking neighbors, the Tajiks became sedentary early on and spoke a Persian language. In the third and second centuries BC, the territory of Tajikistan saw the rise of the Greco-Bactrian culture, which was eventually replaced by the Kushan Empire. In the seventh century AD, the Arab conquests introduced Islam, which had a profound influence on the subsequent development of the Tajik culture. Arabic replaced Persian as the language of power, but the latter remained the medium of record-keeping, learning, daily conversation, and poetry. In the ninth and tenth centuries, the Tajik lands came under the control of the Saffarid and then the Samanid dynasties, and the eleventh and twelfth centuries saw the rise of the Ghaznevid Kingdom and the Empire of Khorezm. The rise of these two Turkic dynasties introduced the Turkic language, which eventually replaced Arabic as the language of the court. In 1219, the region suffered a devastating Mongol invasion led by Genghis Khan that established Mongol dominance for the next two centuries. In the late fourteenth century, the Tajik lands were incorporated into the empire of Timur and his descendants.

Beginning in the sixteenth century, Tajikisktan formed part of the Khanate of Bukhara and was influenced by the rise of the powerful Saffavid Dynasty in Iran (Persia). The Saffavids adopted Shia as their official religion, while the Central Asian population remained Sunni, and relatively isolated from the rest of the Muslim world. In the eighteenth century, Afghan forces took over low-lying parts of the Tajik region, including the ancient city of Balkh. Russian incursions in the second half of the nineteenth century brought Tajiks into the sphere of Russian influence. The Khanate of Bukhara was made a protectorate of the tsarist empire in 1868–1869. In the mid-1890s, the British government, as part of its great power rivalry with Russia, recognized the Amu Darya River as the southernmost frontier of Russian control—which left a large portion of the Tajik-speaking population outside the Russian Empire and thus excluded them from the future Tajikistan. Today, almost 5 million Tajiks live in Afghanistan and Uzbekistan. The Russian Revolution of 1917 spurred rebellion among the Tajiks, and it was not until 1921, with the Russian Empire's collapse and Soviet Russia on the rise, that Soviet troops finally captured Dushanbe, the current Tajik capital. The region became the center of guerrilla resistance to the early Soviet regime as mountain rebels, commonly known as the Basmachi, revolted in the 1920s.

Present-day Tajikistan was established as the Tajik Autonomous Soviet Socialist Republic, as part of the newly formed Uzbek Soviet Socialist Republic, in the fall of 1924. Tajikistan became a full member of the Soviet Union and the seventh union republic in 1929. Repressive campaigns in the 1930s purged ethnic Tajiks from the ranks of local republican government in favor of ethnic Russian settlers. The forced collectivization of agriculture in the 1930s involved large-scale irrigation projects that

and ended on June 14, 1997, when the Tajik government and the coalition of the opposition groups signed a peace treaty. Of course, like any other armed conflict, the war fluctuated in intensity during its five-year course. Yet, the civil war was devastating for the entire country, severely affecting the two parties to the conflict (the Tajik government and religious-nationalist opposition) as well as Tajik society in general. It ended as a result of the inability of either party to dominate the country and neutralize—or at least marginalize—the other. Against a background of widespread popular resentment of the conflict and a strong desire to end the devastation, the existing social, political, and military impasse forced the two parties to accept a peace treaty providing for the minimum demands of both sides. Because neither of the opposing political groups of the conflict era has the power and social backing to initiate a new round of conflict to achieve its maximum demands, and because the Tajiks do not support such a plan for reasons already mentioned, the peace treaty has so far held, generally speaking.

The roots of the conflict laid in the dissatisfaction of a large and growing number of Tajiks right after independence, when the Tajik Soviet elite turned nationalist to remain in power (Peimani 1998, 28–30). In particular, the opposition groups by and large represented the politically, economically, and socially deprived regions of Tajikistan (such as its southern regions), which felt excluded from the post-independence political system dominated by the ex-Soviet elite, of whom many were ethnic Uzbeks from Khojand. Forming a coalition of nationalist and Islamic groups, the opposition groups faced the Tajik elite backed by both Russia and Uzbekistan. Other Central Asian countries rendered their support to a varying extent, because they were all concerned about the takeover of Tajikistan by the coalition forces' unfriendly—if not outright hostile—approach. Uzbekistan was concerned about the expansion of the anti-establishment movement to its country from neighboring Tajikistan. Certain parameters made that scenario a distinct possibility, including strong historical and ethnic ties between the two countries, a significant Tajik community in Uzbekistan, and a prevailing and growing sense of dissatisfaction with the ruling elite among the Uzbeks. The Uzbek government also justified its intervention in Tajikistan in support of its ethnic brethren living in that country. Forming a large minority in Tajikistan, the Uzbeks felt threatened by the ethnically Tajik-dominated opposition forces aiming to end the privileged status of the ethnic Uzbeks, their stronghold (Khojand), and their strong influence in the Soviet-inherited political system. The Uzbek community of Tajikistan threatened on many occasions to secede from that country and join Uzbekistan, a feasible scenario in view of its concentration in the areas bordering Uzbekistan in the Ferghana Valley.

Uzbekistan provided military assistance to the Tajik government in its war against the Tajik coalition forces, and Russia became the largest backer of the Tajik government. The Tajik security forces still in formation in the 1990s were simply too weak to stand on their own. The Russian military presence in Tajikistan, remaining in the post-independence era upon mutual agreement, enabled Moscow to assist Dushanbe significantly, although its forces did not officially enter the conflict in favor of the Tajik government. Practically all other Central Asian countries backed the Tajik elite in one form or another because of their concern about the spillover of the Tajik civil war to

An anticommunist demonstration in Dushanbe, Tajikistan on October 4, 1991. (Pascal Le Segretain/Sygma/Corbis)

their countries and also their obvious opposition to the removal of the Tajik Soviet elite from power by opposition groups with clear implications for them as the Soviet elites turned nationalist.

The end of the civil war opened a new era in Tajikistan's post-independence period. Political stability has improved since 1997, but in order to gain control of certain areas, the Tajik government has made compromises and forged alliances among regional factions and clans that retain substantial political influence. Particularly important is the rivalry between politicians of the northern and southern regions. The 1997 peace accord guaranteed 30 percent of government positions to northern politicians to temper the dominance of the southern clans. That guarantee, however, expired in 2004. The old opposition parties have been either suppressed or forced to join the Tajik government and its different institutions, as provided by the peace accord. Even though the peace accord has not been implemented to the full satisfaction of the parties to the civil war, it has held so far and has been respected by them, by and large. In recent years, new opposition political parties have emerged, some of them embracing extremism. The largest of these extremist organizations is Hizb ut-Tahrir (Party of Liberation), a fundamentalist Islamic group active in many Arab countries. The Hizb ut-Tahrir is a branch of the movement established by Taqiuddin al-Nabhani, an Islamic scholar, in 1953, and it aims at establishing an Islamic state (caliphate) throughout Central Asia. However, it does not advocate violence as a means to that end (Human Rights Watch 2004, 24). The group is distinct from another fundamentalist group, the Islamic Movement of Uzbekistan (IMU), which promotes armed violence as the only means of overthrowing the Uzbek government and anyone supporting it. Yet, in practice all the Central Asian governments treat the Hizb ut-Tahrir as an armed opposition group on a par with the IMU. The Hizb ut-Tahrir is therefore illegal in Tajikistan and elsewhere in the region, although it is not in a position to pose a serious challenge to the authority of the Tajik government. Nevertheless, it has been under severe suppression by the Tajik authorities, who have arrested and imprisoned many of its members and sympathizers for their alleged violent anti-government activities, including armed violence. The Tajik leaders are concerned about the group's potential to grow in the region's poorest country, whose largely dissatisfied population offers an army of potential recruits.

The Islamic Movement of Uzbekistan (IMU) is an Uzbek anti-government group based in Uzbekistan's part of the Ferghana Valley (Human Rights Watch 2004, 16). It was established by a small group of extremists in 1998 with the goal of overthrowing the Uzbek government and establishing an Islamic state in Uzbekistan. The movement has also operated in Tajikistan and Kyrgyzstan, the other two countries that share the Ferghana Valley, and has often crossed the border into those countries to escape the Uzbek security forces or to conduct subversive activities inside them, including killing their border guards and bombing government buildings. The IMU also maintained bases in Tajikistan and the Taliban-controlled regions of Afghanistan, from which it organized several raids into Kyrgyzstan and Uzbekistan in 1999 and 2000. The movement suffered significant losses in 2002 when, after the September 11, 2001 attacks in the United States, the U.S. government launched operations in Afghanistan. Despite its relative inactivity in recent years, the movement continues to be listed as a terrorist threat. The Tajik government blames the IMU fighters for a number of armed attacks in 2005 and 2006, including two bombing incidents in Dushanbe, an attack on a Tajik interior ministry facility in Qayroqqum, and the murder of a defense ministry official (Kimmage 2006). After a few years of limited activities attributed to suppression by the Uzbek government, the IMU's increasing activities in Uzbekistan and its neighbors since 2004 (Weitz 2004, 465–490) have created concerns for all the regional countries affected by its activities.

Overall, the domestic situation in Tajikistan is stable, but that is a result of oppressive government policies. President Imomali Rahmanov easily won reelection in the presidential election of 1999 and 2006, in which opposition parties were persecuted and media were censored. The parliamentary elections of 2005 gave President Rahmanov's party, the People's Democratic Party, a strong majority but were widely considered flawed and unfair. Despite such drawbacks, the inclusion of an Islamic party (Islamic Renaissance Party) and several other parties in the parliamentary elections represented an improvement in political process, since Tajikistan is the only Central Asian country in which a religiously affiliated party is represented in parliament. Changing his surname from Rahmanov to Rahmon in 2007, President Rahmon seeks political supremacy in the country, and considering the success of his party in the parliamentary elections of 2005, he will most likely win a third term in 2013. Such successes, however, mean further political crackdown. Media freedom is curtailed, with official television and radio stations under strict government censorship and opposition newspapers regularly subjected to forced closure. The government has recently begun to renege on earlier promises and agreements. The former opposition fighters who were included in the regular forces under the 1997 accords have almost all been dismissed under various pretexts. On the regional and local levels, the government also reneged on the agreement to fill one-third of government posts with opposition candidates. Many opposition parties have difficulty obtaining official registration to participate in elections. Political crackdown intensified after the 2005 Yellow Revolution in Kyrgyzstan that resulted in the ouster of the Kyrgyz president. The Tajik government became concerned about foreign sponsorship of civil society groups and required foreign embassies and aid organizations to report to the government their contacts with local political and civil activists. In 2006–2007, the country was periodically rocked by explosions, the most recent of which took place in Dushanbe in mid-November 2007. Such explosions are usually blamed on the IMU, but some analysts also speculate that the Tajik government itself might stand behind such incidents in order to maintain a heightened sense of danger among the populace and justify its repressive measures (Eurasianet 2007).

External Conflicts since Independence

In its external affairs, Tajikistan has not experienced major conflicts with the potential for escalation to armed ones since its independence. However, its relations with its neighbor Uzbekistan, the most populous and militarily the strongest regional country, have been tense and unfriendly—to say the least—with periods of open hostility. This is notwithstanding the Uzbek government's backing of the Tajik government during the civil war.

Various factors have contributed to this state of relations, which could potentially escalate to major military conflict, pitting the two neighbors against each other in various forms. One has been disputes over territories and borders. The Tajiks have a claim to their traditional strongholds—the cities of Bukhara and Samarkand—before their incorporation into the Russian Empire, and the Uzbeks have claims to Tajikistan's city of Khojand, which is predominately Uzbek—in addition to these countries' disputes about their border areas. Neither side has seriously pursued those claims, even though there have been many unofficial statements to that effect. Yet, the possibility of the secession of Khojand during the civil war was a serious source of concern for the Tajiks as the Khojandis threatened on many occasions to secede and unite with Uzbekistan should the nationalist-Muslim coalition seize power in Dushanbe (Peimani 1998, 29).

Another factor has been what the Tajik government describes as the interference of Tashkent in its internal affairs. They include Tashkent's alleged backing of anti-Tajik government opponents, including the Khojandis, their provision of safe havens and training camps for such opponents, and their support of coup attempts. In 2006, the Tajik government accused its Uzbek counterparts of having more than ten training camps for supporters of Colonel Mahmud Khudoiberdiev, who was behind a failed coup attempt in Tajikistan (Kimmage 2006). The latter allegedly masterminded the abortive 1999 coup staged by the Uzbek Khojandis (Hiro 1999, 19). Dushanbe and Tashkent have also accused each other of spying (Kimmage 2006).

Yet another factor responsible for these cold relations has been gas imports from Uzbekistan. Tajikistan is dependent on imported fuel, and Uzbekistan has been its major long-term effect on the region, seeking as it did to change the region's ethnic and linguistic structure to make it completely loyal to the Soviet state. Hence, it resorted to ethnic engineering and Russification to substitute the culture and history of Central Asia with an artificial sense of belonging to distinct ethnic and linguistic groups (Shykh-Attar 1992, 17–21). The final objective was to create a completely loyal Russian-speaking Soviet people in place of many national groups.

The main goal of the policy of ethnic engineering was the creation of "ethnically based" Central Asian republics. The Soviet authorities divided the region several times until they created five "ethnically based" republics, each named after one specific, "dominant" ethnic group. The Soviet government intentionally left large numbers of ethnic minorities in each republic as it divided monoethnic regions among different republics by drawing their borders along that line. The policy also required the imposition of a "national language" on each republic in place of the three main regional languages of pre-Soviet era. These were Persian, the administrative and cultural language of most Central Asians; Arabic, their religious language; and Joghatai Turkic, the Turkic people's oral and literary language. Various measures were employed to change this linguistic makeup, such as giving importance to four local languages of the Turkic republics in the place of Joghatai Turkic, and gradually replacing with the Cyrillic alphabet the Persian script used by all Central Asians. The policy of ethnic engineering paved the way for intra- and interstate conflicts geared to ethnic and linguistic discrimination and territorial claims. The latter are a major current problem endangering security in the region.

Several policies the Soviet leaders put in place to achieve their Russification scheme have implications for Central Asia today and in the foreseeable future. One was the settlement of many Russians—and, on a smaller scale, Ukrainians and Volga Germans—in Central Asia in order to change its ethnic composition (Atta'ie 1993, 158). Such people were given sensitive civil and military positions. The fostering of local Russified elites through indoctrination and training of young Central Asians was another policy. Yet another policy was the weakening of the indigenous languages and the promotion of Russian—the so-called supraethnic language—as the main regional language and the means of communication for all Soviet citizens. To facilitate Russification, the Cyrillic alphabets were imposed on the regional languages.

There is no question that Russia has been the most influential nation on the recent history of Turkmenistan. Its impact on Central Asia, including on Turkmenistan, will be felt for a long time in many fields—in particular, the social, economic, political, military/security, and environmental spheres. As a result of Russian rule, the Central Asian nomads, mainly inhabitants of present-day Kazakhstan, Kyrgyzstan, and parts of Turkmenistan, became largely settled and urbanized peoples. The Soviet policy of literacy for all citizens eliminated illiteracy. The Soviet authorities established secular governments in Central Asia, including Turkmenistan, and introduced industries to the region—of course, on a much smaller scale than they did in the Slavic parts of the Soviet Union.

Russian rule of Central Asia also had a major negative dimension. The Russians' view of Central Asia as a hinterland for their country's European part was translated into distorted economic development for the region, evident in limited industrialization and a chiefly cotton-based agriculture unable to provide food for the Central Asians. That made the Central Asians heavily dependent on large imports from other parts of the USSR, a problem from which they suffer today to a varying extent, along with the destructive effects of the Aral Sea environmental disaster, caused by massive cotton production and the diversion of local rivers for irrigation purposes. Furthermore, the politically motivated division of the region, by leaving many large ethnic minorities in every republic, has created a suitable situation for bloody ethnic and territorial disputes in the post-Soviet era. All of Central Asia will be negatively affected by these policies in the years to come.

Unlike Kazakhstan, Turkmenistan does not share borders with Russia, but many factors have ensured Russian influence in that country. Some of these are shared by all Central Asians, such as the preeminence of the Russian language in Central Asia and the extensive ties inherited from the Soviet era and formed since the Soviet Union's fall in the economic, industrial, social, and military/security areas. Other factors include the Russian community of Turkmenistan, accounting for about 10 percent of the population. Yet, perhaps the single most important factor since independence has been Turkmenistan's near-exclusive reliance for gas exports on the Russian gas pipeline network, which connects to Turkmenistan via neighboring Kazakhstan. Ashgabat is increasingly relying on gas exports as one of its two major sources of revenue, along with cotton exports. Consequently, Russia is in a strong position vis-à-vis Turkmenistan, a source of concern for the Turkmens.

Ties with Russia, through whose pipelines the Turkmens conduct almost all their gas export, have been affected by pricing disputes since independence. Ashgabat has accused the Russians of offering low prices for Turkmen gas, which they resell to Europe at much higher prices. Such pricing disputes have taken place several times, including in July 2006. However, owing to the lack of an alternative pipeline, Turkmenistan has not sought to turn the disputes into major conflicts. Obviously, Ashgabat cannot afford to alienate Russia as long as it is dependent on Russian pipelines.

The United States

As elsewhere in Central Asia and the Caucasus, the United States has become an important nation in Turkmenistan in the post-Soviet era. The Turkmens, concerned about over-reliance on Russia, determined to secure their practical independence, and in search of foreign economic assistance, established ties with the Washington upon independence. Being rich in gas and, to a much lesser extent, oil, Turkmenistan has been one of the two Central Asian countries, along with Kazakhstan, of special interest to the American government; it is also in need of U.S. investments and technology for developing its energy resources.

The United States has pursued significant economic activities in Turkmenistan, geared mainly to the production of fossil energy. Despite its official adherence to a policy of neutrality, the Turkmen government has followed the regional trend in the aftermath of the September 11, 2001 attack on the United States by granting the United States military landing and overflight rights in support of its operation in Afghanistan. Because Turkmenistan is a neighbor of Afghanistan, its cooperation with the absence of a legal regime, the unsettled status of the energy-rich Caspian Sea is the major issue in Turkmen foreign policy.

Conflicts over Offshore Caspian Oil Fields

Disputes over the ownership of certain Caspian offshore oil fields have provoked major conflicts between Turkmenistan and Azerbaijan. Caused by the absence of a legal regime for the Caspian Sea, such disputes have been a major source of tension between the Caspian littoral states of Azerbaijan, Iran, Kazakhstan, Turkmenistan, and Russia since the Soviet Union's collapse. The inability of the five littoral states to agree on a legal regime has since created uncertainty about the ownership of many Caspian offshore oil fields and has prevented their development even as it has created a situation ripe for tension and hostility among the littoral states.

Until 1999, Iran and Russia opposed dividing the Caspian Sea into national zones, in favor of dividing it based on the condominium principle. Eager to develop their offshore oil and gas fields to address their deep financial problems, the other three states insisting on division of the Caspian Sea into unequal national zones. Russia joined them in 1999 when it found large offshore oil reserves close to its Caspian coastline. Lacking the support of other Caspian states, Iran has accepted in principle the division of the Caspian seabed into equal national zones, a position backed only by Turkmenistan, although it still favors a condominium arrangement. Seeing no merit in that type of division, Russia has sought to address the issue through bilateral

Oil rig in the Caspian Sea. (Orkhan Aslanov)

agreements with its neighbors. It signed agreements with Azerbaijan in September 2002 and Kazakhstan in May 13, 2002, which solved most but not all territorial disputes as it addressed only the division of the seabed (Eurasianet 2002a). Like Iran, Turkmenistan has not sought to settle the division issue through bilateral agreements with its Caspian neighbors, Iran, Azerbaijan, and Kazakhstan. Nor has it recognized the legality of the Russian bilateral agreements with Azerbaijan and Kazakhstan.

Turkmenistan has disputes with Iran and Azerbaijan for the mentioned reasons, but its disputes with Iran have been inactive and nonhostile. Having extensive and growing political and economic relations, both sides have tried to find a peaceful solution. However, disputes over the ownership of certain offshore oil fields have severely damaged Turkmen-Azeri relations, resulting in Turkmenistan's closing its embassy in Baku in June 2001 (Eurasianet 2001). In particular, the ownership of Azeri, Chiraq, and Guneshli, as well as Serdar (according to the Turkmens) or Kyapaz (according to the Azeris), has pitted the nations against each other since the mid-1990s. The first three operating oil fields have formed Baku's largest offshore oil fields, providing the bulk of its annual oil exports.

The dispute between Turkmenistan and Azerbaijan reached a very hostile stage in July 2001, when their rhetoric included gestures toward military threats. They accused each other of illegal exploration, development, or operation of the disputed oil fields, to some of which Iran had claims. Iran and Turkmenistan on the one side, and Azerbaijan, on the other, also accused each other of violating their territorial waters with military and nonmilitary marine vessels. In such a situation, the sale of two American military boats to Azerbaijan worsened Ashghabat's ties with Baku and also alarmed Tehran. The former expressed deep concern about the transaction, which it portrayed as a threat to its national security and a provocative action to initiate an arms race. In its reaction to the development, the Turkmen government revealed its purchase of Ukrainian military boats, which in turn provoked a harsh Azeri reaction. In 2003 and 2004, these tensions slightly decreased as the governments agreed to continue diplomatic negotiations. In 2009, the two sides have yet to find a satisfactory solution to their dispute.

Conflicts with Uzbekistan

During the Soviet era, Turkmenistan and Uzbekistan were part of the Central Asian economic region and shared most of its transportation, pipeline, or telecommunications infrastructure. Following their independence, relations between the two countries have at times been far from friendly and tension-free. Various factors have contributed to this situation, including border disputes. Thanks to the Soviet division of Central Asia into five ethnically based republics without regard to the historical and ethnic realities, the two neighboring countries have disputes over certain regions. The resulting existence of large ethnic minorities in the two countries (e.g., about 800,000 Turkmens in Uzbekistan) has created grounds for ethnic problems. These countries' nationalist policies toward their respective ethnic minorities have been responsible for rising tensions. In the post-Soviet era, both countries have sought to promote their own respective languages and to elevate the status of their own ethnic kin. In consequence,

Despite Uzbekistan's lack of a common border with Russia, many factors have ensured Russian influence in Uzbekistan since 1991. As elsewhere in the region, such factors include the preeminence of the Russian language and extensive ties—inherited from the Soviet era and formed since the Soviet Union's fall—in the economic, industrial, and military/security fields. In addition to the two countries' memberships in the SCO and the CSTO, their military/security relations have been strengthened through Russian arms sales to Uzbekistan and various military/security agreements made between the two countries since 1991. Formed in the pre-independence era, the Russian community of Uzbekistan, accounting for about 8 percent of the Uzbek population, has guaranteed a degree of presence and influence for Russia in that country that will last for some time. Like other regional Russian communities, many of its members are highly educated, the result of the Soviet policy of ensuring the domination of the ethnic Russians in Central Asia. In short, Uzbek-Russian relations seem to be on an expanding track after about a decade of more or less cool ties caused mainly by Tashkent's interest in developing extensive ties with the Western countries. Evidence suggests growing Uzbek-Russian relations, at least in the near future, despite the Uzbeks' intention to maintain economic and political ties with many other countries, including the United States.

The United States

The United States was an important nation in Uzbekistan until 2005. The same reasons that justified other Central Asian countries' establishing ties with Washington motivated the Uzbeks to forge relations with the United States while maintaining ties with Moscow. Such reasons include a desire to avoid heavy reliance on Russia and therefore secure Uzbekistan's independence, apart from a need to expand relations with major nonregional powers and economic considerations. Uzbekistan's energy resources, mainly gas, were not significant enough to act as a strong incentive for the United States. However, Uzbekistan's strength as a regional power, its determination to limit Moscow's influence in its affairs, and its interest in close relations with the U.S. government created an incentive for Washington to develop close ties with Tashkent. Limited Uzbek-U.S. military cooperation and Uzbekistan's membership in NATO's Partnership for Peace further expanded Uzbek-American relations. Those relations became closer in the wake of September 11, 2001, when Tashkent offered an air force base (Karshi-Khanabad) to the American military for its operation in Afghanistan. However, the outbreak of the color revolutions created suspicion on the part of the Uzbek government regarding long-term U.S. objectives in Central Asia, a concern shared by other Central Asian governments. The Andijan incident ended the Uzbek-U.S. friendship and limited their relations. Having shut down the American air base, the Uzbek government joined other SCO members in their July 2005 meeting to demand a clear timetable for the withdrawal of the American military from Central Asia (Blank 2005). Following a regional trend, Tashkent has expanded its relations with China, Russia, and Iran while sharply lowering those with the United States. As a sign of its growing relations with Russia, Uzbekistan rejoined the CSTO in 2006.

CONFLICTS IN THE POST-INDEPENDENCE ERA

Internal Conflicts since Independence

As in other Central Asian countries, the overall dissatisfactory situation of the post-Soviet era, including significantly lower living standards, unemployment, poverty, and rampant corruption, paved the way for the rise of dissent aimed at the Karimov administration. However, various factors have prevented the emergence of popular opposition, including the absence of anti-government groups with a mass following, the systematic suppression of the opposition, and perhaps the negative experience of the civil war in neighboring Tajikistan, in which opposition groups opposed the Tajik state. Against this background, Uzbekistan has faced no major domestic conflicts. However, it has experienced politically motivated violence and localized, small-scale armed conflicts since the late 1990s.

The Islamic Movement of Uzbekistan (IMU) The Islamic Movement of Uzbekistan (IMU) is an armed fundamentalist group whose main objective is to overthrow the Uzbek regime (Human Rights Watch, March 2004, 16). Based mainly in the Uzbek part of the Ferghana Valley, the IMU has occasionally sought refuge in the valley's Kyrgyz and Tajik sections to avoid the Uzbek security forces or to conduct subversive activities. The Ferghana Valley is a fertile, potentially rich (but currently poor) region divided among Kyrgyzstan, Tajikistan, and Uzbekistan. The IMU has conducted bombings outside the Ferghana Valley, including a series of bombings in early 1999 in Uzbekistan's capital, Tashkent (Hiro 1999a), that demonstrated the vulnerability of the Uzbek state. However, the Uzbek part of the Ferghana Valley has been the main arena for the IMU's armed violence. In the early years of the twenty-first century's first decade, the IMU was significantly weakened by the Uzbek government's systematic suppression and by the loss of some of its fighters in Afghanistan in 2002 during the course of the U.S.-led coalition operation against the Taliban and its allies. However, the group's increased activities in Uzbekistan, Kyrgyzstan, and Tajikistan since 2004, as reflected in various bombings, for instance, suggest its reorganization (Weitz 2004, 465–490).

Benefiting from drug trafficking, the IMU is believed to have assisted the drug traffickers at least on occasions, although the two groups pursue different objectives in Central Asia: political and criminal, respectively. Leading to skirmishes with the Kyrgyz and the Tajik border troops along the common borders, incursions of the IMU and the international drug traffickers into Kyrgyzstan and Tajikistan have been quite common since the 1990s. A recent significant case occurred on May 12, 2006, along the Kyrgyz-Tajik border (Yermukanov 2004). A few reported cases have been major—for example, the Batkan incident in 2000, in which a large contingent of heavily armed international drug traffickers (according to non-Kyrgyz government sources) or well-armed IMU forces with their local Kyrgyz followers (according to the Kyrgyz government) engaged the Kyrgyz security forces, including its military, near the Kyrgyz district of Batkan (Peimani 2000, 4). In late 2008, there were reports of IMU expansion of its operation beyond Uzbekistan. According to the Pakistani government, the

the United States had been involved in the Andijan incident and had attempted to engineer a color revolution in Uzbekistan. The Uzbek government saw the United States as a destabilizing force seeking to replace it with a docile, pro-U.S. regime by provoking a revolution with the assistance of U.S. NGOs. Following the incident, the Uzbek government demanded the closure of the U.S. air force base within six months and obtained it in November of that year (VOA 2005a).

Before that incident, the removal of the governments in Georgia, Ukraine, and Kyrgyzstan through color revolutions caused relations to deteriorate between the Central Asian governments and Washington. Viewed in Central Asia as U.S.-inspired and U.S.-engineered coups to put pro-American leaders in power, the Georgian Rose Revolution (2003) and the Ukrainian Orange Revolution (2004) sent shock waves throughout the region. The outbreak of the March 2005 Yellow Revolution in Kyrgyzstan, interpreted in many CIS countries in the same way as the other two revolutions, merely deepened suspicion about the United States' long-term objectives in Central Asia and the Caucasus. Leaders became wary, and they cooled their political ties with Washington and restricted or closed down U.S. NGOs, especially those in Central Asia, considering them contributors to a situation ripe for color revolutions. The Central Asian governments have also made licensing and license renewal of NGOs difficult, forcing those viewed as major contributors to revolution to shut down their operation in Central Asia. A well-known example of this is the Soros Foundation, which was forced to cease its operation in Uzbekistan in April 2004 (UNOCH 2005).

One reaction to the mentioned events has been a growing interest among the Central Asians in closer relations with Iran, China, and Russia, now seen as more reliable friends than the United States. The Central Asians, including the Uzbeks—but excluding the Turkmens, who adhere to a policy of neutrality—have shown enthusiasm for activities within the Shanghai Cooperative Organization (SCO), of which they are all members. (Iran's current observer seat will likely be upgraded to full membership in the near future.) Reflecting the Central Asians' concern about the U.S. government is the demand made in its July 2005 meeting by all its members—including Kazakhstan, Kyrgyzstan, and Uzbekistan all hosting American forces—for a clear date for U.S. military withdrawal from Central Asia (Blank 2005).

In addition, Tashkent's interest in expanding relations with Moscow became evident in many events, including Uzbek president Islam Karimov's visit with Russian president Vladimir Putin after the Andijan incident. A major development in this regard occurred on November 14, 2005, when Russia and Uzbekistan concluded an alliance agreement against terrorist threats, an agreement that reportedly also committed them to helping each other preserve their national security (VOA 2005b).

Finally, Uzbekistan rejoined the Collective Security Treaty Organization (CSTO) in 2006. The Uzbeks withdrew in 1999 from the organization, then known as the CIS Collective Security Treaty, when their relations with the United States were expanding. On December 13, 2006, Uzbek president Islam Karimov signed into law a bill ratifying a protocol restoring Uzbekistan's membership of the CSTO (Turkish Weekly 2006).

THE RUSSIAN-UZBEK ANTI-TERRORIST TREATY

Russia and Uzbekistan concluded a security cooperation treaty on November 14, 2005. Signed by then Russian president Vladimir Putin and Uzbek president Islam Karimov, the treaty provides for their cooperation against what they referred to as terrorist threats. The two sides are therefore committed to help each other in case of threats to their national security. The treaty, signed after the May incident in Andijan, not only revealed the concern of the Uzbek regime about threats of internal armed conflict and the expansion of extremist/terrorist organizations in Uzbekistan, but also indicated the end of Tashkent's honeymoon with Washington, and its increasing closeness to Russia. Such closeness is atypical of Uzbekistan's relations with Russia, which since independence have been marked mainly by increasing aversion to security cooperation with Moscow within a context of growing ties to Washington. Such aversion has been reflected in many cases, including Tashkent's withdrawal from the Collective Security Treaty Organization (CSTO) in 1999. Apart from a mutual interest in fighting armed extremist groups operating in their countries, a common concern about the long-term objectives of the United States in Central Asia has encouraged closer ties and security cooperation between Russia and Uzbekistan. Although the Uzbeks carefully guard their independence and are concerned about Russia's bid to reestablish itself in their region, evidence suggests their continued and expanded security cooperation with Moscow, including their renewed membership in the CSTO and their membership in the Shanghai Cooperation Organization (SCO).

THE OUTLOOK FOR FUTURE CONFLICTS

The potential exists for internal and external conflicts in Uzbekistan in the foreseeable future.

Internal Sources of Conflict

Since 1991, the overall dissatisfactory situation in Uzbekistan has created suitable ground for the rise of popular dissent that could develop into mass movements. However, the possibility of a widespread anti-government movement capable of challenging the Uzbek regime is slim in the foreseeable future. Yet, localized mass events like Andijan will be a distinct possibility, especially in such deprived regions as the Ferghana Valley.

The IMU and Hizb ut-Tahrir will be in a position to recruit from among the dissatisfied Uzbeks, continuing their operations. In fact, both could well expand should the current situation continue. The reorganization and expansion of the IMU, despite years of suppression, substantiates this assessment. Moreover, the prevailing situation could well give birth to other extremist groups capitalizing on the growing popular discontent.

Nevertheless, there is little likelihood in the near future that organized mass movements led by extremist groups will be capable of destabilizing the Uzbek regime.

External Sources of Conflict

Sources exist for external conflict in Uzbekistan's near future. Owing to the multidimensional nature of the conflict between Uzbekistan and Tajikistan, as discussed previously and in the country profile of Tajikistan, the likelihood of major crises and armed conflicts between the two countries will remain high in the absence of a process for addressing their disagreements in a satisfactory manner. In such a situation, any dispute, against the background of years of hostility and distrust, could trigger the rapid expansion of a major conflict, especially because Tajikistan is mindful of its neighbor's interference in its affairs.

Border and water disputes are two distinct possibilities in Uzbekistan's relations with all its Central Asian neighbors. Unless Uzbekistan settles its border disputes with them in a mutually acceptable manner, conflicts over such issues and their escalation to small-scale armed conflicts are a realistic possibility, if not a probability. Especially if the current situation continues, Uzbekistan's particularly cold relations with Tajikistan and Turkmenistan could put the nations involved on a collision course. In the case of Uzbek-Kyrgyz relations, certain factors apart from territorial issues, such as Kyrgyzstan's sheltering of Uzbek refugees as it did during the Andijan incident, could also lead to armed conflict. Disputes over common water resources could also pit Uzbekistan against Kazakhstan and Turkmenistan in particular, because of the growing need for water.

BIBLIOGRAPHY

Abolhassan Shirazi, Habibollah. 1991. *The Nations of Central Asia.* Tehran: The Institute for Political and International Studies.

Akiner, Shirin. 2005. "Violence in Andijan, 13 May 2005: An Independent Assessment." *Silk Road Paper* (July), 10. www.silkroadstudies.org/new/inside/publications/0507Akiner.pdf (accessed May 5, 2008).

Allworth, Edward. 1989. "Encounter." In *Central Asia: 120 Years of Russian Rule,* edited by Edward Allworth, 1–59. Durham, NC: Duke University Press.

Allworth, Edward A. 1990. *The Modern Uzbeks: From the 14th Century to the Present: A Cultural History.* Stanford, CA: Hoover Press Publications.

Atta'ie, Farhad. 1993. "A Retrospective Glance at the History and the Current Situation of the Central Asian Republics." *The Journal of Central Asia and Caucasus Review* 1, no. 3 (Winter), 151–164.

Blank, Stephen. 2005. "Making Sense of the Shanghai Cooperation Organization's Astana Summit." *Central Asia–Caucasus Analyst,* July 27, 2005. www.cacianalyst.org/view_article.php?articleid=3504 (accessed May 10, 2008).

Bregel, Yuri. 1991. "Turko-Mongol Influences in Central Asia." In *Turko-Persia in Historical Perspective,* edited by Robert L. Canfield, 53–77. Cambridge: Cambridge University Press.

Christou, Alana. 2007. "The Aral Sea." http://aquaticpath.epi.ufl.edu/waterbiology/studentprojects/AralSea-Alana.pdf (accessed October 6, 2008).

Conquest, Robert. 1970. *The Nation Killers: The Soviet Deportation of Nationalities*. London: MacMillan.

D'Encausse, Hélène Carrère. 1989a. "Civil War and New Governments." In *Central Asia: 120 Years of Russian Rule*, edited by Edward Allworth, 224–253. Durham, NC: Duke University Press.

D'Encausse, Hélène Carrère. 1989b. "The Fall of the Czarist Empire." In *Central Asia: 120 Years of Russian Rule*, edited by Edward Allworth, 207–223. Durham, NC: Duke University Press.

D'Encausse, Hélène Carrère. 1989c. "Organizing and Colonizing the Conquered Territories." In *Central Asia: 120 Years of Russian Rule*, edited by Edward Allworth, 151–171. Durham, NC: Duke University Press.

Fuller, Graham E. 1991. *The "Center of the Universe": The Geopolitics of Iran*. Boulder, CO: Westview Press.

Hiro, Dilip. 1999a. "Bomb Blasts in Tashkent." *Middle East International*, March 12, 1999, 16.

Hiro, Dilip. 1999b. "Failed Revolt." *Middle East International*, December 25, 1999, 19.

Human Rights Watch. 2004. *Creating Enemies of the State: Religious Persecution in Uzbekistan*. March 29, 2004. New York: Human Rights Watch.

Human Rights Watch. 2006. "Uzbekistan." *Human Rights Watch World Report 2006*. New York: Human Rights Watch. http://hrw.org/english/docs/2006/01/18/uzbeki12288.htm (accessed May 14, 2008).

Kimmage, Danile. 2006. "Analysis: Extremist Threats, and Doubts, in Kyrgyzstan, Tajikistan." *Radio Free Europe/Radio Liberty (RFE/RL)*, July 24, 2006. www.rferl.org/featuresarticle/2006/07/212f8957-a0bf-4963-aacb-0efe6fbf28a5.html (accessed August 1, 2008).

Menges, Karl H. 1989. "People, Languages, and Migrations." In *Central Asia: 120 Years of Russian Rule*, edited by Edward Allworth, 60–91. Durham, NC: Duke University Press.

Oliver, Mark, and Agencies. 2005. "'700 dead' in Uzbek violence." *The Guardian*, May 16, 2005. www.guardian.co.uk/international/story/0,1485270,00.html (accessed August 15, 2008).

Peimani, Hooman. 1998. *Regional Security and the Future of Central Asia: The Competition of Iran, Turkey, and Russia*. Westport, CT: Praeger.

Peimani, Hooman. 2000. "Drug-Trafficking in the Fergana Valley and Instability in Central Asia." *The Times of Central Asia* (Bishkek), November 2, 2000, 4–5.

Ratter, Igor. 1993. "Will Central Asia Explode?" *The Journal of Central Asia and Caucasus Review* 2, no.1 (Summer), 195–204.

Rywkin, Michael. 1990. *Moscow's Muslim Challenge: Soviet Central Asia*. Armonk, NY: M. E. Sharpe.

Saray, Mehmet. 1994. "Political, Economic [a]nd Cultural Relations between Turkey [a]nd Central Asian Republics." *Eurasian Studies* 2 (Summer), 47–52.

Sarli, Araz Mohammad. 1994. "The Emergence and Collapse of Turkmen States." *The Journal of Central Asia and Caucasus Review* 2, no. 3 (Winter), 71–82.

Shykh-Attar, Ali-Reza. 1992. *The Roots of Political Behavior in Central Asia and the Caucasus*. Tehran: Centre of Central Asian and Caucasian Research in the Institute for Political and International Studies.

Spoor, Max. 1998. "Aral Sea Basin Crisis: Transition and Environment in Former Soviet Central Asia." *Development and Change* 29, no. 3 (July), 409–435.

Takmil-Homayoon, Nasser. 1993. "A Glance at Asia: Understanding Central Asia." *The Journal of Central Asia and Caucasus Review* 1, no. 3 (Winter), 21–47.

Turkish Weekly. 2006. "Uzbekistan Restores Collective Security Treaty Organization Membership." *Turkish Weekly*, December 13, 2006. www.turkishweekly.net/news/41654/ uzbekistan-restores-collective-security-treaty-organization-membership.html (accessed October 4, 2008).

United Nations Development Programme (UNDP). 2005a. "Demographic Trends." *Human Development Report 2005,* 232–235. New York: UNDP.

United Nations Development Programme (UNDP). 2005b. "Survival: Progress and Setbacks." *Human Development Report 2005,* 250–253. New York: UNDP.

United Nations Office for the Coordination of Humanitarian Affairs (UNOCHA). 2005. "Central Asia: Soros Foundation to Continue Despite Setback." *IRIN,* January 2, 2005. www.irinnewws.org.

Voice of America (VOA). 2005a. "America Evacuated Its Air Base in Uzbekistan." *VOA News in Persian,* November 21, 2005.

Voice of America (VOA). 2005b. "Signing an Alliance Agreement between Russia and Uzbekistan." *VOA News in Persian,* November 14, 2005.

Weitz, Richard. 2004. "Storm Clouds over Central Asia: Revival of the Islamic Movement of Uzbekistan (IMU)?" *Studies in Conflict and Terrorism* 27, 465–490.

Yermukanov, Marat. 2004. "Border Incidents Sour Kazakh-Uzbek Relations." *Central Asia–Caucasus Analyst,* June 16, 2004. www.cacianalyst.org/view_article.php?articleid=2457 (accessed July 30, 2008).

In August, Azeri president Haidar Aliyev suggests a new approach to settling the issue of the Caspian Sea legal regime during talks in Baku with visiting Russian deputy foreign minister Viktor Kalyuzhnii. Accordingly, the five Caspian littoral states should first reach an agreement on dividing the seabed into national sectors and only then proceed to discussion of whether and how to divide the waters and the surface.

In September, Azerbaijan, Armenia, and Georgia become allies of the United States in its war in Afghanistan.

In October, street protests widen in Tbilisi as the Georgians hit the streets in outrage at the attempt of the Georgian State Security Ministry to enter the independent Rustavi 2 television station.

In November, the Armenian National Security Ministry rejects as "complete rubbish" and "an outright provocation" the claim made by a former Azeri prisoner that Armenian security officials tried to recruit him to assassinate Azeri president Haidar Aliyev's son, Ilham.

In December, Georgian defense minister David Tevzadze requests Georgia's incorporation into NATO's general air defense system as he addresses a NATO forum in Brussels.

2002

Throughout the year, Georgia, Armenia, and Azerbaijan start military cooperation with the United States in its "War on Terror." Georgian-Russian relations deteriorate drastically over Moscow's accusations of Tbilisi's tolerance of Chechen militants in its Pankisi Gorge.

In January, Georgia and Russia agree to launch a joint operation in the Pankisi Gorge to neutralize "criminals" and "extremists" during talks in Tbilisi between visiting Russian security council secretary Vladimir Rushailo and his Georgian counterpart, Nugzar Sadzhaya.

In February, the U.S. government sends about 200 special operations troops to Georgia to train Georgian troops for their anti-terrorist operation in the Pankisi Gorge.

In March, Russian defense minister Sergei Ivanov warns that the rising tensions in Abkhazia may delay the closure of the Russian military bases in Georgia.

In April, the Foreign Ministry of the unrecognized Nagorno Karabakh Republic denies Azerbaijan's claims that chemical and biological weapons are being stockpiled in Karabakh and Armenia.

In May, a mutiny by Georgian Interior Ministry troops ends as all 60 involved troops return to their base near Telavi in eastern Georgia after days of desertion. According to Giorgi Shervashidze, commander of the Interior Ministry troops, the desertion of servicemen and several officers was to protest the beating of a fellow serviceman.

In October, Abkhaz officials claim that about 50 Chechen fighters pushed out of the Pankisi Gorge by the Georgian anti-terrorism operation to have taken refuge in the upper parts of the Georgian-controlled Khodori Gorge. The six members of the CST sign a charter in Chisinau to expand and rename the alliance the CIS Collective Security Treaty Organization (CSTO).

In November, in his address to the Euro-Atlantic Partnership Council session in Prague, Georgian president Eduard Shevardnadze formally announces his country's intention to become a NATO member.

In December, the first U.S.-trained Georgian commando battalion graduates with 558 personnel.

2003   In January, Georgian president Eduard Shevardnadze opposes extending the mandate of the Russian peacekeeping force deployed under the CIS aegis in Abkhazia unless Russia halts its recently resumed train service between the Russian Black Sea town of Sochi and the Abkhazian capital, Sokhumi.

In February, Armenia sends 34 peacekeepers to Kosovo as part of the Greek peacekeeping contingent.

In March, the Georgian parliament ratifies the U.S.-Georgian military cooperation agreement.

In April, Russia's Duma deputies criticize the U.S.-Georgian military cooperation agreement, describing it as "an exceptionally unfriendly and even hostile act" that creates a serious imbalance of forces in the southern Caucasus and thus poses a threat to international security.

In August, President Haidar Aliyev appoints his son, Ilham, prime minister as the first step in his plan for Ilham to succeed him as president.

In October, two weeks before the presidential election, President Haidar Aliyev resigns and withdraws his candidacy in favor of his son, who wins the election, which is marred by irregularities. Ilham Aliyev's victory provokes two violent clashes in Baku on October 15 and 16 between government security forces and supporters of the opposition Mussavat Party, who claim victory for their leader, Isa Gambar.

In November, the alleged irregularities in the parliamentary elections of Georgia provoke anti-government protests, leading to the resignation of President Eduard Shevardnadze. The incident becomes known as the Rose Revolution.

In December, in Tbilisi, the vice chairman of the U.S. Joint Chiefs of Staff, General Peter Pace, announces that his country will allocate $40 million for a new training program for the Georgian armed forces (Sustainment and Stability Operation Program). The program provides for 70 U.S. instructors to train two marine and two logistics battalions.

2004   Throughout the year, many bloody clashes take place between the Georgian and the South Ossetian separatist forces. Armenia sends 46 noncombat troops to Iraq, including bomb disposal experts, doctors, and transport specialists.

In April, Georgia's air force commander accuses Russia of shooting down an unmanned Georgian spy plane flying over the breakaway republic of Abkhazia. The first meeting of the EU-Georgia Cooperation Subcommittee on Justice, Freedom and Security is held in Brussels.

In May, Russia sends a 300-strong unit from the army's railway force to Abkhazia as tension expands between Russian and Georgia over the breakaway republic.

In July, in Brussels, the first meting of Troika representatives of the Political and Security Committee (PSC) of the Georgia-EU Council is held.

In August, Georgia attacks South Ossetia's capital of Tskhinvali in a bid to restore its sovereignty over the breakaway republic. In support of the latter, the Russian military repels the Georgian forces and launches a massive land, sea, and aerial attack on the military and military industrial facilities of Georgia. It also recognizes the independence of Abkhazia and South Ossetia. The Abkhaz military pushes back the Georgian troops from the only part of Abkhazia under Tbilisi, the Khodori Gorge.

Georgia and Russia sever their diplomatic ties. Georgia leaves the CIS.

In September, the European Union, through its rotational leader (French president Nicholas Sarkozy), concludes a cease-fire agreement with Georgia and Russia, which both sides accuse each other of not honoring. Russia makes its full withdrawal from Georgia, subject to Tbilisi's conclusion of a nonaggression pact with Abkhazia and South Ossetia. Azeri president Ilham Aliyev pays an official visit to Moscow, the first south Caucasian leader to set foot in Moscow since the August Georgian-Russian war. During his visit to Tbilisi, U.S. vice president Dick Cheney says the United States firmly backs NATO membership for Georgia.

Chapter 11

Armenia

GENERAL STATISTICS

Area	29,785 km²
Population	2,999,000 (2007 est.)
Population Density	101 inhabitants per km² (2007 est.)
Major Cities	Gyumri Vanadzor Yerevan (capital)
Gross Domestic Product (GDP)	$3.6 billion (2004 est.)
Total Active Armed Forces	60,000: 300,000 reservists (2007) and 34 troops stationed in Serbia; some 3,500 Russian troops stationed in Armenia.
Annual Military Expenditure	$376,500,000 (2007)
Military Service	24-month universal conscription.
International Organization Membership	CIS (1991) Council of Europe (2001) CSTO (1992) NATO Partnership for Peace (1994)

NATO Individual Partnership Action
Plan (2005)
OSCE (1992)
UN (1992)

HISTORY OF ARMENIA

Armenia is a landlocked, mountainous country in the southern Caucasus that borders Azerbaijan, Iran, Turkey, and Georgia. It is a multiparty nation-state with an ancient and historic cultural heritage. Populated since prehistoric times, this region saw the rise of the ancient Kingdom of Urartu (first millennium BC), in which Armenians, an Indo-European tribe, played an important role. In later years, Armenians resisted Assyrians before being ruled by Iran (Persia) until Alexander the Macedonian overran the region in the fourth century BC. Armenia then became a province of the Seleucid Empire. When Rome conquered this empire in 189 BC, Armenia was split in two, prompting the Armenian king Artashes I to declare Greater Armenia independent from Greek domination.

Armenia reached its zenith during the reign of King Tigranes II the Great (95–55 BC), who extended his influence into Syria, Anatolia, and Caucasian Albania and made Armenia the strongest state of the region. This heyday, however, proved short-lived, for the Armenians were soon defeated by the Romans and were forced to give up territory and form an alliance with Rome. Over the next centuries, Armenia served as a buffer zone between the Roman and Iranian (Persian) Empires. In the early fourth century, Armenia became the first nation to accept Christianity as its state religion, a turning point that shaped Armenian history and culture.

Although Armenia was a battleground between Iran and Rome (and Rome's successor, the Byzantine Empire), it nevertheless developed a sophisticated culture and national identity. Its unique alphabet was created by Mesrob Mashtots in the fifth century AD. As Iran's power declined, Armenia gravitated toward Byzantine control and enjoyed relative independence until the arrival of the Arabs in the seventh century AD. Suffering as a province in the Abbasid Caliphate, Armenia also suffered later from the Turkic invasions in the eleventh century and the Mongol invasion in the thirteenth century. Although the Armenian mainland was devastated by continued warfare, a new state, the Kingdom of Cilicia—popularly known as Little Armenia—was established on the coast of the Mediterranean Sea in the eleventh century. This soon developed into a major center of trade and played a prominent role during the Crusades before being destroyed in the fourteenth century. Over the next 400 years, the Armenians were torn between the Ottoman Empire and the Iranian empires, whose territories in the Caucasus expanded and contracted as a result of wars. In both empires, the Armenians were granted considerable autonomy within their own enclaves and became excellent traders and merchants.

In the nineteenth century, after its expansion into the southern Caucasus, the Russian Empire took control of the Armenian mainland, contributing to an Armenian cultural renaissance. The rise of Armenian nationalism in the late 1800s planted the seeds of Turkish-Armenian ethnic conflict, lasting to this day. According to Armenian sources, thousands of Armenians fell victim to this conflict in the last decade of the nineteenth century, and between 600,000 and 1.5 million Armenians perished or were killed during World War I, when the Ottoman authorities forcibly exiled its entire Armenian population of some 1.75 million people to Syria and Mesopotamia out of fear that Armenia would side with Russia to divide the Ottoman territory. Turkish sources deny this account and attribute the heavy loss of Armenian lives, which they estimate to be much lower, to the hardships of World War I and famine. Despite these disputing claims, it is certain that tens of thousands of Ottoman Armenians emigrated to Iran, Russia, Syria, Lebanon, France, and the United States during World War I. Their offspring now form the Armenian diaspora throughout the world.

Although the Russian imperial army gained most of Ottoman Armenia during World War I, this gain was lost after the Bolshevik Revolution of 1917. As the Russian Empire collapsed, Armenia enjoyed a brief but tumultuous period of independence in 1918–1920. Territorial claims led to Armenia's conflicts with neighboring Georgia and Azerbaijan in 1919–1920. More consequential, however, was the Turkish-Armenian conflict. At the end of the World War I, the victorious Allied powers sought to divide the Ottoman Empire, and the Treaty of Sèvres (1920) promised to enlarge the Armenian republic with former provinces of the Ottoman Empire. However, the treaty was rejected by the rising Turkish National Movement, which, under the leadership of Mustafa Kemal Pasha, known as Atatürk (Father of Turks), overthrew the Ottoman government and declared itself the rightful authority of Turkey. In 1920, Armenia and Turkey fought a brief war, which ended with the Treaty of Alexandropol. That treaty forced Armenia to disarm most of its military forces, cede almost half of its prewar territory, and give up all the territories granted to it by the Treaty of Sèvres. The invading Bolshevik Red Army occupied the weakened Armenian Republic in late 1920. The Treaty of Alexandropol was soon superseded by the Treaty of Kars, signed between Turkey and the newly established Soviet Union. Accordingly, the Soviet Union agreed to Turkish control of the Kars, Ardahan, and Iğdır regions, all of which were formerly part of Russian Armenia.

In 1922, Armenia merged with Azerbaijan and Georgia to form the Transcaucasian Federated Socialist Republic, which survived until 1936, when each of the three countries became independent Soviet republics. The Soviet decision in 1923 to grant the Armenian enclave of Nagorno-Karabakh to Azerbaijan proved of much consequence. During the Soviet rule, Armenia enjoyed relative security and economic growth despite the repression and terror campaigns of Joseph Stalin. An agricultural state in the early twentieth century, Armenia underwent rapid industrialization and urbanization. By the 1980s, a massive nationalist movement arouse in Armenia that focused on the recovery of the Nagorno-Karabakh region. This movement eventually became the basis for a popular organization, the Armenian National Movement, which led the republic to full independence in 1991.

MAJOR PEOPLES AND NATIONS IN ARMENIA'S HISTORY

As a land link between Asia and Europe, the Caucasus has been of strategic importance to many powers in the last 3,000 years. Among other factors, Armenia's strategic location in the southern Caucasus has motivated many nations to pass through it during their eastward or westward migrations, to conquer it, and to settle there. Consequently, many nations have played an important role in Armenian history. Iran, Turkey, and Russia have exerted the greatest influence on Armenia, but neighboring Georgia, for centuries the only other Christian state in the region, has also contributed to the development of the Armenian state and society. Relations with Georgia are of particular importance for Armenia, because under the economic blockade imposed by Turkey and Azerbaijan, Georgia offers Armenia its only land connection with Europe and access to its Black Sea ports. However, Armenia's reliance on Russia, with whom Georgia has very tense relations, complicated Armenian-Georgian contacts, which are further complicated by the development of close relations between Azerbaijan and Georgia and Turkey and Georgia (for details on Armenian-Georgian relations, see the country profile of Georgia). In recent years, the United States has become actively involved in the Caucasus, and the Armenian diaspora in the United States has played a crucial role in helping the fledgling Armenian state in the first few years following independence.

Turkey (The Ottoman Empire) and Iran (Persia)

During its long history, Armenia has faced off with many conquerors, but the two most influential ones proved to be the Ottoman Empire and Iran (Persia). The Iranian (Persian) empires and their subsequent Iranian states conquered, subjugated, or otherwise extended their influence over Armenian lands for hundreds of years. The Central Asian Turkic tribes, who conquered parts of the Caucasus in their westward migration starting in the eleventh century, also significantly affected the region for years afterward. The resulting Turkification process set the stage for the historical and linguistic link between Turkey and the Caucasus (Sarli 1994, 75–76; Saray 1994, 47–48). As discussed in the country profile of Azerbaijan, the Turkification process of the Caucasus over a few centuries Turkified the Azeris, while the Armenians and the Georgians survived it and maintained their national characteristics, including their distinct languages.

Historically, Armenia had close ties with the Iranian (Persian) states. Between the sixth and the fourth centuries BC, Armenia and the southern Caucasus were under Achaemenid Persian rule. In the third century, Armenia was controlled by the Parthian Arsacid Dynasty, which laid the foundation for the Artaxiad (Artashesian) Dynasty in Armenia. After a brief revival under Tigran the Great, Armenia fell under influence of the Sassanid Iranians (Persians) between the third and seventh centuries. The Arab conquest in the seventh century, with the subsequent establishment of the caliphate, and the Seljuk and Mongol invasions in the eleventh and thirteenth centuries reduced Iran's influence in the Armenian highlands. This process, however, was reversed with the emergence of the Iranian Safavid Dynasty (the fifteenth to eighteenth centuries). The reemergence of Iran as a major power helped restore its influence in the region. During the Ottoman-Iranian (Persian) Wars, the Safavid shahs (Kings) campaigned in

Armenia and resettled tens of thousands of Armenians, including many artisans and merchants, to various parts of Iran, in particular Isfahan (then Iran's capital), where they helped revive trade and contributed to the Iranian economy. The Safavid rulers granted prestigious status to skilled Armenians and facilitated their integration through various means, employing them in financially rewarding positions and building churches for them in their main cities of settlement. Interestingly, facilitation also included building the Julfa district in Isfahan to resemble Armenia's city of Julfa, which still exists. The migration of the Armenians to Iran was encouraged and continued during the reign of the later Safavid rulers and also during the subsequent short-lived Afsharid Dynasty (1736–1802). Such migration continued on a smaller scale until the annexation of the Armenian lands by Russia in the nineteenth century, but picked up again during World War I and the early years of the Bolshevik Revolution, when many Armenians left the Ottoman Empire and Armenia for neighboring countries.

In the eighteenth century, the Russian Empire sought to expand its sphere of influence to the eastern Caucasus, then under Iranian control. The Russian efforts to penetrate that region proved effective in the early nineteenth century when Iran, weakened by internal problems, was forced to give up territories as a result of two major wars against Russia. The first of these wars, the Russo-Iranian War of 1804–1813, resulted in the Treaty of Gulistan (1813), which confirmed the Russian annexation of modern-day Azerbaijan, Daghestan, and eastern Georgia (Amirahmadian 2000, 32). Iran retained its control over Armenia for another 15 years. Its effort to regain the lost territories resulted in another unsuccessful Russo-Iranian War (1826–1828), which ended in the Treaty of Turkmanchai (1828), forcing the Iranian rulers to renounce their claims over the Yerevan Khanate (most of present-day central Armenia) and the Nakhjevan (Nakhchivan) Khanate (most of today's Nakhchivan Autonomous Republic).

During the Soviet Era, Armenia remained isolated from the outside world and maintained only very limited contact with Iran. However, Armenian-Iranian relations have been expanding and virtually tension-free since Armenia's independence in 1991. Against a background of historical ties, political realities, economic imperatives, and security considerations, Yerevan and Tehran have been inclined to seek close relations. As a result, despite religious and ideological differences, the two countries have remained friendly. Because Armenia is landlocked and surrounded by two hostile countries to its east and west (Azerbaijan and Turkey) and an unreliable neighbor to the north (Georgia), its southern neighbor (Iran) is its only reliable access to the open seas and to regional and international markets, as well as a secure supplier of fossil energy. The two nations have implemented several multimillion-dollar energy projects. In 2007, for instance, they began cooperation on the construction of a railway line and an oil refinery that would process Iranian crude oil. A strategically important component of Armenian-Iranian relations has been completion of a pipeline to supply Armenia with Iranian gas; its first and second phases went online in 2007 and 2008, respectively. The project aims to alleviate Armenia's heavy dependence on Russia for its gas when the growing tension in Georgia's ties with Russia makes it unwise to depend on importing Russian gas through Georgia, which borders both Russia and Armenia. Through the Iran-Armenia pipeline, gas is imported on favorable terms for Armenia, which pays for it with electricity generated by the fifth unit of the Armenian Hirazdan power station, constructed and fully financed by Iran.

THE IMPACT OF GEORGIAN-RUSSIAN CONFLICTS ON ARMENIA

Certain recent developments have raised doubts about the feasibility of significant trade between Armenia and Russia in the predictable future. In particular, the spy crisis of September/October 2006 and the Georgian-Russian war of August 2008 made Armenia an unwilling partner to, and a victim of, deteriorating Georgian-Russian relations. Unless those relations improve drastically in the near future, the prospect of which is next to nil, the war's fallout could likely lead to major long-term changes in Armenia's trade and energy relations with Russia, with a potentially negative effect on their political ties. As a landlocked country having no border with Russia and experiencing hostile relations with Azerbaijan that borders Russia, Armenia must rely on its neighbor Georgia, which has a common border with Russia, to conduct its Russian trade. Fluctuations in Georgian-Russian relations since 1991 had a limited impact on the Armenians' trade with Russia until September 2006, when the alleged spy incident changed the situation, leading to the imposition of extensive sanctions on Georgia by Russia. Moscow's decision to sever all land, sea, and air trade links with Georgia suddenly denied Armenia access to Russia. The possibility of third-party trade with Russia via the Georgian Black Sea ports was not extensive enough to ensure normal Armenian-Russian trade and was also unpredictable, and thus unreliable. Although the Russians' total blockade of Georgia was not meant to be permanent, the predictable continued worsening of Georgian-Russian relations made Georgia (through which Armenia also received Russian piped gas) an unreliable trade route for Armenia.

The August war of 2008 ended the Armenian-Russian trade via Georgia for what is predicted to be a long period of time because of Russia's sudden severing of official ties between Georgia and Russia and the unlikeliness of any opening of land, sea, and air trade routes through which Russian trade with Armenia could take place in the foreseeable future. Theoretically, Armenia could still use Georgia's ports to conduct its trade with Russia through Ukraine, which is accessible via the Black Sea. However, that would be an expensive option as well as an unreliable one, with Russian-Ukrainian relations also deteriorating. Furthermore, it would not be a solution for losing Russian gas via Georgia, for the fate of Russian gas exports to Armenia via its pipeline through Georgia in the post-August war era is simply unknown. In such a situation, Yerevan may well be forced to substantially decrease its trade with Russia in favor of other trading partners, and to increase its gas imports from its friendly neighbor Iran.

Armenia also needs Iran as a regional power to deter a possible new war with Azerbaijan over Nagorno-Karabakh, with the possibility of dragging Turkey into the conflict. For Iran, close and cordial relations with the three Caucasian states have been important. Besides serving Iran's economic interests, the Caucasus provides a land link between Iran and Europe, needed by Iran to reduce its heavy reliance on Turkey. Preventing the region's domination by a hostile United States has also been another incentive for Tehran to forge friendly ties with the regional countries. In light of the

regained control over many Armenian industrial units by settling Yerevan's debts to Russia in return for acquisition or purchase of industries within the context of the Armenian government's privatization program. The Russians already own the four blocs of the Hirazdan thermal power plant, six hydropower stations of the Sevan-Hirazdan cascade, 55 percent of ArmRosGazprom (Armenia's only gas operator), and, since 2005, major energy distribution (pipeline) networks. Additionally, a five-year deal was signed in 2003 under which RAO Interworld UES, the Russian power-producing giant, took over management of the Armenian nuclear power station in Metsamor. Such developments mean that Moscow has secured its long-term influence in Armenia. Apart from these, almost a million Armenian citizens who emigrated during the hard days of 1993–1995 continue to work abroad and transfer hundreds of millions of dollars back to Armenia every year, of which a large portion comes from Russia.

Outside the economic realm, Armenia remains dependent on Russia for political support. The presence of Russian military facilities in Armenia contributes to Yerevan's sense of national security and certainly prevents its hostile neighboring countries, namely Azerbaijan and Turkey, from pursuing more belligerent policies. Being the main backer of and arms supplier to Armenia, Russia has been a necessity for the security of Armenia in its conflict with Azerbaijan. These realities enable Russia to play a major role in the Azerbaijan-Armenia conflict over Nagorno-Karabakh—yet another means for Moscow to exert its influence in Armenia.

The United States

As in the other CIS countries, Washington has become an actor in Armenia since the latter's independence. Certain factors have inclined the Armenians to maintain political and economic ties with the United States, including their efforts to integrate their economy in the world economy and to receive various types of economic assistance to address their numerous inherited economic shortcomings, in addition to those generated by their transitional economy.

Another factor responsible for friendly relations has been the activities of the Armenian diaspora residing in the United States. The diaspora consists of the descendants of the thousands of Armenian refugees who fled to the United States during and after World War I. This well-established, well-organized, prosperous ethnic community has been a proactive lobby, influencing American politicians in favor of Armenia to a significant degree. Thus, in the fall of 2007, the Armenian diaspora actively lobbied the U.S. Congress to adopt a resolution recognizing what the Armenians consider as the Armenian genocide by the Turks. The resolution was passed by the House Foreign Affairs Committee by a vote of 27–21 in October 2007, but stalled after causing a major political scandal not only within the United States, but also in U.S. relations with Turkey. Nonetheless, Washington's interest in Azerbaijan's oil and gas resources, and thus in maintaining close ties with that country, has limited the Armenian diaspora's ability to secure a pro-Armenian policy to assist Yerevan in its territorial dispute with Azerbaijan. The Armenian diaspora has certainly been instrumental in creating a positive image of Armenia in the United States and has provided Armenia with tens of millions of dollars in funds and investments.

The United States and Armenia have not experienced serious upheavals in their relations. However, despite being friendly and predictable, those relations have not grown to the same extent that American ties with Azerbaijan and Georgia have. Washington's growing relations with Azerbaijan, prompted mainly by interest in the Azeri oil resources, have been a major factor limiting Armenian–U.S. relations. By the same token, Armenia has refrained from becoming too close to the United States, desiring close ties with both Iran and Russia for various political, economic, and military/security reasons. Since independence, Yerevan has pursued a balanced foreign policy to avoid international isolation and overidentification with any single country. It has therefore established friendly relations with Russia and Iran while simultaneously forging ties with the United States. In fact, its ties with the former are more extensive and multidimensional, a reflection of Yerevan's recognition of the regional realities requiring such ties with the two regional powers. Iran, for example, offers to Armenia practically the only reliable access to international markets and open seas, preventing the landlocked country from full encirclement by its enemies (Azerbaijan and Turkey) and its unreliable northern neighbor, Georgia, with lucrative oil-related ties with Baku, which could burst into chaos and war over its breakaway republics. Russia maintains a military force in Armenia, a deterrent to a possible Azeri attack assisted by Turkey.

Consequently, Armenia's friendly ties with the United States have a different significance for each of them. Washington seeks to prevent Armenia from turning into a full-fledged Russian ally, attempting to secure its friendship, along with that of the two principal U.S. allies in the region (Azerbaijan and Georgia), in order to maintain its influence in this strategic region bordering two sources of concern for Washington: Iran and Russia. However, the Armenians consider their ties with Washington a means to address their numerous economic difficulties through various types of assistance in funds and technology, which, so far, have not fully materialized. Moreover, they have considered such relations as a means of strengthening their position vis-à-vis Azerbaijan and of helping them balance their ties with Russia and Iran, and thus secure their independence.

Within this context, in 2002 Yerevan and Washington began military cooperation on a small enough scale to avoid upsetting Moscow (Magdashian 2002). The Armenians sent small military units for noncombat duties to Afghanistan and Iraq in support of the U.S.-led coalition (Zakarian and Danielyan 2004). However, unlike Azerbaijan and Georgia, the Armenians refused to host American military personnel after September 11, 2001. The American government has also provided training and funds for the Armenian effort to locate and deactivate mines. Armenia's membership in NATO's Partnership for Peace has provided another ground for military cooperation. The deadlocked Nagorno-Karabakh conflict has also created grounds for U.S. influence in Armenia, along with Russia. Moreover, Washington's involvement in the Minsk Group (MG) has helped expand Armenian-American relations. Created in 1992 by the Conference on Security and Cooperation in Europe (subsequently renamed the Organization for Security and Cooperation in

Europe, OSCE), the MG seeks a peaceful negotiated settlement to the Nagorno-Karabakh territorial dispute.

INTERNAL CONFLICTS SINCE INDEPENDENCE

Unlike its two south Caucasian neighbors (Azerbaijan and Georgia), Armenia has not experienced major internal conflicts. In particular, its stability has not been weakened by any armed or unarmed opposition group, nor has it had any separatist movements. This is largely because throughout the Soviet era, Armenia remained a very homogenous nation with very small minority groups. Nonetheless, internal civil strife has not been foreign to Armenia; in fact, its past two decades have been quite turbulent. In 1988, a disastrous earthquake rocked the north of the country, killing at least 25,000 and affecting one-third of the population. In October 1999, a group of armed gunmen from the nationalist Dashnak movement staged a coup d'état, storming the building of the parliament, taking dozens of deputies hostage, and killing Prime Minister Vazgen Sargsyan, Parliamentary Speaker Karen Demirchyan, Deputy Speakers Yuri Bakhshyan and Ruben Miroyan, and Emergencies Minister Leonard Petrosyan. The gunmen surrendered a day later, after they were allowed to speak on national television and were promised a fair trial and safe passage. They were all arrested, tried, and sentenced to life in prison. The assassination was followed by a period of political instability, during which the opposition parties unsuccessfully attempted to gain power and force Armenian President Robert Kocharyan to resign. Instead, Kocharyan was re-elected in 2003, although the presidential election was marred by widespread allegations of ballot rigging.

In the last ten years, Armenia has experienced substantial macroeconomic growth. Gross Domestic Product (GDP) growth totaled 12.1 percent in 2007, mostly thanks to the manufacturing, construction, food processing, and tourism sectors. Armenia has also greatly benefited from a large and powerful diaspora, especially in the United States, and from remittances from thousands of Armenians working abroad. According to the National Statistical Service of Armenia, the foreign trade turnover of Armenia in 2007 neared $3 billion, with export volume amounting to $835 million and imports totaling $2.1 billion. Nevertheless, the average monthly nominal wage remains relatively low at 74,028 drams ($228).

Internal stability was most recently shaken in the spring of 2004, when opposition organized several weeks of protests that revealed the population's dissatisfaction with the government's policies. However, these protests remained relatively small and did not represent a major threat to the Armenian authorities. According to regional observers, their small scale indicated the opposition's failure to tap into the popular discontent with the current situation, characterized by corruption, high unemployment, and decreasing access to social services. The Armenian opposition is divided and is perceived by many as seeking to regain power rather than to reform the country, an image that limits its popularity. In March 2007, Prime Minister Andranik Markarian died suddenly of a heart attack, which caused a reshuffling in the government. Serge Sarkisian was eventually nominated for prime minister. His Republican Party, which supports Robert Kocharyan's government, successfully campaigned against the opposition candidates and secured over 30 percent of the votes in the parliamentary election in May 2007. The presidential election of February 20, 2008, provided the opposition with another chance to challenge Kocharyan and Sarkisian. It pitted Levon Ter-Petrosian, who made a dramatic comeback as an opposition leader, against Prime Minister Serge Sarkisian. According to official results of the election, which international observers judged to be generally democratic, Sarkisian won over 53 percent of the vote, whereas Ter-Petrosian gathered 21.5 percent. Nevertheless, the election failed to resolve political tensions, and two days after the poll, tens of thousands of Armenians gathered in Yerevan to protest the official results.

EXTERNAL CONFLICTS SINCE INDEPENDENCE

Armenia has experienced a major territorial conflict with its neighbor, Azerbaijan, since independence (De Waal 2003). The conflict actually started a few years before Armenian independence in 1988, when Armenia and Azerbaijan found themselves in conflict over the ownership of Nagorno-Karabakh. An Armenian-dominated enclave inside Azerbaijan, this territory was historically part of Armenia but was turned into the Nagorno-Karabakh Autonomous District and granted to Azerbaijan by the Soviet authorities in 1923. This decision planted the seeds of a territorial conflict, pitting the Armenians and the Azeris against each other in the last years of the Soviet Union, when the weakening of the Soviet political system and its governing ideology paved the way for the emergence of ethnic and territorial disputes throughout the USSR.

Territorial disputes between Armenia and Azerbaijan over Nagorno-Karabakh surfaced in the 1980s, when Mikhail Gorbachev's policy of glasnost allowed for open expression of nationalistic sentiments (Croissant 1998). Violence, including armed incidents, perpetrated by Armenian and Azeri nationalists alike and targeting Azeri and Armenian ethnic minorities in their respective countries, surfaced in 1988 and continued during the last years of the Soviet Union. The conflict escalated into a full-scale civil war in Azerbaijan when Nagorno-Karabakh declared independence from Azerbaijan on December 10, 1991. The Karabakhi Armenians, fully backed by the Armenian government, successfully faced the Azeri government seeking to prevent the region's secession. In the course of a bloody and devastating war, Armenian forces became actively involved in the fighting, although Armenia never formally declared war against Azerbaijan. A cease-fire, but not a peace agreement, ended the conflict in 1994. Refugees displaced by the armed conflict numbered nearly a million. An estimated 400,000 Armenians living in Azerbaijan fled to Armenia and Russia. At an estimated 600,000 people—7 percent of the total population—Azerbaijan's internally displaced population is one of the largest per capita of any state in the world (Amnesty International 2007). The armed conflict left about 20 percent of the Azeri territory under Karabakhi Armenian control, including Nagorno-Karabakh proper, the strategic Lachin Passage (an Azeri territory connecting the region to Armenia), and the adjacent Azeri land and villages that serve as a protective buffer zone for the Armenian forces. Today, the Nagorno-Karabakh

Azerbaijan (1945–1946) in its occupied Iranian land failed to become a popular state and collapsed after the Soviet withdrawal in 1946, prompted by U.S. pressure in part (Riazanovsky 1984, 534).

Unlike the Russian era, the Soviet era had a major impact on Azerbaijan's social and linguistic structures. The Soviet regime imposed Russian on the Azeris, as it did on other Caucasians, promoting Russian as the official, "supraethnic language." The Soviet regime settled many Russians and other Slavs in Azerbaijan, to occupy sensitive positions, who now form the nonregional minorities in that country.

Russia still exercises substantial influence in Azerbaijan because of certain factors that include the two countries' shared land and sea borders, Azerbaijan's need to use Russian roads, railroads, and air space for transportation, and the still-eminent status of the Russian language. Moreover, Russia's status as the principal backer of and arms supplier to Armenia enables Moscow to play a major role in the Azeri-Armenian conflict over Nagorno-Karabakh.

Azeri-Russian relations have not been close and tension-free since 1991. They were especially unstable and unfriendly, if not downright hostile on occasions, during the presidency of Abulfazal Elchibey in the early 1990s. His clear pan-Turkist and anti-Russian policies created concern in Russia, not only because of their implications for turning Russia's southern neighbor into an enemy, but also because of their potential impact on Russian minorities in the northern Caucasus, including Chechnya, Ingushetia, and Dagestan. Chechnya's bid for independence at the time made the situation even more dangerous for Russia—one reason the Russians implicitly backed the Armenians in their war with Azerbaijan. However, the removal from power of Elchibey and the ascension to power of Haidar Aliyev helped ease the situation. Apart from occasional tension, Azeri-Russian relations have since been stable, although not close (owing to the growing U.S. political, economic, and military presence in Azerbaijan). The construction and operation since 2006 of the Baku-Tbilisi-Ceyhan oil pipeline (BTC) have served only to further damage relations between Baku and Moscow, its purpose being to enable Azerbaijan and eventually Kazakhstan and Turkmenistan to bypass both Iran and Russia to export their oil.

The United States

The United States has become an important nation in Azerbaijan in the post-Soviet era. Azeri-American relations have expanded to comprise political, economic, and military/security matters. To counterbalance Russia and to ensure their independence, the Azeris have encouraged these relations. The American government has been keen on these relations for two chief reasons. One is Azerbaijan's oil resources, seen as a potential backup to those of the Persian Gulf along with the resources of Kazakhstan and Turkmenistan (Azerbaijan is a new supplier of oil to the growing international markets). U.S. companies now dominate the Azeri oil and gas industry. Closely related to this, Azerbaijan could also offer a transit route that bypasses both Iran and Russia for the oil exports of the newly-independent Caspian states through its neighbor Georgia, sharing borders with Turkey and the Black Sea. Thus, Azerbaijan offers both land and sea transit routes. As discussed in the chapter "Oil in the Caucasus," the BTC

INAUGURATION OF THE BTC/BTE AND CONFLICTS IN THE CAUCASUS

The inauguration of the controversial Baku-Tbilisi-Ceyhan oil pipeline (BTC) on July 13, 2006, was not only economically significant but prepared the ground for predictable conflicts relating to oil exports. The construction of this approximately $4 billion pipeline was justified not by its economic sense, but by its political objective, for both Iran and Russia provide much cheaper and more sensible alternatives for oil exports for Azerbaijan as well as other Caspian oil exporters. Yet, the policies of Washington and its European allies, particularly the United Kingdom, have been the limitation and eventual end of the role of Iran and Russia in the Caspian oil and gas industries, including their exports. This policy has especially targeted Iran, whose role in the regional oil and gas industries is very small. It now mainly amounts to a limited involvement in oil exports through swap deals and limited involvement in oil development projects, despite its proximity to the Caucasus and Central Asia, owing to the categorical opposition of the American government, which seeks to deny Iran economic gains and political influence in those regions. Within this context, the BTC is meant to bypass Iran and Russia regarding Azerbaijan's oil exports and eventually those of other Caspian oil exporters, particularly Kazakhstan.

The Baku-Tbilisi-Erzurum gas pipeline (BTE) (also known as the South Caucasus pipeline and the Shah Deniz pipeline) was completed in July 2007 with the same intent. Built in the same corridor as the BTC, the US$ 1 billion project connects Azerbaijan's Shah Deniz gas field to Turkey's Erzurum via Georgia for the export of Azeri gas to international markets, and to help fulfill Turkey's and Georgia's need for gas. If a connecting undersea pipeline across the Caspian Sea were laid, it could also potentially enable Turkmenistan, which now depends on Russia and Iran for gas exports, to export gas. Unsurprisingly, the BTC and the BTE have been a source of concern for both Tehran and Moscow, which view the pipelines as a clear threat to their interests and a sign of the growing presence of the United States in their neighboring regions. In view of Iran's and Russia's obvious efforts to promote their interests in those regions, the two pipelines' operation will certainly contribute to conflicts between Iran and Russia, on the one hand, and the United States and its allies, who are active in those regions, on the other. No doubt, these conflicts will have a negative impact on peace and stability in the Caspian region.

is a blatant manifestation of this function, increasing the importance of Azerbaijan for Washington. Another reason for Washington's ties with Baku is the strategic importance of Azerbaijan, arising from its shared border with Russia and Iran, two sources of concern for Washington.

Azeri-American relations have been largely tension-free. Baku followed the regional trend after September 11, 2001, granting the U.S. military landing and overflight rights in support of its operations in Afghanistan and Iraq. It has also sent small military units to both countries in solidarity with Washington. Apart from diplomatic relations, Azerbaijan's membership in certain organizations and programs in which the

A gas-compressing factory at Neft Dashlari, built by the U.S. company Pennzoil, symbolically demonstrates the American interest in Azerbijan's fossil energy industry. (Remi Benali/Corbis)

United States is involved (e.g., NATO's Partnership for Peace) has provided another vehicle for expanding ties.

Additionally, the unsettled Nagorno-Karabakh conflict has provided grounds for American, as well as Russian, influence in Azerbaijan. Washington's involvement in the Minsk Group (MG) has helped expand Azeri-American relations. Created in 1992 by the Conference on Security and Cooperation in Europe (now renamed the Organization for Security and Cooperation in Europe, OSCE), the MG seeks a peaceful negotiated settlement of the Nagorno-Karabakh dispute.

INTERNAL CONFLICTS SINCE INDEPENDENCE

Azerbaijan has had a turbulent post-independence history. The country inherited from the Soviet era a devastating civil war. Between late 1991 and mid-1993, when late President Haidar Aliyev returned to power, Azerbaijan experienced numerous political, economic, social, and security problems caused by the sudden collapse of the Soviet Union and the civil strife that ensued. Failure to deal with the Nagorno-Karabakh conflict brought down the first president of independent Azerbaijan, ex–Communist Party leader Ayaz Mutalibov, in 1992. His successor was the first non-communist elected president, Abulfazal Elchibey (Elçibay) of the People's Front of Azerbaijan. Besides its corruption and poor performance in the war against Armenian separatists, the Elchibey government did not enjoy popular support while having hostile relations with Azerbaijan's northern (Russia) and southern (Iran) neighbors, both of which were on friendly terms with Armenia. Added to their worries about Azerbaijan's pro-Western orientation, Iran and Russia were particularly concerned about Baku's agreement with a consortium of Western companies for the exploration of the rich Caspian offshore oil fields that effectively excluded the two regional powers. Failures in the war and growing discontent led to an armed uprising of troops led by Colonel Surat Huseynov in Ganca. As the government diverted the Azeri troops from the front line to deal with Huseynov's rebellion, the Armenian forces advanced to occupy several Azeri districts in the proximity of Nagorno-Karabakh. As the rebel forces approached Baku, President Elchibey fled the capital, but before his departure invited former Communist Party leader Haidar Aliyev to resolve the situation. Aliyev became chairman of the Azeri parliament in June 1993 and later assumed the presidency after winning elections in October of the same year.

Aliyev ended Elchibey's unbalanced foreign policies of pan-Turkism, open hostility toward Iran and Russia, and overreliance on Turkey despite Ankara's weaknesses, to address numerous transitional problems. Aliyev's pursuit of a more balanced foreign policy, which provided for tension-free relations with Tehran and Moscow and friendly ties with Washington, helped Azerbaijan end its regional isolation, secure a cease-fire with the Armenian Karabakhis, and focus on its own internal affairs. Aliyev restored a degree of normalcy and stability to the war-torn country and improved the devastated Azeri economy by attracting foreign investment in Azerbaijan's oil industry and thus increasing its oil exports and government revenues. This allowed him to win the presidential election in October 1998. However, his years in power failed to solve the territorial conflict over Nagorno-Karabakh, which threatened his authority. For example, in 1995 a coup attempt by the commander of the military police, Rovshan Javadov, was averted, resulting in Javadov's death and the disbanding of Azerbaijan's military police. In addition, rampant corruption became a salient characteristic of the Azeri government during Aliyev's presidency, which became increasingly autocratic and intolerant of political dissent. The oil boom also contributed to a dangerous social polarization, for only a small percentage of the population benefited from oil exports even as the majority experienced lowering living standards, low income levels, unemployment, and poverty. Aliyev's death in 2003 did not result in a major change of direction in either domestic affairs or foreign policy, which was marked by a growing orientation to Washington—a major source of concern for both Moscow and Tehran.

Azerbaijan's post-independence political system has been dominated by the Haidar Aliyev family and their friends, who have also controlled its economic life since 1993. Before his death in December 2003, Haidar Aliyev arranged for his son's succession by turning Azerbaijan into a royal republic (discussed below). Undoubtedly, as was the case under Haidar Aliyev, the current Azeri government under Ilham Aliyev does not enjoy the support of the majority of the Azeris. Additionally, it suffers from a major legitimacy problem because of the undemocratic process of succession. However, because of the weaknesses of the opposition parties and their failure to gain a strong popular backing, the Aliyev government faces no organized political challenge strong enough to destabilize it. The major opposition groups (Mussavat and Azerbaijan's Popular Front) themselves lack popular legitimacy because of their membership in the corrupt government of President Abulfazal Elchibey (1992–1993), who presided over the loss of Azerbaijan's land to the Armenian separatists (Peimani 1998, 35–36).

AZERBAIJAN'S OIL RESOURCES: BLESSING OR CURSE?

Among the South Caucasian states, Azerbaijan is the only one blessed with a significant amount of oil and, to a lesser extent, natural gas, something seen by the Azeris and many others as a guarantee securing a bright future for that country. Yet, far from ensuring prosperity, peace, and stability, Azerbaijan's oil wealth could actually help destabilize the country. Azeri oil resources could at best secure Azerbaijan 15 to 20 years of oil export at over a million barrels a day, which could generate a significant amount of annual revenue for the Azeri government. This revenue, if spent prudently, could help build the foundation of a strong economy to address the numerous economic, infrastructural, and educational shortcomings of Azerbaijan while eradicating poverty and unemployment. Such a scenario, if successful, would likely contribute to stability by addressing, to a great extent, sources of internal instability related to the so-far unsuccessful transition from the Soviet economy to a type of free enterprise. However, at least two factors shed doubts on the feasibility of such a success. One is the rampant corruption that effectively limits the revenue available for investment in problem areas. Another is the apparent "Dutch disease" affecting the Azeri's economy, by which the growth of the oil industry—the only viable industry and the main revenue generator— comes at the expense of other sectors lagging far behind. The significant oil revenue does not generate economic growth and employment in a major way in other sectors, but rather it practically creates disincentives for their growth and exports. Unless these two problems are addressed, the booming oil industry will certainly contribute to social polarization and internal instability as a result of the expected uneven distribution of income, high unemployment and underemployment, and poverty.

Civil War over Nagorno-Karabakh

The civil war over the disputed region of Nagorno-Karabakh (Amirahmadian 2000, 27–50; De Waal 2003) has been Azerbaijan's most important conflict since independence. This armed conflict between the Azeri government and the separatists of Nagorno-Karabakh pitted Azerbaijan against neighboring Armenia, which backed the separatists. In this sense, it was both an internal and an external conflict whose unsettled status opened the gates for its resumption in the form of a civil or interstate war.

The conflict started a few years before Azerbaijan's independence in 1988, when the two Soviet republics of Azerbaijan and Armenia found themselves in conflict over the ownership of Nagorno-Karabakh, an Armenian-dominated enclave inside Azerbaijan (Croissant 1998). Armed violence perpetrated by both Armenian and Azeri nationalists finally escalated into a civil war in Azerbaijan as the Karabakhi Armenians, fully backed by the Armenian government, sought to secede from Azerbaijan and join Armenia. The conflict outlived the Soviet Union and continued until 1994, when a cease-fire, but not a peace agreement, ended the war without addressing its root causes. The armed conflict left about 20 percent of the Azeri territory under Karabakhi Armenian control, including Nagorno-Karabakh, the Lachin Passage (an Azeri territory connecting the former to Armenia), and the adjacent land. The Karabakhis run their controlled territories as an independent state with the unofficial support of Armenia.

Notwithstanding many mediatory efforts, including those of the OSCE (Freire 2003), the two sides have failed to settle the conflict peacefully. Their positions are simply incompatible, leaving practically no room for compromise. Whereas Azerbaijan demands the return of its occupied territories, the Armenian Karabakhis, backed by Armenia, want to unite the territories with Armenia. Although it is well known that Armenia is Nagorno-Karabakh's backer and supplier, Armenia does not officially recognize Nagorno-Karabakh's independence, because it is politically impossible to do so, for no country recognizes the occupied land's current status; rather, all consider it part of Azerbaijan.

This has put all parties in limbo. Azerbaijan is not militarily strong enough to regain its lost land through war, nor do the regional or the international moods support such a scenario. Armenia cannot go ahead with the unification, despite the blessing of the Armenians and the Armenian Karabakhis. The Armenian Karabakhis are frustrated with the status quo, containing the threat of war, which, along with their unrecognized status, discourages major foreign and Armenian investments in their territory. The ongoing no-war-no-peace situation is not tenable, but a durable peaceful settlement seems illusory.

The Presidential Election of 2003

The presidential election of October 15, 2003, made a mockery of the democratic process and revealed extensive corruption, the fragility of the Azeri political system, and Azerbaijan's proneness to major domestic conflicts. The election was part of the plan of President Haidar Aliyev to transfer his power to his son, Ilham Aliyev, before his death (December 12, 2003). To that end, in August 2003, President Aliyev appointed his son prime minister. Two weeks before the presidential elections of October 15, the senior Aliyev resigned as president and withdrew his candidacy in favor of his son, who won by a large margin an election that was neither free nor fair, according to domestic and foreign observers (HRW 2004a; AI 2004a). To ensure that outcome, the Azeri government carried out a well-organized campaign of fraud that covered various types of voting irregularities—ballot-box stuffing, multiple voting, and intimidation of voters and election observers.

In the aftermath of the election, two violent clashes took place in Baku on October 15 and 16 between government security forces and supporters of the opposition Mussavat Party (MP), who protested the electoral result and claimed victory for their leader, Isa Gambar (HRW 2004a, b). The security forces used brutal and excessive force to deal with the unarmed protestors, who responded by attacking the Azeri police and military personnel, destroying their vehicles and damaging government buildings. The clashes left one dead and hundreds of protestors and dozens of police and army personnel injured (AI 2004a; HRW 2004b). After the violence, hundreds of political activists, mainly MP members, were arrested for allegedly instigating, organizing, or participating in the violence (AI 2004a, b). The Azeri government also continued its

Supporters of the opposition Mussavat (Equality) Party protest in November 2005 in Baku, Azerbaijan. Tensions were high in the capital as residents went to the polls to elect a new parliament. (Oleg Nikishin/Getty Images)

crackdown on the opposition by reportedly intimidating and dismissing from their jobs many opposition activists and their family members (AI 2004a).

EXTERNAL CONFLICTS SINCE INDEPENDENCE

Conflict with Armenia

Azerbaijan's main external conflict has clearly been with Armenia, its first and foremost enemy. As mentioned earlier, the separatist movement in Nagorno-Karabakh pitted Azerbaijan against Armenia, the main backer of the Karabakhi Armenians. Armenia has since supported the Karabakhis economically, financially, and militarily and is the reason they have survived despite the Azeri government's cutting of all supply routes to their region. It is not a secret that Yerevan supports the unification of Nagorno-Karabakh with Armenia, although it has not taken official steps to that end because of the international community's disapproval. This is despite the fact that, in practice, Nagorno-Karabakh is now part of Armenia, and its residents are considered Armenian, not Azeris, by Yerevan, as reflected in the domination of the Armenian government by the Karabakhi Armenians. Dominating post-independence Armenian politics, ex-Armenian president Robert Kocharyan is a Karabakhi and a former leader of the Karabakhi Armenians.

Relations with Georgia

Georgia and Azerbaijan have a long history of mutual ties that can be traced back to medieval times. In 1918, after a century of direct Russian rule, both countries emerged as independent republics but became engaged in territorial disputes over the Zakatala district. Georgia was also alarmed by Azerbaijan's support of the short-lived South Western Caucasian Republic, which would have included historical Georgian provinces in the southeastern Caucasus. Nonetheless, Azerbaijan and Georgia maintained relatively peaceful ties throughout their brief independence, which ended with the Soviet occupation. After 70 years of Soviet rule, Georgia and Azerbaijan proclaimed independence in 1991 and have since maintained cordial relations. Azerbaijan's vast oil and gas reserves have motivated Georgia, effectively blockaded by Russia, to turn to its southern neighbor for help. In February 1993, Georgia concluded a major treaty of friendship, cooperation, and mutual relations with Azerbaijan, which pledged to provide energy resources to Georgia on the condition that Tbilisi would not re-export Azeri oil or natural gas to Armenia. In the late 1990s, the two countries became involved in major geopolitical projects that brought international investment and influence. Both countries are partners in the Baku-Supsa and the Baku-Tbilisi-Ceyhan oil pipelines, as well as the Baku-Tbilisi-Erzerum gas pipeline. They are currently working on the Baku-Tbilisi-Kars railway line, which will provide a transport corridor from the Caucasus to Europe. Both states are members of GUAM, the Organization for Democracy and Economic Development. Despite such close relations, Baku and Tbilisi also have points of disagreement, mainly related to the Georgian-Azeri border. The two countries are also involved in a contentious dispute over the ownership of the David Gareja monastery complex, which, according to the Georgians, has historically belonged to Georgia.

Relations with Turkmenistan

Azerbaijan's relations with Turkmenistan have been unfriendly and hostile on occasions because of ownership disputes over certain Caspian offshore oil fields.

Disagreement about division of the Caspian Sea has been a major source of dispute among the Caspian littoral states (Azerbaijan, Iran, Kazakhstan, Turkmenistan, and Russia) since the Soviet Union's fall. Failure to agree on a legal regime for dividing the Caspian Sea has created uncertainty about the ownership of many Caspian offshore oil fields and has prevented their development while creating a situation ripe for tension and hostility among the littoral states.

Until 1999, Iran and Russia opposed dividing the Caspian Sea into national zones in favor of dividing it based on the condominium principle. The other three states, eager to develop their offshore oil and gas fields to address their deep financial problems, insisted on its division into unequal national zones. Russia joined them in 1999 when it found large offshore oil reserves close to its Caspian coastline. Lacking the support of other Caspian states, Iran has accepted in principle the division of the Caspian seabed into equal national zones (a position backed only by Turkmenistan), although it still favors a condominium arrangement. Russia has sought to address the

Chapter 13

Georgia

GENERAL STATISTICS

Area   69,702 km²

Population   4,646,003 (July 2007 est.)

Population Density   64 inhabitants per km² (2007 est.)

Major Cities   Batumi
                                            Kutaisi
                                            Tbilisi (capital)

Gross Domestic Product $7.6 billion (2005 est.)

Total Active Armed Forces   32,000

Annual Military Expenditure $906 million (2007)

Military Service   Compulsory and voluntary active duty
                                            military service for men 18 to 34 years
                                            of age, with an 18-month conscripted
                                            service obligation (2005).

International Organization   CIS (1993)
Membership   Council of Europe (1999)
                                            GUAM (1997)
                                            NATO Partnership for Peace (1994)

NATO Individual Partnership Action
Plan (2004)
NATO Intensified Dialogue (2006)
OSCE (1992)
UN (1992)

HISTORY OF GEORGIA

Georgia has a long history that can be traced back more than 3,000 years. Georgians are believed to have descended from indigenous inhabitants of the Caucasus, and historical and archeological evidence indicates that humans have inhabited this region since the earliest times. Starting in the tenth millennium BC, hunters and gatherers established permanent settlements in the southern Caucasus, and several major cultures flourished in the territory of present-day Georgia. The increasing sophistication of these early Georgian cultures led to the emergence of the tribal confederations at the end of the second millennium BC in western Georgia. In his *Odyssey*, Homer mentions King Aietes and his mighty kingdom of Colchis (western Georgia).

The kingdom of Iberia (eastern Georgia) arose in the fourth century BC, but by 66 BC the Roman general Gnaeus Pompeius Magnus (Pompey the Great) had brought much of Georgia under Roman sway. Christianity was proclaimed a state religion in the early fourth century AD. In the later centuries, Georgia was contested by Iran (Persia) and Byzantium before being occupied by the Arabs in the seventh century and the Seljuk Turks in the eleventh century. Between 975 and 1008, the Bagrationi Dynasty (from southeastern Georgian principality of Tao-Klarjet) succeeded in uniting various Georgian principalities into a powerful Kingdom of Georgia. During the reigns of King David II Aghmashenebeli ("The Builder") (1089–1125) and Queen Tamar (1184–1213), Georgia reached the peak of its golden age, establishing a vibrant culture and controlling an empire that encompassed much of the Caucasus.

In the thirteenth century, Georgia was devastated and divided by the Mongol invasion. The kingdom attempted to revive itself under King Giorgi V ("The Brilliant") in the fourteenth century, but was sacked several times by Timur (Tamerlane) between 1386 and 1400 and entered a period of decline and political fragmentation. In the sixteenth century, the Ottoman Empire and Iran (Persia) competed for Georgian territory, dividing it into two spheres of influence in 1555; the west of Georgia was controlled by the Ottomans, and the east by Iran. In the early 1600s, Iranian Shah Abbas I controlled eastern Georgia and transferred tens of thousands of Christian Georgians to Iran, where their descendents still reside. Simultaneously, the Ottomans dominated the western regions of Georgia, where the kings of Imereti and princes of Mingrelia resisted the Ottoman encroachment. In 1783, King Erekle II (1762–1798) of Kartli-Kakheti (eastern Georgia) negotiated the Treaty of Georgievsk with Catherine the Great of Russia, recognizing the supremacy of the Russian Empire in return for protection from the Turks and the Iranians. King Erekle II and his heirs were guaranteed the throne, and the Georgian church was allowed to remain independent. However, in 1801, in violation of the Treaty of Georgievsk, Emperor Alexander I of Russia unilaterally abolished the Georgian kingdom and annexed it to the Russian empire. The Bagrationi royal family was detained and exiled, and the autocephaly of the Georgian church abolished. The remaining western Georgian principalities were gradually annexed by the Russian Empire between 1804 and 1864, as was Georgia's eastern part, under Iranian control (including Tbilisi), as a result of two series of Russo-Iranian wars. Throughout the nineteenth century, the Russian Empire, seeking to extend its territory southward, was engaged in bitter conflict with the Ottomans and successfully acquired several historical Georgian provinces, inadvertently accomplishing "the gathering of the Georgian lands" that inspired so many Georgian rulers.

The Russian authorities played an important role in modernizing the region, and the nineteenth century was the period of relative prosperity, commercial development, and educational encouragement for Georgia. Russian rule, however, also had a negative side, revealed in continued Russian colonialism in Georgia; cultural repression became a particular cause of resentment. A strong sense of national identity reemerged in the nineteenth century, helped along by the liberation of the serfs in 1864, a new urban working class, and an educated middle class. By 1898, the Third Group, a radical political party with Marxist leanings, counted Joseph Dzhughashvili (later to rename himself Joseph Stalin) among its members. The 1905 Russian Revolution led to guerrilla struggles in Georgia that were harshly suppressed by tsarist soldiers.

After the February Revolution of 1917 and the fall of the Russian Empire, Georgia became a member of the short-lived Transcaucasian Federation with Armenia and Azerbaijan before declaring independence in 1918. Georgia briefly accepted the protection of German forces during World War I, and after the defeat of the Triple Alliance, British troops occupied Georgia until 1920. However, in 1921, the Red Army entered the country and declared it a Soviet republic. Georgia was not spared the rigors of Sovietization, and widespread purges of Georgian society were perpetrated by Stalin's henchmen in the 1930s. The years of Soviet rule also industrialized and urbanized the theretofore mostly agrarian country. Still, the oppressive Soviet regime could not dampen the Georgian sense of nationalism, which fed numerous nationalist movements among the educated elite. By the 1980s, with the start of Mikhail Gorbachev's reforms, the Georgian national liberation movement only intensified, culminating in Georgia's declaration of independence in 1991.

MAJOR PEOPLES AND NATIONS IN GEORGIA'S HISTORY

The Caucasus has been a strategically important region for various regional and nonregional powers over the last three millennia, particularly because it is the only land link between Asia and Europe, and because of its mineral resources and fertile land. Unsurprisingly, in addition to other considerations, these characteristics have created a strong incentive for many rising nations to conquer it as part of their expansionist policies, or to settle there during their migration from Asia to Europe (or vice versa). As a result, the Caucasus has been affected over time by a large number of nations. However, Iran, Russia, and Turkey have significantly affected the present and future of the Caucasians, including the Georgians; other countries, primarily Armenia, have had noteworthy impact on the Georgians as well. The post-Soviet era has enabled the United States to emerge as an influential power in the region, including in Georgia.

Armenia

Despite almost three millennia of coexistence and common bonds against foreign threats, the Georgians and Armenians have a long history of mutual suspicion and conflict, especially recently. These conflicts are both political and social. Historically, Armenians were successful merchants and business leaders in Georgia, and by the nineteenth century, trade remained the monopoly of the Armenians. That led to their economic dominance and caused tensions in their relations with the impoverished Georgian nobility, which eventually found itself heavily indebted to them. Furthermore, by the late nineteenth century, the newly emancipated peasantry, now migrating to cities, began to compete with the more sophisticated urbanite Armenians and naturally viewed them with suspicion. Tensions existed also in the realm of religion, for the Georgian Orthodox and Armenian Gregorian churches preached different creeds and distrusted each other. Frequent accusations of misappropriation of churches and forced conversion of parishioners were, and still are, made by both sides. As a result, the prevalent stereotype of the Armenian was the shrewd, devious merchant out to trick and defraud Georgians. Such sentiments have survived well into the twenty-first century and sometimes lead to outlandish, if not outright xenophobic, incidents in Georgian politics.

Although ethnic tensions targeting Armenians do not occur over all of Georgia, the Armenians in Javakheti (southeastern Georgia) have remained apprehensive of the Georgian authorities after the nationalistic policies of Zviad Gamsakhurdia in the early 1990s. The local Armenians have since established the Javakhk organization, which actively campaigns for a referendum on the autonomous status of the Javakheti region. In 1998, the Javakhk and the Georgian troops avoided a war when the Georgian army units conducting exercises in that region encountered armed groups of Armenians who reportedly possessed heavy weaponry, including artillery, having mistaken the exercises for a government attack.

Disputes between government officials and Armenians frequently take place in Javakheti. In October 2005, hundreds of local residents in Akhalkalaki, an administrative center of Samtskhe-Javakheti region, protested the closure of trade facilities by the financial police. Tensions flared up after police fired several shots into the air and used force to disperse the rally. The latest incidents include one on March 9–11, 2006, when clashes between the Georgian and Armenian youth in Tsalka left one dead and many injured. Although the public defender's office ruled out ethnic motives in the incident and called it hooliganism, the Armenian community in Tsalka and Akhalkalaki organized protest rallies and seized the local court and university building, voicing demands for autonomy.

Ethnic Armenians have refused to serve in the Georgian army because of discrimination and abuses to which they are subjected by the Georgians. There are indications

Georgian President Eduard Shevanadze (right) walking outside the Georgian parliament building in Tbilisi. Shevardnadze was dragged from the parliament by his bodyguards as protesters seized control of the chamber on November 22, 2003 during the Rose Revolution that ended his presidency. (Viktor Drachev/AFP/Getty Images)

officers on spy charges, in reaction to which Moscow suspended all land, sea, and air transportation with Georgia and began rounding up and deporting many legal and illegal Georgian migrants from Russia, a move with serious negative economic and security implications for Georgia.

In spite of his initial limited success, Saakashvili now faces the same problems that haunted his predecessor and contributed to Shevardnadze's downfall. Georgia is currently beset with numerous difficulties, including: widespread corruption and government inefficiency; the secessionist demands of Abkhazia and South Ossetia, which have declared themselves independent states, recognized and militarily backed by Russia; various economic problems; and widespread poverty. The new government's reform programs have failed to alleviate the social misery that afflicts the Georgian population. Furthermore, some government reforms have served only to alienate people. For example, Saakashvili's administration has prohibited street vendor trade and introduced Western-style vending machines, but this type of modernization has also embittered people who have no other means of subsistence.

Increased discontent with the Saakashvili administration became evident on November 2, 2007, when tens of thousands Georgians demonstrated in the Georgian capital. On November 7, after five days of mass protests, the Georgian police used tear

THE GEORGIA-RUSSIA SPY CRISIS

The troubled relations between Georgia and Russia experienced a major blow in September–October 2006, when the Georgian government arrested four Russian military officers, charging them with espionage in conjunction with another officer not in Georgian custody. Demanding the handover of the fifth officer, the Georgian police surrounded the Russian military office in Tbilisi. The event suddenly worsened Georgian-Russian ties, as manifested in exchange of hostile statements by high-ranking officials on both sides, including Georgian president Mikhail Saakashvili and Russian president Vladimir Putin. Whereas Georgia accused Russia of illegal activities in its territory and of efforts to redominate Georgia and restore Russia's lost superpower status, Russia described the Georgian behavior as unjustifiable, provocative, and prompted by Georgia's ties with a foreign state—by implication, the United States. Summoning home its Georgian ambassador and withdrawing almost all embassy staff, the Kremlin imposed a series of punitive measures on Georgia: suspension of all land, sea, and air transportation between Georgia and Russia, a ban on Georgian exports to Russia, and the location, roundup, and deportation of many legal and illegal Georgian migrants from Russia. Georgia's release and deportation of the Russian officers about four days after their arrest did not end the conflict. In fact, the televised event, designed to humiliate the deportees, only added insult to injury, making the Russians extend their punitive measures against Georgia.

It is unknown what prompted the crisis. Having two military bases in Georgia at the time, Russia's espionage network in that country was an obvious secret. The refusal of both the United States and the European Union to firmly back Georgia does not suggest their strong hand behind the event. Although such foreign influence and Georgia's dissatisfaction with Russia could have played a role in the event, President Saakashvili's concern about his declining approval rating in the wake of the 2008 presidential election could have been a major factor, suggesting his instigation of the crisis to improve his rating by stimulating Georgian nationalism.

gas, batons, and water cannons to clear the streets of Tbilisi, and President Saakashvili declared a state of emergency in the country and shut down opposition TV and radio stations. In an attempt to discredit opposition leaders, the government released "secret video and audio tapes" implicating them in contacts with the Russian intelligence, a charge both the opposition and Russia strongly deny. The actions of the Georgian authorities were widely condemned both inside Georgia and internationally. These events revealed the fragility of the Georgian political and economic situation. The Saakashvili administration has failed to address social problems, and its use of force on November 7, 2007, alienated a large number of Georgians. Having restricted the opposition and deprived it most of its media outlets, President Saakashvili called an early presidential election for January 2008 to ensure a second term. The election was barely over when the opposition alleged that the vote had been rigged, citing unexplained delays in preparing the final vote tally as a likely indication of this.

Gudauta base in Abkhazia in the 1990s. Lacking control over Abkhazia, Tbilisi could not confirm this withdrawal and regularly accused Moscow of maintaining troops there. In any case, the fact that Moscow housed peace-keeping troops on the base made the withdrawal practically meaningless. Between 1993 and 2007, the two sides negotiated the withdrawal of the Russian forces from the remaining Russian bases in areas under the Georgian government's control. One was in Akhalkalaki, located in a predominantly Armenian region of Samtskhe-Javakheti, and another was in Batumi, the capital of Ajaria, now under Tbilisi's control. The Russian government accepted in principle the eventual withdrawal of its troops from Georgia in 1999, but resorted to various strategically motivated excuses not to agree on an irreversible, definite date for the withdrawal. Many objectives, including preserving its influence in its former republic, Georgia's clear pro-American direction since the ascension to power of President Mikhail Saakashvili in 2004, and the growing U.S. military presence in this Russian neighbor, further weakened Russia's incentive to pull out its troops from Georgia. Nevertheless, the Russian army evacuated bases in Akhalkalaki and Batumi in 2007, transferring the Batumi base to the Georgian military in November 2007, a year ahead of schedule. After the Georgian-Russian war of August 2008, Russia's deployment of large military units in Abkhazia and South Ossetia, and its intention to maintain its troops in close proximity to the two breakaway republics inside the Georgian territory as a security precaution, if proves to be sustainable, will certainly create grounds for major conflicts between Tbilisi and Moscow.

Chechens in the Pankisi Gorge

Another troublesome issue in Georgian-Russian relations has been the presence of Chechen armed groups in the Georgian region bordering Chechnya. In 1999, under newly-elected president Vladimir Putin, Russia initiated a second round of war in Chechnya to regain control of Chechnya, which it lost in 1996 after a devastating four-year war. The Chechen militants used not only the neighboring territories of the Russian republics of Ingushetia and Dagestan to attack the Russian troops in Chechnya, but also the northern parts of Georgia bordering Chechnya, mainly the Pankisi Gorge (Valley). Consequently, the expansion of the Chechen war to Georgia became a distinct possibility, for the presence of the Chechen militants in that country infuriated the Russians. This issue led to a dangerous confrontation between Russia and Georgia in 2002, when Moscow accused Tbilisi of tolerating the armed Chechen militants (Mulvey 2002). Facing Moscow's threat to attack the Pankisi Gorge to end the presence of the Chechen militants, the Georgian government denied the accusation, attributing the latter's presence to its inability to secure the region. In that year, the Georgians accepted American military advisers to train their forces for operations in the Pankisi Valley. The Georgian government's efforts to deal with the issue did not satisfy the Russian government, whose troops were hit throughout 2002 by the Chechen forces operating in the valley and from within Chechnya and neighboring Dagestan and Ingushetia. On occasion, Russia threatened to use force to deal with the Chechen militants operating from the Pankisi Gorge.

The Russo-Georgian conflict continued in 2003, although on a smaller scale. Georgia admitted that armed Chechens previously had operated in the Gorge, but insisted that its troops had driven them out of there. Nevertheless, on occasion, including in June of that year, Russian president Vladimir Putin implied the presence of the Chechen militants in the Pankisi Gorge. This was denied by Georgian intelligence chief Lieutenant General Avtandil Ioseliani, who invited his Russian counterpart to visit that region (Karakulova 2003). In 2002 and 2003, Georgia added fuel to the fire by allowing the extradition by Russia of some, but not all, of the Chechens in Georgia's custody who were wanted as terrorists by Russia. The issue subsequently subsided with the cessation of the frequent Chechen attacks from Georgia. However, the issue was not totally forgotten when the Georgian-Russian war of August 2008 broke out, in view of the presence of Chechen refugees in Georgia, of whom some were considered terrorists by Russia.

Georgian-U.S. Ties

The principal troublesome issue in Georgian-Russian relations has been the expansion of Georgia's relations with the United States. Since independence, Tbilisi has viewed friendly ties with Washington as a means to counterweight Russia and to limit its influence in its country still tied to Russia in many ways by two centuries of Russian control. Apart from securing U.S. support for the closure of the Russian military bases in its land, Tbilisi has also considered the United States as a power capable of helping Georgia regain control of its two breakaway republics. Russia has backed the two republics since the early 1990s and has been militarily present in their territories. Moscow substantially increased that military presence after the Georgian-Russian war of August 2008 and now recognizes the two as independent states. For these reasons, as well as for economic ones, Tbilisi has been eager to expand relations with Washington under both Eduard Shevardnadze and Mikhail Saakashvili.

Unsurprisingly, the Georgian government's policy of close relations with the United States since 2001, particularly in its military dimension, has caused both anger and fear in Moscow. The Kremlin considers the growing political influence and military presence of Washington in Georgia—as well as in other former Soviet republics and former Warsaw Pact states—to be part of Washington's plan for the gradual encirclement of Russia by hostile and potentially hostile states housing U.S. military. The ascension to power of President Saakashvili increased Russian concern, as he is openly pro-American and encourages much closer relations with Washington; he has advanced a plan for membership in NATO and the European Union. The process of his ascension to power itself has further intensified Russia's concern about the intentions of both Georgia and the United States in the region.

Legitimizing Mikhail Saakashvili as a national leader, the January 2004 presidential election took place as the last stage of a process that was undemocratic in nature, but not in form, leading to the removal from power of the elected Georgian president, Eduard Shevardnadze. Although Shevardnadze's shrinking popular support was not a matter of dispute, the manner in which his era ended is widely seen in the CIS

STRATFOR Global Intelligence Update (SGIU). 2002. "Terror War Expands to Georgia: U.S. Sends Troops to Former Soviet State to Take on al-Qaida," February 22, 2002. Reprinted by Yorkshire Campaign for Nuclear Disarmament. http://cndyorks.gn.apc.org/news/articles/terrorwarexpands. htm (accessed July 28, 2008).

Suny, Ronald Grigor. 1994. *The Making of the Georgian Nation*, 2nd ed. Bloomington and Indianapolis: Indiana University Press.

United Nations Development Programme (UNDP). 2005a. "Demographic Trends." *Human Development Report 2005*, 232–235. New York: UNDP.

United Nations Development Programme (UNDP). 2005b. "Survival: Progress and Setbacks." *Human Development Report 2005*, 250–253. New York: UNDP.

Wheatley, Jonathan. 2005. *Georgia from National Awakening to Rose Revolution: Delayed Transition in the Former Soviet Union. Surrey, UK:* Ashgate Publishing.

international neutrality status (RIA Novosti 2005). In March 2006, Georgia withdrew from the CIS Council of Defense Ministers as a step toward its membership in NATO (*Pravda* 2006). The council is a consultative body aimed at encouraging military cooperation among the CIS countries. Georgian president Mikhail Saakashvili justified the decision by saying that Georgia could not be part of two military alliances at the same time (ibid.). Although Georgia's rapid membership in the U.S.-dominated NATO was unlikely at the time, the move indicated its determination to leave the Russian-dominated CIS in the near future to become fully integrated in the Western bloc, as also demonstrated in its bid to join the European Union. Georgia's plan to leave the CIS became a reality in the aftermath of the Georgian-Russian war of August 2008. On August 12, President Saakashvili announced his decision to leave the CIS (CNN 2008). The Georgian parliament adopted certain resolutions to that effect on August 14, 2008, based on which the Georgian foreign ministry sent a note on the same day to the CIS executive committee notifying it of Georgia's withdrawal from the CIS (Ministry 2008).

FUNCTION

The CIS was established to help the ex-Soviet republics, with their extensive multidimensional ties, in coordinating their post-independence activities in major areas of importance to all of them, particularly the foreign and economic fields. It also meant to provide a peaceful framework for those republics to sever the Soviet-created ties between and among each other and to establish their own sovereign states with independent institutions and economies. These important issues for all the former Soviet republics were clearly reflected in the CIS charter, signed by the CIS members on December 21, 1991 (theRussiaSite.org 2007). Thus, the charter recognized the current borders between and among the CIS members, as well as the nations' independence, sovereignty, and equality, while providing for the establishment of a free-market ruble zone and a joint defense force.

Theoretically, the CIS provides a forum for political, economic, military/security, and parliamentary cooperation among its member states. Its various councils are meant to facilitate such cooperation. They include the Council of the Heads of States, the Council of the Heads of Governments, the Council of Foreign Ministers, the Council of Defense Ministers, the Council of Border Troops Commanders, and the Inter-Parliamentary Assembly. Yet, in practice, cooperation among the CIS member states has been limited since its creation. In fact, it has been on a descending path for the overwhelming majority of the members. The sudden collapse of the USSR created for a while the need for cooperation among their heavily interconnected countries. However, coming out of the initial shock of the post-independence era, most of the CIS states no longer have a strong incentive for multidimensional cooperation with each other within a regional organization with limited capabilities to address their needs, particularly financial ones.

The practical, but not nominal, importance of the CIS institutions has diminished over time. This is because with a varying degree of advancement, efficiency and self-sufficiency, the CIS member states have all established their political, economic, and military/security sectors. This achievement has effectively ended or, at least significantly reduced, their need for the CIS supranational institutions. For example, its military entity, the Coordinating Staff (CF), was important for the majority of the member states lacking a military of their own in the 1990s, especially during the early years. Yet, thanks to the formation of military forces by all of them, the CF has lost its practical importance. Additionally, the growing military ties between many CIS countries and non-CIS members—first and foremost with the United States, as well as with U.S.-dominated NATO—have also decreased the CF's importance for many CIS member states. Apart from addressing the shortcomings of their early years of independence, the eroding enthusiasm of these states for the CIS is a result of their expanding relations with the non-CIS countries, including those in Asia and the West.

An outcome of this reality has been a clear lack of interest on the part of the majority of the CIS countries in establishing a full-fledged free trade zone as envisaged in the CIS charter, for whose realization the CIS states signed the Economic Union Treaty in September 2003 (Zhalimbetova and Gleason 2001). Toward that end, many agreements were subsequently signed on various economic issues, including free trade (April 1994), payments (October 1994), customs (January 1995), legal harmonization (January 1996), customs classification lists (February 1996), and railway tariffs (October 1996), all of which mainly remained on paper and thus proved ineffective (ibid.). Although originally planned for a 2005 launch, after years of delay the CIS members could not even agree on a 2012 launch date in their June 2005 meeting (Corso 2005).

Additionally, their differing, if not conflicting, interests on the one hand, and a clear desire among just about all of them to avoid redomination by Russia on the other, serve as a strong disincentive, further reducing their interest in being active in an organization dominated by Russia. In reality, the only two CIS states with enthusiasm for turning the CIS into a united and fully functional grouping are Russia and Belarus. They have taken steps for an eventual reunification in an unspecified time in the future, as they formed the Union of Russia and Belarus in 1997 (Chernyshova 2003). In short, the practical importance of the CIS for its member states has decreased significantly, notwithstanding the conclusion of many agreements among its members concerning integration and cooperation in many areas.

As a regional organization, the CIS is not a cohesive union of its member states. Nor is there any indication that it is heading that way, thanks to the strong reluctance of the majority of its members for that type of organization. The memory of the Soviet era and the fear of domination by Russia has been one factor in this regard. Need for extensive foreign investment and technology to deal with the enormous number of inherited problems of the Soviet era as well as those of the transition period has been another. The absence of adequate resources within the CIS for such purposes has therefore encouraged an outward look inside the CIS, at the expense of weakening the incentive of many CIS countries to work toward strengthening the organization. This deficiency has reflected the limits of the CIS and the inability of the organization to provide a forum for expanding multilateral relations among its members. Thus, those

Corso, Molly. 2005. "C.I.S. Struggles for Cohesion." *Power and Interest News Report (PINR),* June 6, 2005. http://pinr.com/report (accessed January 11, 2009).

InfoNIAC.com. 2007. "Russia Questions Further Existence of the CIS Post-Soviet Organization." *Infoniac.com,* March 18, 2007. www.infoniac.com/news/russia-nato.html (accessed October 6, 2008).

Kupchinsky, Roman. 2005. "CIS: Monitoring the Election Monitors." *Eurasianet,* April 2, 2005.

Lewis, William H., and Edward Marks. 1998. "Searching for Partners: Regional Organizations and Peace Operations." McNair Paper No. 58, Institute for National Strategic Studies, National Defense University. June 1998. Washington, D.C.: NDU Press.

Ministry of Foreign Affairs of Georgia. 2008. Statement of the Ministry of Foreign Affairs of Georgia on Georgia's Withdrawal from CIS. August 18, 2008, www.mfa.gov.ge/index.php?lang_id=ENG&sec_id=36&info_id=7526 (accessed October 5, 2008).

Mu, Xuequan, ed. 2007. "Russia, Belarus, Kazakhstan to Launch Customs Union in 2011." *China View,* October 7, 2007. http://news.xinhuanet.com/english/2007-10/07/content_6838587.htm (accessed October 6, 2008).

Olcott, Marta Brill. 2000. "Getting It Wrong: Regional Cooperation and the Commonwealth of Independent States." February 2000. Washington, D.C.: Carnegie Endowment for International Peace.

Pravda. 2006. "Georgia Opts Out of Ex-Soviet Military Cooperation Body." *Pravda,* March 2, 2006.

Pravda. 2008. "Putin to Ukraine: Don't Bite the Hand That Feeds You." *Pravda.ru,* October 3, 2008. http://english.pravda.ru/world/ussr/03-10-2008/106520-putin_ukraine-0 (accessed October 5, 2008).

RIA Novosti. 2005. "Turkmenistan Declares Its Associated Membership in CIS—Georgian President." August 27, 2005.

RIA Novosti. 2006. "CIS Observers Barred from Ukraine Election Monitoring." January 24, 2006.

theRussiaSite.org. 2007. *Charter of the Commonwealth of Independent States,* trans. John Fowler. April 1, 2007. http://therussiasite.org/legal/laws/CIScharter.html (accessed January 11, 2009).

Weinstein, Michael A. 2005. "Intelligence Brief: Uzbekistan–C.I.S." *Power and Interest News Report (PINR),* September 1, 2005.

Zhalimbetova, Roza, and Gregory Gleason. 2001. "Eurasian Economic Community (EEC) Comes into Being." *Central Asia–Caucasus Analyst* (Washington), June 20, 2001.

Major realized projects include the Mashhad-Bafg railroad, which became operational at the end of 2004, shortening the distance between Central Asia and the Persian Gulf by 800 kilometers, as Mashhad is connected via an existing railroad (Mashhad-Sarakhs) to Tejan in Turkmenistan at one end and via another (Bafg-Bandar Abbas) to the Persian Gulf port of Bandar Abbas (ECO 2008). However, other projects missed the deadline of 2007, the most important being the Istanbul-Tehran-Turkmenbashi-Tashkent-Almaty railroad, also known as the Iron Silk Road, connecting Central Asia to Europe via Iran and Turkey as part of the Trans-Asian Railway's main line. The ECO's Baku Declaration of May 5, 2006, stressed the importance of the railroad for facilitating the trade of the ECO states (ECO 2006). In early 2009, it seems that the ECO has missed its scheduled date of completion and full operation in the second half of 2008 (UNESCAP 2007).

Nor were all the envisaged telecommunications projects completed by 2007. However, many of them have been completed as of this date (April 2009). Major related projects include a transmission line to transfer 100 megawatts of power from Iran to the city of Gawadar in Pakistan's Baluchistan Province, realized in September 2008 and scheduled to become operational in mid-October 2008 (Fars News Agency 2008).

There are many other areas of interest for the ECO. They include energy development, both for meeting the growing needs of its member states and also for export to non-ECO markets, regional cooperation on agriculture and industry, and health. Member states have been engaged in bilateral and multilateral projects in these fields, but cooperation in these areas has been limited.

The ECO has been growing since its founding in 1985. The expansion in 1992 boosted the organization by enlarging its domestic market, with an apparent positive impact on the bilateral trade of its members. The expansion also provided the ECO with additional opportunities for economic activities thanks to the need of the Central Asian states and Azerbaijan to address their inadequate infrastructure, underdeveloped agriculture, limited industrialization (Kyrgyzstan, Tajikistan, and Turkmenistan), and outdated industries, added to their daily needs for consumer goods and food. Despite this situation, the founding states' enormous potential for growth, and the need for cooperation and trade among its members, the ECO is still in its infancy. It has yet to realize its potential, develop into a full-fledged regional organization, and use its full capacity to positively and significantly affect the economic growth of its members. In particular, the organization is far from reaching its objective of fostering regional economic integration, as indicated in very limited amount of trade between ECO members, with few exceptions (such as the booming trade between Iran and Turkey and between Iran and Turkmenistan). Accordingly, in the years following 2000, only "about six percent of each ECO member's [foreign] trade ha[s] been with other ECO zone countries" (Golpira 2006).

Many factors have been responsible for this situation, including political disagreements between ECO members (such as between Iran and Pakistan and between Azerbaijan and Turkmenistan) and their pursuit of opposing foreign policies, which effectively decrease their incentives for bilateral cooperation. Washington's pressure on ECO members to limit Iran's economic gains in their relations with that country is another factor. Yet another factor has been difficulty in mobility for ECO nationals. Thus, despite agreements for the simplification of visa procedures, especially for business people, crossing borders is not easy. Such political issues have been a major reason for the nonimplementation of many ECO agreements and for delays in the completion of projects. Political issues and the ECO's structural and organizational deficiencies aside, many ECO member states still lack adequate, appropriate, and sufficiently modern infrastructure and institutions to enable them to fully make use of their own resources and those in the ECO region, a necessity for ensuring the rapid and sustainable development of their economies. Such shortcomings are also a major technical barrier to expanding trade and economic cooperation. The ECO has sought to address these barriers since its inception, but with limited success. The ECO needs a boost to expand cooperation among its member states. Perhaps the December 11, 2007 agreement, signed in Ashgabat between the ECO and the SCO to facilitate cooperation between the two regional organizations in economics and trade, transportation, energy, environment, tourism, and unspecified "other areas," could be one of the many required triggers for that boost (ECO 2007).

BIBLIOGRAPHY

Economic Cooperation Organization (ECO). n.d. *Organizational Structure.* www.ecosecretariat.org (accessed April 1, 2008).

Economic Cooperation Organization (ECO). 1995. *Transit Trade Agreement.* March 15, 1995. Tehran: ECO.

Economic Cooperation Organization (ECO). 1997. *Treaty of Izmir.* September 14, 1997. Tehran: ECO.

Economic Cooperation Organization (ECO). 2002a. *ECO Prospects and Challenges in Transport & Communication Sector.* September 2002. Tehran: ECO.

Economic Cooperation Organization (ECO). 2002b. *1st Summit Communiqué—Tehran Communiqué.* February 16–17, 2002. Tehran: ECO.

Economic Cooperation Organization (ECO). 2006. *Baku Declaration.* May 5, 2006. www.ecosecretariat.org/ftproot/High_Level_Meetings/Summits/9th_summit/Baku_declaration_2006.htm (accessed October 5, 2008).

Economic Cooperation Organization (ECO). 2007. "Memorandum of Understanding between the Secretariat of Shanghai Cooperation Organization and Economic Cooperation Organization, December 11, 2007." www.ecosecretariat.org (accessed October 5, 2008).

Economic Cooperation Organization (ECO). 2008. "Development of ECO Railway Important Projects: Bafq-Mashad Railway." www.ecosecretariat.org/Directorates/Trans/2005_bafgh.htm (accessed October 6, 2008)

Fars News Agency. 2008. "Iran, Pakistan to Launch Electricity Transmission Line." September 30, 2008. http://english.farsnews.com/newstext.php?nn=8707091214 (accessed October 8, 2008).

Golpira, Hamid. 2006. "Whither ECO?" *Tehran Times,* November 2, 2006.

Islamic Republic News Agency (IRNA). 2004. "Iran, Afghanistan to Invest 2 Billion Dollars in Transportation Sector." *IRNA,* November 21, 2004. www.payvand.com/news/04/nov/1178.html (accessed October 2, 2008).

Peimani, Hooman. 1998. *Regional Security and the Future of Central Asia: The Rivalry of Iran, Turkey, and Russia.* Westport, CT: Praeger.

Railway Gazette. 2008. "Opening Up Afghan Trade Route to Iran." January 28, 2008. www.railwaygazette.com/features_view/article/2008/01/8694/opening_up_afghan_trade_route_t o_iran.html (accessed October 2, 2008).

United Nations Economic and Social Commission for Asia and the Pacific (UNESCAP). 2007. "Review of Developments in Transport in Asia and the Pacific." http://intranet.unescap.org/ ttdw/review/files/Review2007_dataandtrends.pdf (accessed October 2, 2008).

Chapter 16

Collective Security Treaty Organization (CSTO)

HISTORY

In the aftermath of the Soviet Union's disintegration in 1991, Russia and a few other former Soviet republics joined to establish a regional security organization. At that time, only the three Slavic former Soviet republics (Russia, Ukraine, and Belarus) housed the bulk of the Soviet military forces and assets, especially in terms of advanced equipment and weapon systems. That left very limited resources (personnel and assets) for other former Soviet republics, especially after the withdrawal of many Soviet units from their newly independent countries, most of which were then deployed in Russia. In practice, Russia was the only ex-Soviet republic with a full-fledged military force. Ukraine and Belarus had significant forces compared to other ex-Soviet republics, all of which were in the process of forming their military forces with the limited assets and personnel inherited from the USSR. In view of these realities, and the need for security, many former Soviet republics, now CIS states, found logical and practical the idea of a regional security organization of such states with many natural ties to each other.

Against this background, six CIS countries gathered in Uzbekistan's capital, Tashkent, on May 15, 1992, to sign a treaty by which they established the CIS Collective Security Treaty (CST), also known as the Tashkent Collective Security Treaty (Kaczmarski 2005). The signatories were Armenia, Kazakhstan, Kyrgyzstan, Russia, Tajikistan, and Uzbekistan. A few other CIS states joined the CST during the following year: Azerbaijan and Georgia on December 9, and Belarus on December 31. Belarus had incentives to join the CST, being a firm supporter of a Soviet-type union of CIS countries (reflected in its treaty with Russia to that effect). Minsk and Moscow formed the Union of Russia and Belarus in 1997 as a step toward their ultimate reunification at an unspecified time in the future (Chernyshova 2003). For Azerbaijan and Georgia, the heavy toll of their devastating civil wars, which pitted their central governments against their respective breakaway republics, all backed by Russia directly or indirectly, pushed them to join the CST, for they hoped to secure Russia's assistance in dealing with those republics.

The CST treaty stipulated its member states' commitment to refrain from using force or threatening its use in the conduct of their foreign policy toward each other. Furthermore, it obligated the signatories to regard an aggression against one CST member as an aggression against all members, requiring their rendering to the affected member all necessary types of supports to neutralize the aggressor. Finally, the treaty banned its signatories from joining other military alliances or regional groupings of states.

The CST members agreed to extend the life of the military organization every five years. Hence, six of its original members (Armenia, Belarus, Kazakhstan, Kyrgyzstan, Russia, and Tajikistan) signed a protocol on April 2, 1999, to renew the organization for another five years. The other three members (Azerbaijan, Georgia, and Uzbekistan) refused to sign and thus withdrew from the CST (Cornell et al. 2004, 70; Simon 2004). Their withdrawal was the result of their gradual shift to the United States in search of allies in the CIS region in the post-Soviet era, and of their growing wariness of Russia, which they saw as planning to restore its lost influence in its former republics, now independent states. On October 7, 2002, in Chisinau, the six CST members signed a new charter, the Treaty of Chisinau, to reorganize the CST, which was renamed the Collective Security Treaty Organization (CSTO) and headquartered in Moscow (Kaczmarski 2005). The CSTO has since tried to turn itself into an active organization of relevance to its membership's needs as they face the growing Western military presence in the CIS countries, in particular that of U.S. and U.S.-led NATO forces. The Russian-led organization has aimed at developing itself into an alternative to those forces. Suspicions about long-term American objectives in the CIS countries, and especially its alleged masterminding of the color revolutions in Georgia, Ukraine, and Kyrgyzstan, have created a more cooperative mood toward Russia in many CIS counties, despite their strong ties with Washington. The Central Asian countries have found motivations for improving and expanding their relations with Moscow. As a consequence, Uzbekistan rejoined the CSTO as a full member on June 23, 2006. On December 13, 2006, Uzbek President Islam Karimov signed into law a bill ratifying a protocol restoring Uzbekistan's membership in the CSTO (Interfax-AVN 2006). This was an expected move, in light of Uzbekistan's deteriorating relations with Washington because of the Andijan incident in May 2005, an armed incident backed by the United States, according to the Uzbek government (Akiner 2005).

MEMBERSHIP

According to its charter, membership in the CSTO is open to any country sharing both its principles and purposes. Countries must also be prepared to undertake the membership obligations set forth in the CSTO charter, as well as those international agreements and treaties falling within the CSTO mandate.

The CSTO had six members (Armenia, Kazakhstan, Kyrgyzstan, Russia, Tajikistan, and Uzbekistan) when it was established in 1992. Its membership increased to nine in

1993, when Belarus, Georgia, and Azerbaijan joined the organization. Yet, it decreased to six in 1999 as a result of the withdrawal of Georgia, Azerbaijan, and Uzbekistan. Uzbekistan's successful bid to regain full membership in 2006 increased the number of CST member states to seven. Georgia's and Azerbaijan's rejoining will be simply out of the question in the foreseeable future unless a major shift in their political systems ends their pro-U.S. orientation and reorients them toward Russia. At least in early 2009, there is no strong evidence for the likelihood of such a development in the near future, particularly in the case of Georgia, which fought a devastating war with Russia in August 2008. Having received the U.S. government's backing, as promised by Vice President Dick Cheney during his September 2008 visit (Myers 2008), Georgia's bid to join NATO as a full member removes the possibility of the Georgian government even considering rejoining the CSTO in the foreseeable future.

FUNCTION

The CSTO is a regional military/security organization built on the concept of collective security. Based in Moscow, its affairs are conducted by four major organs: the Council on Collective Security, the Council of Ministers for Foreign Affairs, the Council of Ministers of Defense, and the Committee of Secretaries of the Security Council (CSTO 2002). Its permanent working organ is the Secretariat of the Organization (ibid.). The CSTO describes itself as a defensive military organization with no aggressive policy or plan toward any country (ibid.). Accordingly, its members do not consider any state an enemy. The organization encourages political measures to prevent and end military conflicts threatening its members should they occur. According to the CSTO charter, dealing with such situations by military means should be the last resort, used only in the event of the failure of nonmilitary measures.

However, although the CSTO does not currently have a list of enemies accepted by its entire membership, the organization has expressed concern about the military affairs of certain states, implicitly describing them as enemies or potential enemies. As a recent example, in September 2007 CSTO Secretary General Nikolai Bordyuzha termed the constant rises in defense spending in Azerbaijan and Georgia a threat to the entire region (Bissenova 2007).

The CSTO is a regional organization mandated to coordinate and expand cooperation among its member states in the fields of military and political affairs. To meet that end, it provides for the development of multilateral structures and mechanisms of cooperation for ensuring the national security of its members. Furthermore, it provides for assisting its members through various means in the event of a security threat endangering their sovereignty, independence, security, or territorial integrity. Such means include readiness to offer military support to any of its members facing a military threat or an act of aggression.

The CSTO is a military/security alliance with a mandate focused on certain activities. These activities make the organization distinct from those of the CIS Military Cooperation Coordination Headquarters. In 2003, a senior CSTO officer, Lieutenant General Vasily Zavgorodni (head of the working group of military coordinators in the

Collective Security Council administration) made the following statement regarding the mandate of the CSTO in his interview with Interfax-AVN Military News Agency:

> The main goals of the Collective Security Treaty Organization are to ensure management of the Collective Quick-Deployment Forces in Central Asia and forces on other collective security theaters, and to combat international terrorism, drug trafficking, etc. The CIS Military Cooperation Coordination Headquarters mostly coordinates military activity of the Armed Forces of the CIS member nations, so we are not competitors. (Interfax-AVN 2003,)

Held on April 29, 2003, the Dushanbe summit of the CSTO released a statement to clarify the common opinion of its member states. Accordingly, it confirmed the "need to strengthen foreign-policy interaction and military-political cooperation between the member-countries" (ibid., para.). It also stressed the "readiness of [its] member-countries to contribute to the strengthening of regional and international security (ibid., para.). The summit also agreed to set up the CSTO military headquarters in Moscow to be operational beginning January 1, 2004 (ibid., para.).

The CSTO has so far adhered to its policy of nonhostility. However, there is no question that the emerging and expanding disagreements between Russia and the United States over international and regional issues, particularly those related to the CIS countries, are setting the stage for blatant hostile relations between the CSTO and the Western countries and their military organization, NATO. The U.S.-dominated alliance's expanding presence in the southern CIS countries has been a major source of concern in Moscow. The growing wariness of Washington on the part of other CSTO members and the expanding suspicion in those countries about long-term American objectives in Central Asia and the Caucasus also suggest the creation of a consensus within the CSTO to oppose American military and political influence in their regions.

Russia took advantage of this situation to bring back Uzbekistan into the CSTO in 2006. The CSTO meeting in Moscow of the CSTO heads of state, June 22–23, 2005, provided the opportunity for it. The summit meeting was held concurrently with the meetings of the CSTO countries' ministers of foreign affairs, defense ministers, and secretaries of the national security councils. The Uzbek government accused Washington and some of its European allies of allegedly masterminding or being involved in the May 2005 armed conflict in Andijan, but Washington and its European allies (the European Union) condemned the alleged use of excessive force and human rights abuses by the Uzbeks in dealing with the incident. In such a situation, all the high-ranking Russian officials attending the Moscow meeting unconditionally backed Uzbekistan and condemned categorically what they described as a clear act of terrorism in Andijan (Socor 2005). These officials, who offered to help the Uzbeks suppress terrorism by all means, included Minister of Foreign Affairs Sergei Lavrov, Defense Minister Sergei Ivanov, Security Council Secretary Igor Ivanov, and CSTO Secretary General Nikolai Bordyuzha (ibid.).

Repeating what his top officials had said, Russian president Vladimir Putin also criticized the U.S.-led coalition in Afghanistan for tolerating the growing export of

Afghan heroin to Russia and for failing to suppress "terrorist training bases, including those supported by certain intelligence services," which, according to Putin, led to the export of terrorism to Uzbekistan (ibid.). Russia and the CSTO's full backing of the Uzbek government in its dealing with the Andijan incident and their offer of assistance helped improve and expand ties between Uzbekistan and Russia and pave the way for the readmission of Uzbekistan to the CSTO in 2006.

Apart from facilitating the readmission of Uzbekistan, the Moscow meeting of 2005 also provided an opportunity to revitalize the CSTO. Toward that end, the meeting approved a framework plan for CSTO development in two stages (through 2010 and beyond). It also approved plans to upgrade the Collective Rapid Deployment Forces in Central Asia, also creating an interstate commission tasked with handling deliveries to and servicing of military equipment for CSTO members at preferential prices. The last item was aimed at preventing the members from purchasing weapons from the NATO countries, mainly the United States. Furthermore, the Moscow meeting made a major decision with a clear impact on the consolidation of the organization and the integration of its member states under Russian authority, endorsing the separation of the CIS Joint Air Defense System, formed nominally of ten CIS countries, from the CSTO-planned United Air Defense System, consisting of only six members.

The CIS Joint Air Defense System is composed of the CIS countries under their individual national commands, whose military exercises are coordinated by a center in Russia. This entity regards each member state's airspace as distinct and sovereign. Contrary to this, the United Air Defense System consists of the air defense forces of six CSTO members under a single Russian planning system and command. This body considers the air space of its members a single CSTO airspace. The justification for this planned system lay in the close ties of some CIS countries and even their expressed interest in joining NATO, which, according to Russia, requires a system for the CSTO members.

The CSTO has recently taken certain measures to turn itself into a full-fledged military organization, two of which are especially important. During the Dushanbe CSTO summit meeting of October 6, 2007, the presidents of the CSTO member states signed an agreement to establish a CSTO peacekeeping force (Gabuev and Solovyev 2007). The CSTO defense ministers had already approved the plan at a meeting in Bishkek on September 28, 2007, which was approved by their foreign minister on October 4, 2007 (ibid.). The CSTO Moscow headquarters was quoted as saying that the force was mandated to carry out any operation within the CSTO territory without "any outside interference," including UN sanctions, "if a situation arises to threaten stability and internal security of any CSTO state" (ibid.). In addition to operations within the CSTO territory, the CSTO will be able to "create peacekeeping brigades with an international status" whose "zone of peacekeeping activities could be in any hot spot in the world," according to CSTO Secretary General Nikolay Bordyuzha (ibid.). The October 2007 agreement also provides for the CSTO members to purchase Russian weapons at the same price that Russia does (ibid.).

Additionally, the CSTO signed an agreement with the Shanghai Cooperation Organization (SCO) also on October 6, 2007, in Dushanbe (*Daily Times* 2007). The agreement further consolidates the CSTO as a military organization to enable its membership to face the rising challenges of NATO's plans to expand in Central Asia and the Caucasus, even though SCO General Secretary Bolat Nurgaliyev and CSTO general secretary Nikolai Bordyuzha denied having any plan toward that end (ibid.). Instead, they stressed that the agreement was a means to "broaden cooperation between our similar organizations in security issues, in fighting crime and illegal drug traffic" (ibid.).

The CSTO has conducted military exercises as part of its preparedness to perform its duties under its charter. In this regard, its August 24, 2006, military exercise, Rubezh–2006, is noteworthy. Launched in Central Asia, the joint forces of four member states (Russia, Kazakhstan, Kyrgyzstan, and Tajikistan) conducted counterterrorism war games (Chossudovsky 2006). There was speculation that the military exercise, in addition to its stated mentioned objectives, was also a reaction to the military threats posed by Washington in the region, such as a possible U.S. attack on Iran. The most significant CSTO military exercise to this date is Rubezh–2008, conducted in Russia and Armenia during the summer and fall of 2008. Started in July 2008, the four-stage exercise, which involved about 4,000 servicemen from Armenia, Russia, and Tajikistan, was the "first large-scale joint manoeuvre" of CSTO, according to Armenian Defense Minister Seyran (ARKA 2008). Reportedly, other CSTO members are "represented by military staff from respective defense ministries" (PIMS 2008).

The CSTO has yet to become a full-fledged military alliance of committed members. Added to their membership in NATO's Partnership for Peace, the political, economic, and even military/security ties of most of its members to the United States make questionable their level of commitment to the CSTO for as long as they are maintained. Of an obvious major bearing on their CSTO membership, their military/security ties with the United States include hosting its military (Kazakhstan and Kyrgyzstan), participating in the U.S.-led coalitions in Iraq and Afghanistan (e.g., Armenia), and granting overflight and emergency rights to the U.S. Air Force (Kazakhstan and Tajikistan). The consolidation and emergence of the CSTO as an integrated military alliance with committed members contradicts this type of relations. So long as its members allow this situation to continue, the CSTO cannot logically develop under Russia as an alternative to the U.S. military and the NATO alliance. Uzbekistan has severed its military ties and decreased its political ties with the United States. In early 2009, there is no evidence to substantiate the rumors that the Uzbek government is considering allowing the U.S. military to use the German air base in Termez for its operations in Afghanistan. Even if this turns out to be true, it could be nothing more than a tactical move out of concern about the expanding civil war in neighboring Afghanistan, not a policy reversal toward Washington, in light of the Uzbek government's view that the United States is planning a color revolution in its country—the reason for reducing its ties with Washington in May 2005. Uzbekistan's Central Asian and Caucasian counterparts also have yet to take steps to end their military and political cooperation with the United States for the purpose just discussed. In early 2009, there is not any hard evidence suggesting the feasibility of such a move in the near future, although the growing concern about Washington in Central Asia could well convince those states to revise their foreign and military policies in the future.

BIBLIOGRAPHY

Akiner, Shirin. 2005. "Violence in Andijan, 13 May 2005: An Independent Assessment." *Silk Road Paper* (July 2005), 10. www.isdp.eu/files/publications/srp/05/sa05violencein.pdf (accessed October 4, 2008).

ARKA News Agency. "Armenian Defense Minister: Rubezh 2008 First Large-Scale Joint Military Exercises." ARKA, July 23, 2008. www.arka.am/eng/defence/2008/07/23/10404.html (accessed October 4, 2008).

Bissenova, Alima. 2007. "Azerbaijan Rejects Criticism of Military Spending." *Central Asia–Caucasus Analyst,* October 16, 2007. www.cacianalyst.org/?q=node/4713 (accessed September 28, 2008).

Chernyshova, Natasha. 2003. "Russia and Its Neighbours: Russia-Belarus: The Union That Never Happens." *Institute for War & Peace Reporting–Belarus Reporting Service,* no. 03, February 12, 2003.

Chossudovsky, Michel. 2006. "Russia and Central Asian Allies Conduct War Games in Response to US Threats." *Global Research,* August 24, 2006.

Collective Security Treaty Organization (CSTO). 2002. *Charter of the Collective Security Treaty Organization.* United Nations Treaty Collection, Vol. 2235, I-39775. http://untreaty.un.org/unts/144078_158780/5/9/13289.pdf (accessed January 11, 2009).

Cornell, Svante, Roger M. McDermott, William D. O'Malley, Vladimir Socor, and S. Frederick Starr. 2004. *Regional Security in South Caucasus: The Role of NATO.* Washington, D.C.: Central Asia-Caucasus Institute.

Daily Times. 2007. "Security Alliances Led by Russia, China Link Up." *Daily Times,* October 6, 2007. http://www.dailytimes.com.pk/default.asp?page=2007%5C10%5C06%5Cstory_6-10-2007_pg4_3 (accessed October 5, 2008).

Gabuev, Alexander, and Vladimir Solovyev. 2007. "Gendarme of Eurasia," *Kommersant,* October 8, 2007. www.kommersant.com/p812422/CIS_CSTO_Russia_Lebedev/ (accessed September 30, 2008).

Interfax-AVN. 2003. CIS Collective Security Council. FBIS Transcribed Text. April 29, 2003. www.fas.org/irp/world/russia/fbis/ciscollecsecycouncil.html (accessed October 3, 2008).

Interfax-AVN. 2006. "Uzbekistan Restores Collective Security Treaty Organization Membership." *Interfax-AVN,* December 13, 2006 (accessed October 3, 2008).

Kaczmarski, Marcin. 2005. "Russia Creates a New Security System to Replace the C.I.S." *Power and Interest News Report,* December 21, 2005. www.pinr.com/report.php?ac=view_report&report_id=416&language_id=1 (accessed October 3, 2008).

Myers, Steven Lee. 2008. "Cheney Backs Membership in NATO for Georgia." *The New York Times,* September 4, 2008. www.nytimes.com/2008/09/05/world/europe/05cheney.html (accessed October 3, 2008).

Partnership for Peace Information Management System (PIMS). 2008. "'Rubezh 2008': The First Large-Scale CSTO Military Exercise." *PIMS,* October 2008. www.pims.org/news/2008/08/06/rubezh-2008-the-first-large-scale-csto-military-exercise (accessed October 5, 2008).

Simon, Jeffrey. 2004. "Partnership for Peace: Charting a Course for a New Era." *Strategic Forum,* no. 206, March 2004.

Socor, Vladimir. 2005. "CIS Collective Security Treaty Organization Holds Summit." *Eurasia Daily Monitor* 2, no. 123, June 24, 2005. www.jamestown.org/single/?no_cache=1&tx_ttnews%5Btt_news%5D=30576 (accessed January 11, 2009).

exploration, in construction of oil and gas pipelines, and in the field of high-tech information and telecommunication technology, the SCO states agreed to establish "at the earliest possible" time expert working groups on issues of fuel and energy, modern information, and telecommunication technology. The attending SCO heads of government also signed the Agreement on Interbank Cooperation (SCO 2005). In October 2006, Russia reportedly raised in a very broad sense the idea of creating an SCO "energy club" (Gazeta.kz 2006).

The SCO is committed to building trust and goodwill among its members. To achieve that end, it seeks to promote closer relations among its members, not just in the security field but also in the political, economic, scientific, technical, energy, environmental, cultural, and educational realms. Steps toward these objectives have not been very impressive so far, except for the growing political closeness of the SCO members. Yet, even in this field, the members are still far from having similar political views, especially with respect to international affairs. For instance, concerns about the long-term objectives of Washington in Central Asia and the Caucasus are definitely a common denominator among all the SCO states and are thus a strong reason for their cooperation. This has been evident in their 2005 demand for a clear timetable for the departure of the U.S. military (Blank 2005). Nevertheless, Kyrgyzstan, Kazakhstan, and Tajikistan have military ties with the United States, including a U.S. Air Force base in Kyrgyzstan and the granting of overflight and emergency landing rights to the U.S. military by Kazakhstan and Tajikistan. Uzbekistan also has ties with NATO by renting an air base to Germany (Termez Air Base). In late 2008, there were rumors that Uzbekistan may let the U.S. military use this facility, for which no supporting evidence was provided.

The SCO is in its infancy. The organization is still in the process of shaping and reshaping itself into a strong regional organization dealing with security issues. However, there is no question that if the current trend continues, it will emerge as a major regional organization capable of affecting both regional and international affairs, thanks to a variety of factors, including its impressive size and population. The current SCO members control about 30 million square kilometers with a population of 1.455 billion people, or about a quarter of the total population of the world. Other contributing factors are the nuclear arsenals and the conventional military capabilities of Russia and China, and their industrial capacity. China's seemingly unstoppable economic strength, the oil and gas resources of the SCO membership, and the SCO's proximity to the European Union and the fast-growing Asia/Pacific region are additional factors.

Because they are large and populous nations, the future membership of Iran, India, and Pakistan, if it becomes a reality, will certainly further strengthen the SCO. This is a function of their significance as regional powers and their political and economic capabilities, apart from the nuclear status of India and Pakistan and the conventional military strength of Iran, which is mainly based on its indigenous and growing military industry. Such membership will expand the borders of the SCO to the energy-rich Persian Gulf and the Indian Ocean. Iran has the world's second-largest oil and gas reserves, with strong potential for discovering large, untapped reservoirs. Therefore, its membership in the SCO—one of whose members (Russia) has the world's largest

THE UNKNOWN STATUS OF THE U.S. AIR BASE IN KYRGYZSTAN

The fate of the U.S. Air Force base at Manas Airport in Bishkek (Ganci Air Base) is far from certain. The issue of U.S. military bases in Central Asia, including Kyrgyzstan, was raised at the Shanghai Cooperation Organization (SCO) summit in Astana in July 2005. Signed also by Kyrgyzstan, the summit's final declaration demanded that the American government specify dates for its forces' withdrawal from that region. The growing concern among the Central Asian, Chinese, and Russian governments about the U.S. objectives in Central Asia and the Caucasus justified the requested dates to ensure the removal of the bases. The demand practically ended grounds for a long-term stay of the American military in Kyrgyzstan. Within this framework, logically, Kyrgyzstan's increasing the base's annual rent from about $1 million to $200 million sought not just to maximize Kyrgyzstan's gain from the base, but also probably attempted to lay the groundwork for the base's eventual closure, perhaps over financial disputes. In July 2006, the U.S. and Kyrgyz governments agreed on a new annual rent of $150 million, subject to approval by the U.S. Congress. Although approval was given, the region's increasing suspicion of the U.S. military presence, the worsening internal stability of Kyrgyzstan, caused by expanding opposition, and the SCO's demand will all likely contribute to the eventual closure of the U.S. base in the foreseeable future unless major changes take place in these areas. Whereas in June 2008 Washington expressed its intention to expand its military presence at Manas Airport by asking the Kyrgyz government to allocate an additional 300 hectares to the air base, evidence suggests that the base's long-term survival is highly unlikely. This became evident in February 21, 2008, when Kyrgyz President Kurmanbek Bakiev clearly expressed his intention to demand the American government's closure of the base, although without specifying an exact date. In February 2009, President Bakiev's demanding the Kyrgyz parliament to start deliberation on the closure of the American air base without setting a date created additional doubts on the survival of the air base.

gas reserves and a substantial amount of oil—will turn the SCO into the single major force in the international energy market, with corresponding political and economic influence. The fossil energy resources of Kazakhstan and Uzbekistan will only further strengthen this influence.

A major, if not *the* major, importance of the SCO lies in its contribution to the consolidation of the emerging multipolar international system in which the SCO seeks to be a major pole. In light of the American government's efforts since the end of the Cold War to prevent the formation of such a system in favor of a unipolar one, the SCO will likely become a force to challenge and deny the United States such status if the current pace of events continues. This will require the SCO's efforts to retard and eventually reverse the growth of American political, economic, and military influence in the regions of interest to the SCO membership. Added to this general point, the strong U.S. interests in Central Asia and the Caucasus, a major area of operation of the SCO, will turn those regions into an arena of rivalry and conflict. This situation will surely be intensified by the emerging trend of the Central Asian countries, ever since the outbreak of the color revolutions, toward distancing themselves from Washington and becoming closer to China and Russia.

The SCO is not currently a military alliance, but its security nature, which requires military cooperation among its members, will likely push it toward becoming at least an alliance with a clear military mandate. Within the framework of the SCO and outside it, certain parameters have been pushing China and Russia closer to each other. Among others, these include the growing military pressure on these powers that comes from the expansion of the U.S. military presence in their proximity, Washington's withdrawal from the ABM treaty, and its work on a missile defense system. To this list should be added U.S. talks and efforts, now at a low level, to develop new generations of nuclear missiles for limited and tactical applications

The SCO is in the process of consolidation, for all its members see merits in its membership. In particular, both China and Russia are considering the organization a vehicle for strengthening their power, counterbalancing the growing U.S. presence and influence in their proximity, and thus preventing the full domination of Washington in their neighboring regions. In particular, they view the organization as a means of stopping the further expansion of NATO by preventing the membership of the Central Asian and Caucasian nations in the U.S.-dominated military alliance and eventually ending their participation in its Partnership for Peace program. In the aftermath of the Georgian-Russian war of August 2008, this objective is especially important for Russia, as Georgia is pushing for NATO membership—a bid backed by Washington, as clearly stated by U.S. Vice President Dick Cheney during his September 2008 visit to Georgia (Myers 2008), but not yet (April 2009) by all other NATO members. Moreover, Russia considers the SCO a means for reestablishing itself as a superpower, along with other means and measures to restore the economic, political, and military power it lost when the Soviet Union collapsed. Other members are concerned about the long-term objectives of the U.S. government in their region and its efforts to settle there through the formation of pro-American governments, as the "revolutionary" governments of Kyrgyzstan, Georgia, and Ukraine are perceived. For that matter, these members regard the SCO as a vehicle to counter U.S. power, although they are not yet willing to become fully committed to the Russian bloc.

BIBLIOGRAPHY

Akin, Andrew M. 2005. "The Shanghai Cooperation Organization: A Structural Functional Analysis." Ph.D. diss., Troy State University.

Associated Press (AP). 2007. "Russian Official Says Country's Reputation Damaged by Oil Dispute with Belarus," January 13, 2007.

Associated Press (AP). 2008. "Iran Announces It Is Seeking Membership in the Shanghai Cooperation Organization," March 24, 2008. www.iht.com/articles/ap/2008/03/24/asia/AS -GEN-Tajikistan-Iran-SCO.php (accessed October 4, 2008).

Blank, Stephen. 2005. "Making Sense of the Shanghai Cooperation Organization's Astana Summit." *Central Asia–Caucasus Analyst,* July 27, 2005. www.cacianalyst.org/view_article .php?articleid=3504 (accessed September 14, 2008).

Craig, Timothy G. 2003. "The Shanghai Cooperation Organization: Origins and Implications." Master's thesis, Naval Postgraduate School.

Daily Times. 2007. "Security Alliances Led by Russia, China Link Up," October 6, 2007, www.dailytimes.com.pk/default.asp?page=2007%5C10%5C06%5Cstory_6-10-2007_pg4_3 (accessed October 4, 2008).

Daly, John. 2001. "'Shanghai Five' Expands to Combat Islamic Radicals." *Jane's Terrorism & Security Monitor,* July 19, 2001.

Gazeta.kz. 2006. "Russia's Foreign Ministry Develops Concept of SCO Energy Club." *Kazakhstan Today,* December 1, 2006. http://eng.gazeta.kz/art.asp?aid=84086 (accessed October 5, 2008).

Ministry of Foreign Affairs of the People's Republic of China (MFAPRC). *Shanghai Cooperation Organizatio.* MFAPRC official website, July 1, 2004. http://www.fmprc.gov.cn/eng/topics/sco/t57970.htm (accessed April 27, 2009)

Myers, Steven Lee. 2008. "Cheney Backs Membership in NATO for Georgia." *The New York Times,* September 4, 2008. www.nytimes.com/2008/09/05/world/europe/05cheney.html (accessed October 3, 2008).

People's Daily. 2007. "SCO Anti-Terror Drill Holds Decision-Making Practice." People's Daily Online, August 13, 2007. http://english.peopledaily.com.cn/90001/90777/6237722.html (accessed October 5, 2008).

Shanghai Cooperation Organization (SCO). 1997, 2003, 2004, and 2005. "Chronology." SCO official website, www.sectsco.org/html/00030.html (accessed March 31, 2007).

Weitz, Richard. 2006. "Reading the Shanghai SCO Summit." *Central Asia–Caucasus Analyst,* July 12, 2006. http://www.cacianalyst.org/?g=node/4049 (accessed January 3, 2009).

Xinhua. 2006a. "SCO to Intensify Fight against Cross-Border Drug Crimes," April 21, 2006. http://english.people.com.cn/200604/22/eng20060422_260252.html (accessed March 31, 2008).

Xinhua. 2006b. "SCO to Stage Joint Anti-Terror Military Exercise in 2007," April 26, 2006. http://english.scosummit2006.org/en_zxbb/2006-04/26/content_332.htm (accessed October 10, 2008)

Yom, Sean L. 2002. "Power Politics in Central Asia: The Future of the Shanghai Cooperation Organization." *Harvard Asia Quarterly* 6, no. 4, 48–54.

Chapter 18

Organization for Democracy and Economic Development–GUAM

HISTORY

The collapse of the Soviet Union in December 1991 left many former Soviet republics unprepared to operate normally on their own as the result of a variety of political, economic, social, and military/security factors. Hence the need for cooperation became apparent to just about all of them. Although the concept of cooperation was acceptable, there were disagreements on its specifics, including its framework and management. In particular, the newly independent states were concerned about Russia's efforts to dominate their countries in a bid to restore its lost influence. As a result, the creation of the Commonwealth of Independent States (CIS) did not meet the expectations of many of them, who then sought groupings of like-minded states to pursue their national interests.

Within this context, GUAM was founded on October 10, 1997, in Strasbourg, France, during the summit of the Council of Europe, in which the CIS countries were members (GUAM 1997). Its founders were the four CIS countries of Georgia, Ukraine, Azerbaijan, and Moldova; the first letters of their names form the organization's name. GUAM, whose name has since changed a few times to reflect its changing membership, aims to advance the interests of its member states in all major fields, with an emphasis on economic development. In particular, the organization seeks to promote economic growth and address the shortcomings of its members in all the related areas, with an emphasis on their adherence to democracy while preserving and consolidating their independence. This last objective is designed to ensure that their countries will not be dominated by Russia, for which they seek integration in the Western bloc of states, particularly the European Union, apart from reasons arising from the pro-Western orientation of the GUAM founders. GUAM is also seen as a means to counter Russian power in the CIS territories with the backing of Washington— an assessment rejected by the organization itself, but seemingly logical in light of its expanding ties with the Western countries and their political, economic, and military organizations, such as NATO and the European Union (EU). However, GUAM leaders have officially dismissed such claims on many occasions and declared their strong willingness to develop close, friendly relations with Moscow. This attitude recognizes the realities of their countries and their region, which make normal ties with Russia a necessity for political, economic, and security reasons. Nevertheless, this does imply that the GUAM countries have in fact had friendly relations with Russia. On the contrary, two of its members, Georgia and Ukraine, have had turbulent relations with Russia, especially since the ascension to power of their pro-American leaders, Mikhail Saakashvili and Viktor Yushchenko, on the back of the Rose Revolution of 2003 and the Orange Revolution of 2004, respectively. In the wake of the Georgian-Russian war of August 2008, Georgia severed its ties with Russia. Ukraine's ties with Russia have since further deteriorated, because its president sided with Georgia during the war and allegedly supplied weapons to the Georgian military during that conflict, as claimed by Prime Minister Vladimir Putin (*Pravda.ru* 2008).

GUAM has not been very active since its inception. Uzbekistan left the CIS Collective Security Treaty Organization (CSTO) in April 1999, along with Azerbaijan and Georgia (Cornell et al. 2004), for its relationship with Moscow was cooling in favor of Washington. Uzbekistan joined GUAM on April 24, 1999, at the meeting of the presidents of GUAM participating states in Washington. Its membership resulted in the group's change of name to GUUAM, adding a second *U* for Uzbekistan. This enlargement created hope that the organization would become active and continue to grow. However, Uzbekistan's membership proved half-hearted, reflecting fluctuations in its ties with Moscow and Washington rather than commitment to the alliance's objectives. As its ties with the Western countries, and particularly the United States, deteriorated after the Andijan incident of May 2005, Uzbekistan finally withdrew from GUUAM in May 2005 after years of virtual inactivity (*RIA Novosti* 2005). Reflecting Uzbekistan's departure, the GUUAM members changed the name of their organization back to GUAM. As part of a series of efforts to revitalize the organization and increase its membership, its remaining four members changed its name again on May 23, 2006, to the Organization for Democracy and Economic Development–GUAM (GUAM 2006a). In their declaration to that effect, the four presidents of the GUAM states stressed their commitment to the objectives of the organization, as set in 1997, regarding economic development, democracy, and European integration and security, inviting those states sharing such objectives to join them. The secretariat of the organization is in Kiev.

MEMBERSHIP

Known today (2009) as GUAM, the Organization for Democracy and Economic Development–GUAM had four founding members in 1997. Georgia, Ukraine, Azerbaijan, and Moldova constituted its membership until 1999, when Uzbekistan joined the organization, increasing its member states to five and changing its name to GUUAM. As a five-member grouping, GUUAM did not last very long. Uzbekistan's decision to withdraw from GUUAM in 2005 decreased the number of its members to four. In 2006, the renaming of the organization to the Organization for Democracy and Economic Development–GUAM was meant, among other things, to help revive and expand the organization by attracting new members. In early 2009, there is no strong indication of the immediate joining of a new member, nor is there any sign of one in the foreseeable future.

FUNCTION

The Organization for Democracy and Economic Development–GUAM (hereafter GUAM) has a mandate with economic, political, and security components, which are reflected in its organizational structure (GUAM 2006b). Its highest body is the annual summit meeting attended by the GUAM presidents once a year in Yalta, Ukraine. The sessions of ministers for foreign affairs of its member states form its executive body and are convened twice a year. The Committee of National Coordinators (CNC), consisting of one coordinator from each GUAM member state, appointed by its respective foreign minister, is the organization's working body. GUAM also has an information office located in Ukraine's capital, Kiev. Eight working groups conduct GUAM's activities, dealing with certain general issue areas: power engineering, transport, trade and economics, information science and telecommunications, culture, science and education, tourism, and the struggle against terrorism, organized crime, and drugs.

As envisaged by its founders, GUAM is a political and economic alliance having the strategic objective of strengthening the independence and sovereignty of its member states. At its time of establishment on October 10, 1997, the presidents of the four founding countries (Azerbaijan, Georgia, Moldova, and Ukraine) justified its founding as a function of their common interests (GUAM 2001). The four countries shared an interest in developing political and economic relations, bilateral and regional cooperation, and regional and European security, while remaining committed to democratic values, as they claimed. The joint communiqué issued upon its foundation stressed the importance of cooperation among the members and spelled out its final purpose and framework:

> . . . the Presidents [of Georgia, Ukraine, Azerbaijan and Moldova] underscored the need for strengthening quadrilateral cooperation for the sake of a stable and secure Europe guided by the principles of respect for sovereignty, territorial integrity, inviolability of state frontiers, mutual respect, cooperation, democracy, supremacy of law, and respect for human rights.... In this connection, they underlined the prospects of the four nations' cooperation within the framework of the OSCE, other European and Atlantic structures, including the recently established Euro-Atlantic Partnership Council and the Partnership for Peace NATO Program. (GUAM 1997, paras. 4, 5)

The leaders of the four countries agreed to undertake joint efforts to overcome the difficulties confronting Europe in the new millennium. The joint communiqué also specified a major economic ambition of the organization with clear political and security dimensions. Hence, it expressed GUAM's intention to become a major transit rout:

> During the meeting, the Presidents stressed the importance of the four nations['] cooperation in establishing a Euroasian, Trans-Caucasus transportation corridor, considering joint actions taken in this direction a sound foundation for fostering friendship and cooperation, good-neighborly relations and full utilization of existing economic opportunities. (GUAM 1997, para. 2)

The envisaged "Eurasian, Trans-Caucasus transportation corridor" is a stated focus of cooperation of the GUAM membership. On surface, it is simply an economic objective to establish a trade/transit route to connect Eurasia to Europe via the Caucasus and the Black Sea, on which two member states (Georgia and Ukraine) have ports. This is of course a means of facilitating trade among the GUAM members as well as conducting trade of other states through this route, which has access to Asia and Europe via the Caucasus. However, it also has clear security and political dimensions for certain reasons. Such a route, if it becomes a reality—and there is no strong indication of this in 2009—will enable Azerbaijan and Georgia to bypass Russia for their trade with Ukraine and Moldova and also to conduct trade through Ukraine with the rest of Europe. Theoretically, this route will also enable the landlocked Central Asian countries to bypass Russia and Iran for their international trade by accessing Azerbaijan via the Caspian Sea, through which they can reach the Black Sea passing through neighboring Georgia. Such a route could decrease the vulnerability of GUAM and the Central Asian states to pressure by Russia, through which they currently conduct the bulk of their trade out of geographical necessity. This envisaged route would also enable Azerbaijan, Georgia, and the Central Asian states to avoid the Iranian route by providing an alterative to that and, of course, to the Russian route, their only two practical transit options for international trade. Such bypassing has been an objective of the U.S. government in the southern CIS countries since the 1990s.

The envisaged Eurasian, Trans-Caucasus transportation corridor also seeks to rival the North-South Corridor. This corridor is a joint project of Iran, Russia, and India to make use of their access to the open seas (Black Sea, Persian Gulf, and Indian Ocean), their established sea links, and Iran's and Russia's sea and land links via the Caspian Sea and the Caucasus, to offer a shorter, faster, and cheaper alterative for the European-Asian trade than shipping through the Suez Canal. The corridor has been in operation on a small scale for the last few years and is something in which other regional and nonregional countries, including Azerbaijan, are interested. The main target of the Eurasian, Trans-Caucasus transportation corridor is to establish an alternative to this route by connecting the Caspian Sea region to the Black Sea via Azerbaijan and Georgia. Provided this project turns into reality, such a transit route will surely contribute to tension in the bilateral relations of the GUAM states with Iran, Russia, and India. The fate of GUAM's envisaged route is not bright in early 2009, for the Georgian-Russian war of August 2008 seriously raised question about Georgia's ability to function as a secure transit route so long as its hostile relations with Russia provide grounds for military conflicts with Russia.

Between 1997 and 1999, when Uzbekistan left the CIS Collective Security Treaty and joined GUAM to turn it into GUUAM, the organization was not very active. Uzbekistan's membership was perceived as a potential booster, which turned out to be unrealistic. The main organizational achievement of the following period was the signing of GUUAM's charter in its Yalta summit, held on June 6, 2001 (GUAM 2001). The charter formalized the organization and established an institutionalized framework for its activities and its continuity. However, shortly after that, in 2002, Uzbekistan announced its decision to leave the organization eventually and thus stopped attending its meetings at all levels, with the practical effect of its immediate, but unofficial withdrawal. Tashkent made official this fait accompli in May 2005.

Annual summit meetings and more frequent ministerial ones since its founding have all stressed the need for the cooperation of GUAM members and the expansion of the organization's activities. Yet, in practice GUAM has not had a lot to demonstrate as its practical achievements since its establishment. In fact, the organization seems to have been stagnating since 2002. In part, this was reflected in the attendance of only two GUAM heads of state in its 2004 summit meeting in Yalta. Another sign of inactivity has been the lack of any meaningful progress on their various agreements (including a free trade area), which are yet to be implemented.

However, there are suggestions as of its revitalization because of the change of governments in Georgia and Ukraine (Ziyadov 2006). Thanks to their color revolutions, both countries now have pro-American governments whose cooperation with each other has been promoted by their common political orientations. The two countries push for their integration in the Western bloc and cooperation with NATO and the European Union in addition to their already close, and now expanding, ties with the United States.

Although there are not yet (in early 2009) strong indications of a fundamental change in GUAM's life, there has been at least a more upbeat mood at the GUAM leadership level since 2005. This suggests a desire, at minimum, to turn the organization into an active entity. For example, in its summit meeting of April 2005, held in Chisinau, Moldova, when Uzbekistan's departure from the GUUAM became official, Azeri president Ilham Aliyev made the following remark: "Our organization is emerging as a powerful force, participating in resolving problems in the Caspian-Black Sea region . . . . [GUAM] member states share a common approach against terrorism and separatism," as reflected in GUAM's joint declaration (*Civil Georgia* 2005, para.). His Ukrainian counterpart, Viktor Yushchenko, assessed the summit as "a new page" in the organization's history (ibid., para.). He also stressed that GUAM stood on the "three whales"—democracy, economic development, and security/stability (ibid.). The Ukrainian president went beyond statements to set a clear objective for Ukraine as a GUAM member:

"There are four hot spots [Abkhazia, South Ossetia, Transdnestria and Nagorno-Karabakh] in our region. And Ukraine sets giving a boost to resolving at least one of these conflicts as its goal." He also stated that Ukraine has drafted a proposal over Transdnestria conflict resolution, titled "Seven Steps," adding that Ukraine will submit the full plan within three weeks. (Ibid., para.)

In short, the attending leaders stated that their organization was turning into a meaningful vehicle for regional cooperation (ibid). The summit's communiqué reflected the intention of Georgia, Ukraine, Azerbaijan, and Moldova to revitalize their organization (GUAM 2005). It therefore called for implementing all decisions and agreements, including the formation of a free trade area (ibid.). Perhaps prompted by the new mood in GUAM, on May 30, 2006, in Baku, Safar Abiyev and Anatoly Gritsenko, the respective Azeri and Ukrainian defense ministers, discussed the possibility of establishing a GUAM peacekeeping force (*Civil Georgia* 2006). The news suggested a move toward ending the inactivity of GUAM, but this has yet to become a reality. The organization still lacks any major role in the lives of its current members. Nor has it been successful in enlarging the alliance since 2005, despite the hope of its leaders. The engagement of other states in GUAM has so far been mainly confined to ceremonial participation in its meetings. For instance, the presidents of Poland, Romania, and Lithuania, the vice president of Bulgaria, the vice speaker of the Estonian parliament, the Latvian minister of economy, representatives of the United States and Japan, and the heads of diplomatic missions accredited to Azerbaijan attended GUAM's June 19, 2007, summit meeting in Baku (GUAM 2007).

As stipulated in their charter and declarations, the GUAM countries are expected to have common policies on issues of common interest. Furthermore, they should act as a bloc with common objectives in international and regional organizations to advance their national and collective interests. There have been some indications of the GUAM countries' working toward that end in CIS meetings since 2006. As a recent example, during the CIS foreign ministerial meeting of April 21, 2006, Georgia, Ukraine, Azerbaijan, and Moldova acted in concert. Led by Ukraine, these countries formed a bloc expressing their shared views on political and economic issues and thus their opposition to certain Russian policies that damage their interests. Therefore, Georgia and Moldova submitted separately prepared statements about Russia's ban on imports of their wines and other agricultural products imposed on the Russian market (Socor 2006). Also, the three GUAM states supported Ukraine's proposal to condemn the Holodomor, the 1930s famine in Ukraine, as genocide (ibid.).

Since its inception, GUAM has so far (2009) failed to develop itself into a full-fledged regional organization. Recent developments could potentially be the indicators of a clear change for the better, but it is yet unknown whether such developments represent true change or only a few isolated cases of cooperation for tactical purposes.

BIBLIOGRAPHY

Civil Georgia. 2005. "GUAM Leaders Hail Chisinau Summit," April 22, 2005. www.civil.ge/eng/article.php?id=9677 (accessed October 1, 2008).

Civil Georgia. 2006. "Azerbaijan, Ukraine Mull over GUAM Peacekeeping Forces," May 31, 2006. www.civil.ge/eng/article.php?id=12694&search=Azerbaijan,%20Ukraine%20Mull%20over%20GUAM%20Peacekeeping%20Forces (accessed October 1, 2008).

Cornell, Svante, Roger M. McDermott, William D. O'Malley, Vladimir Socor, and S. Frederick Starr. 2004. *Regional Security in South Caucasus: The Role of NATO*. Washington, D.C.: Central Asia-Caucasus Institute.

Organization for Democracy and Economic Development—GUAM. 1997. "Joint Communiqué of the Meeting of the President of Azerbaijan, Georgia, Moldova and Ukraine." October 10, 1997. http://guam-organization.org/en/node/440 (accessed January 11, 2009).

Organization for Democracy and Economic Development—GUAM. 2001. "Charter of the Organization for Democracy and Economic Development—GUAM." June 6, 2001. http://guam-organization.org/en/node/450 (accessed January 11, 2009).

Organization for Democracy and Economic Development—GUAM. 2005. "The Chisinau Declaration of the GUUAM Heads of States 'In the name of democracy, stability and development.'" April 22, 2005. http://guam-organization.org/en/node/438 (accessed January 11, 2009).

Organization for Democracy and Economic Development—GUAM. 2006a. Kyiv Declaration on Establishment of the Organization for Democracy and Economic Development–GUAM, May 23, 2006. http://guam-organization.org/en/node/468 (accessed January 11, 2009).

Organization for Democracy and Economic Development—GUAM. 2006b. Organizational Structure of the GUAM, May 19, 2006. http://guam-organization.org/en/node/269 (accessed January 11, 2009).

Organization for Democracy and Economic Development—GUAM. 2007. 2nd Meeting of the Council of Heads of State, Baku, Azerbaijan, June 19, 2007. www.mfa.gov.az/ssi_eng/international/organizations/guam/Baku_Summit_2007/Baku_GUAM_Summit_Communique_eng.pdf (accessed October 4, 2008).

Pravda.ru. 2008. "Putin to Ukraine: Don't Bite the Hand That Feeds You," October 3, 2008, http://english.pravda.ru/world/ussr/03-10-2008/106520-putin_ukraine-0 (accessed October 5, 2008).

RIA Novosti. 2005. "Uzbekistan Quits Anti-Russian GUUAM," May 6, 2005.

Socor, Vladimir. 2006. "CIS Split at Ministerial Conference." *Eurasia Daily Monitor,* April 25, 2006.

Ziyadov, Taleh. 2006. "The Battle of Forums: Transformation of Regional Organizations in Eurasia." *Central Asia–Caucasus Institute,* July 12, 2006.

NATO and these countries' military forces conduct joint military exercises. Generally speaking, these are small-scale exercises. An example is Cooperative Best Efforts 2003, launched in Armenia in 2003 with the participation of 400 troops from different countries (Cornell et al. 2004, 68).

The Central Asian and Caucasian NATO partners contribute to NATO-led operations. To ensure their ability to take part in such missions, they participate in NATO exercises and training programs. For example, Azerbaijan and Georgia have dispatched small contingents of troops for noncombat duties to Kosovo and Afghanistan (Cornell et al. 2004, 72–73, 75). Armenia has also participated in NATO's Kosovo Force (KFOR) peacekeeping operation (Armenian Assembly of America 2004). Kazakhstan and Tajikistan assist NATO with its operations, including in Afghanistan, for instance, by allowing the use of their countries for the transit of supplies/troops from NATO countries to Afghanistan. To that effect, Tajikistan signed an agreement with NATO in 2004 (McDermott 2004).

Moreover, NATO and the Central Asian and Caucasian states cooperate on certain issues of immediate and long-term interest. Among others, these include defense reform in those countries, preventing the proliferation of weapons, clearing landmines, and disposing of stockpiled munitions, disaster preparedness, and scientific research. Demining is of special importance for a country such as Tajikistan, which was engulfed in a five-year civil war that ended in 1997. The NATO Partnership for Peace Trust Fund Policy was established in September 2000 to assist NATO partners in the safe destruction of stockpiled anti-personnel landmines (NATO 2007b). Tajikistan has benefited from this program, launched after NATO's completion of its demining project in Albania in 2001 (ibid.). Clearance of 569 hectares of contaminated land and disposal of unexploded ordnance has been achieved in Georgia under this program (NATO 2008b). The Trust Fund has undertaken projects to destroy small arms and light weapons, conventional munitions, and rocket fuel oxidizer. One of its ongoing projects is the destruction of large anti-aircraft missiles in Georgia (NATO 2007b).

Anti-terrorism is another area of joint work between NATO and its partners, including the Central Asians and Caucasians. NATO and its partners launched a Partnership Action Plan against Terrorism at the 2002 Prague summit of NATO. This plan has aimed at improved intelligence sharing and cooperation. It has also focused on border security and terrorism-related training and exercises.

The interest of the countries of Central Asia and the Caucasus in the Partnership for Peace Program is not one-sided. This partnership is also of interest to NATO, to which those regions are important because of their rich energy resources—mainly their significant oil and natural gas reserves. Although small compared to those of the Persian Gulf, these reserves are still significant enough to supply a fraction of the increasing demand of the Western countries for imported fuel. NATO's interest is also the result of these regions' three neighboring powers: China, Russia, and Iran. Despite its differing relations with each of them, these states, as rising regional and global powers, are a major source of concern for NATO in the short term and its chief concern in the long term. The rise of Iran as a regional superpower, as some argue, with claims to the regions in its proximity, is a source of concern in view of the unfriendly or unstable ties between Iran and many Western countries and their allies, accounting for almost the entire NATO membership. Another reason for concern for NATO in light of the mentioned state of relations between Iran and the Western countries is Iran's long shared border with the Persian Gulf, which contains the world's largest reservoir of oil and natural gas, on which the Western economies are dependent. In the case of China and Russia, their respective rise and resurgence as global powers are a particular source of long-term concern for NATO because of their weight as large countries having large populations, strategic geographical locations, vast resources, and powerful conventional military capabilities and nuclear arsenals.

Consequently, NATO pays special attention to the regions neighboring Iran, China, and Russia. This was translated into a certain decision at the Istanbul summit in June 2004 regarding the Partnership for Peace Program in Central Asia and the Caucasus. Accordingly,

> A decision was also taken to put special focus on engaging with Partner countries in two strategically important regions, namely the Caucasus (Armenia, Azerbaijan, and Georgia) and Central Asia (Kazakhstan, the Kyrgyz Republic, Tajikistan, Turkmenistan, and Uzbekistan). NATO has assigned a special representative for the two regions as well as two liaison officers. Their role is to assist and provide advice in implementing relevant aspects of Individual Partnership Action Plans, where appropriate, as well as the Partnership Action Plans on Defence Institution Building and against Terrorism. (NATO, December 16, 2006)

However, NATO relations with the Central Asians and the Caucasians have not been all rosy. Central Asians are having second thoughts about their ties with NATO. Uzbekistan's ties with the military alliance have been cooling since May 2005, when NATO joined the United States and the European Union in condemning the Uzbek government's suppression of an armed conflict in Andijan, as discussed earlier. Uzbekistan immediately demonstrated its anger at NATO by declining to send its defense minister to a NATO ministerial meeting in June 2005, which provoked a NATO statement about reviewing its ties with that country (*Central Asia–Caucasus Analyst* 2005). Even though Uzbekistan is still a member of the Partnership for Peace Program, it has minimized its ties with NATO, as acknowledged by NATO in 2008, although the latter is trying to keep a "dialog" with Tashkent to improve their severely damaged bilateral relations (NATO 2008a).

Uzbekistan and other Central Asian countries have had reservations about the overall Western objectives in their region in the wake of the color revolutions in Kyrgyzstan, Ukraine, and Georgia, which had a direct negative impact on their assessment of NATO as a Western military alliance. Furthermore, the poor performance of the Western countries in Iraq, where the U.S.-led coalition operates, and in Afghanistan, where NATO is in charge of the International Security Assistance Force (ISAF), has raised serious doubts about the capability and reliability of the Western countries and NATO, as well as about anti-terrorism as the reason for their presence in West and South Asia. As a result, their "initial enthusiasm over the military might of North Atlantic Alliance and its image as a reliable safeguard against extremism and terrorism seems to be

Part 4

WHAT THE FUTURE WILL HOLD FOR CENTRAL ASIA AND THE CAUCASUS

Chapter 20

Conclusion

Central Asia and the Caucasus had a difficult time during their first decade of independence. Not only did they suffer from a wide range of political, economic, and social problems caused by the sudden fall of the Soviet Union and their unprepared transition, they experienced various types of intra- and interstate conflicts, including armed ones. Armed conflicts included civil wars (Azerbaijan, Georgia, and Tajikistan), skirmishes along their borders (faced by all Central Asian and Caucasian states to a varying extent), and small-scale violent activities of armed extremist/terrorist groups (Kyrgyzstan, Tajikistan, and Uzbekistan). Territorial issues, especially border disputes and ownership disputes over certain Caspian oil fields, created the potential for armed conflicts in the bilateral relations of many of these countries. Civil wars in their neighboring countries (Afghanistan and Russia) also created security problems, bringing about the threat of war when Russia accused Georgia of harboring armed Chechens fighting Russian troops in Chechnya.

In the ninth year of their second decade, these regions are more stable, in a comparative sense. By and large, they face no immediate major challenges to the security and stability of their member states, with the major exception that Georgia has had turbulent relations with Russia, especially since 2005. Between that year and 2008, various issues, including the espionage crisis of September/October 2006 and Russia's imposition of extensive sanctions on Tbilisi, severely damaged Georgian-Russian relations, already worsened—particularly by Russia's backing of the breakaway republics of Abkhazia and South Ossetia. The Georgians' resort to arms to reestablish control over South Ossetia in August 2008 led to a full-scale war between Georgia and Russia, during which the Russian forces paralyzed the Georgian military and destroyed just about its entire military industry. Unsurprisingly, the war has turned the two countries into enemies, laying the groundwork for future armed conflicts between the two neighbors should the current course of relations continue.

Although other Caucasian and Central Asian states do not face a similar fragile security situation at this time, they are all prone to intrastate conflicts as a result of their failed transition, which has created polarized societies ready to burst into conflicts ranging from mass demonstrations to civil war. Furthermore, almost all these states have the seeds of interstate conflicts of various kinds.

MAJOR TRENDS IN CENTRAL ASIA AND THE CAUCASUS

Political Trends

In the second decade of independence, the governments of all five Central Asian states and Azerbaijan have opted for an undemocratic style of statecraft. Despite their differences, all these governments are consolidating their authoritarian regimes with all their components, including extensive human rights abuses. This process is further disassociating their respective peoples from them at a time when their societies are heading toward instability and intrastate conflicts, including violent ones. This is an outcome of their dismal economic growth (with the exception of the oil and gas sectors of the fossil energy exporters) and rampant poverty and low income, which are polarizing their societies along political and economic lines. Armenia and Georgia have pursued a less authoritarian, more open form of governance with greater tolerance of dissent. Yet, these are far from irreversible democracies leaving the possibility of internal instability caused by mass movements—especially in Georgia, where the Rose Revolution increased expectations among the Georgians for an overhaul of the post-Soviet Georgian political system marked with rampant corruption. The Georgian government's oppressive approach to the opposition groups in late 2007 and its resort to a snap election in January 2008—after depriving the opposition groups of their media and limiting their activities—raised doubts about Georgia's commitment to a nonauthoritarian and democratic form of statecraft qualitatively different from those of Azerbaijan and the Central Asian countries.

The rapid drop in the approval rating of President Mikhail Saakashvili suggests the disappointment of Georgians with the "revolutionary" government. The sudden eruption of patriotism among Georgians increased his popularity substantially during the course of the Georgian-Russian war, but this has proven to be unsustainable in the postwar era. His approval rating has been falling rather rapidly, as many Georgian now question the wisdom of their government's resort to arms to end the practical independence of the two breakaway republics. At the same time, subsiding emotions are enabling many Georgians unhappy with the government to rediscover the reasons for their old grievances. Against this background, unless the Georgian government adopts a different course of action, it will be only a matter of time before its country develops an authoritarian system of government.

Economic Trends

The Central Asian and Caucasian economies are now performing much better than in the first decade of their independence. Nevertheless, after years of contraction and dismal growth, their current better performance is still far from what these countries need to address their various economic problems. There is no indication that their performance in the near future will be at rates high enough to cause drastic changes for the better in their economies and eradicate many of the ills of their failed economic transition, including widespread poverty and low income.

It should be kept in mind that the comparatively high growth rates of the better-performing economies since 2000—those of Azerbaijan, Kazakhstan, Turkmenistan, and Uzbekistan—have been largely the result of significant increases in the prices of oil, gold, and cotton. Needless to say, the dependency of these economies on such exports will cause fluctuations in their economic growth as the prices of those items fluctuate. Hence, their high rate of economic growth will not be sustainable unless they diversify their economies and decrease their dependency on the export of so few items. The sharp decline in the price of oil from about $150 a barrel in July 2008 to about $100 a barrel in October 2008, only to further drop to about $50 a barrel in April 2009, serves as an example of the unsustainable nature of their economic growth, which has been mainly funded by oil- and gas-generated income. The other states, whose economies have undergone periods of good performance, are also highly dependent on the export of a few items: for example, cotton and gold, in the case of Kyrgyzstan and Tajikistan. These states, too, are on the path of unreliable growth.

Hostile relations with Russia will certainly have a major negative impact on the economic performance of Georgia, at least in the short run, until the Georgians can compensate for the loss of the Russian market, especially for wine lost before the August war, and also remittances sent by Georgians working in Russia. In fact, the Russian government began to stop Georgians from working in Russia after the spy crisis of 2006, under the pretext of ending illegal financial activities. At minimum, in view of the rapid expansion of hostility between Moscow and Tbilisi in the post-August 2008 war era, logic suggests that those Georgians who still reside in Russia will not be able to live and work there legally or freely, and that the Russian government will completely stop their remittances—at least those transmitted through traceable channels. To this should be added the negative impact of a total stoppage of Russian gas exports to Georgia. In early 2009, it is not clear whether such exports will continue to supply Georgia and also Armenia, which can receive Russian gas only through Georgia.

In the absence of Russian gas, geographical realities leave only two gas suppliers for Georgia: Azerbaijan and Iran. Azerbaijan, being a gas supplier to Georgia since 2004, when Russia cut gas exports to Georgia as the result of "accidents," does not have enough unused capacity to meet all Georgia's gas requirements. Iran is already connected to Georgia via an old Soviet pipeline through which it can supply some of Georgia's requirements, as it started to do in the wake of the Russian "accidents." Georgia has seriously considered importing a much larger amount of gas from Iran through the now-operating Iran-Armenia pipeline. Technically, there will be no need to lay pipe to connect Armenia and Georgia if Russian gas exports to Georgia (and thus Armenia) are completely halted; the existing connecting line could be used for Iranian exports by reversing the direction of the gas passing through the pipeline. This would require some relatively minor modifications to the pipeline (a feasible scenario). Yet, a major obstacle at this point seems not this, but the fact that Russia has bought the Armenian gas pipeline network. It is not yet clear whether that purchase includes the Armenian share of the Iranian-Armenian pipeline, because the Russian and Armenian authorities have made many contradicting statements in this regard. A major shortage of gas, if it becomes a reality, will certainly seriously damage the Georgian economy.

In short, the Central Asian and Caucasian economies, which are neither capitalist nor socialist, but have most of the negative characteristics of both systems, have a long way to go to become robust, free-enterprise economies. There is no evidence to suggest that this status—a necessity for eradicating poverty and low income, the major social causes of political instability—can be achieved in the foreseeable future.

Social Trends

The Central Asian and Caucasian countries are mainly socially fragile, because of many parameters that can be summed up in their failed political and economic transition. The failed transition has created a limbo economy and undemocratic, authoritarian, or totalitarian political systems unable to satisfy the economic, political, and social needs of the majority of their peoples. Their societies are facing rapid social and economic polarization because of uneven economic growth and unfair distribution of income. There is a corresponding political polarization as a result of the political marginalization of the majority and the accumulation of political power in the hands of small, largely unaccountable, mainly corrupt elites. With the partial exception of Armenia, and particularly Georgia, the elites widely abuse the human rights of their peoples. The absence of a large and growing middle class has denied the Central Asian and Caucasian societies the long-term social basis for stability. The seemingly unstoppable social polarization will have a major destabilizing impact on those societies.

Security-Related Trends

Since independence, all the Central Asian and Caucasian countries have experienced various types of conflicts. To a varying extent, internal or external conflicts have affected their countries with short- or long-term consequences for their stability. By and large, these countries do not face today an imminent security threat arising from internal or external sources of conflicts—with the exception of Georgia, which could experience major security threats owing to its dangerously hostile relations with Russia since the Georgian-Russian war of August 2008.

The Central Asian and Caucasian states could all face security challenges and instability in the foreseeable future thanks to their common potential for intra- and interstate conflicts. This is notwithstanding their differences in size, population, resources, industrial advancement, and economic opportunities as the major factors determining their degree of success in advancing their economies and addressing various transitional challenges. Although such conflicts are not inevitable, they could likely occur

some of the major causes of that conflict, such as regional disparities, could create grounds for a civil war should armed groups with a significant social base emerge.

Uzbekistan could also be engulfed in a civil war. Even though existing social and economic problems create a fertile ground for the rise of popular dissent, at least in the less developed and poorer parts of the country, such as the Ferghana Valley, the possibility for the rapid expansion of popular dissent capable of becoming a major movement is not very strong in the foreseeable future. In the absence of armed popular opposition groups or at least large, armed extremist groups, the transformation of such movements into a force strong enough to impose a civil war on Uzbekistan does not seem very likely. The outbreak of such war as a result of the growth of the existing armed groups, although a possibility, is not very likely either, at least in the near future. Since the late 1990s, the country has experienced a low-density armed conflict waged by the IMU, but this conflict has mainly been limited to the Ferghana valley. The possibility is slim that it will spill over to other parts of the country in a significant manner in the next few years. However, the IMU's reorganization, reflected in its expanding activities and its alleged operations in alliance with the Taliban in Pakistan's South Waziristan, bordering Afghanistan, suggest this potential.

Interstate Wars

The potential for interstate armed conflict of varying scale and scope is real in Central Asia. As detailed in the previous chapters, there are many reasons for hostilities and a great deal of suspicion in the relations of Uzbekistan and Turkmenistan, Tajikistan and Uzbekistan, Uzbekistan and Kazakhstan, Uzbekistan and Kyrgyzstan, and Kyrgyzstan and Tajikistan, stemming from Soviet-era issues such as territorial and border disputes, in addition to issues that have emerged since 1991. Although very limited in scale, frequent skirmishes, shootings, and troop concentrations along their borders since independence have indicated the possibility of larger-scale armed conflicts, against a background of many unsettled issues in their bilateral relations.

Hence, escalation of disagreements to major crises with the potential for development into armed conflict is possible in the near future. Yet, although limited armed conflicts, primarily along the borders, are a distinct possibility given the history of the region since 1991, the outbreak of major armed conflicts, including full-scale wars, is less likely, though still a possibility. Major armed conflicts would require more than the existence of disputes in the bilateral relations of the aforementioned states. For such a scenario, the presence of a favorable environment in their countries, particularly a strong nationalist mood, and also in the region would be necessary. To this, one should add another factor: the state of relations of any regional state considering a major war to settle certain disputes with the main regional powers (Iran, China, and Russia), which have varying degrees of influence in the Central Asian states, and also that with the United States having a degree of military presence and extensive oil- and gas-related economic ties with Kazakhstan and Turkmenistan.

As of today, (April 2009), none of the Central Asian states would benefit from a war in Central Asia that could expand to other regional countries, thanks to the existence of various ties, including ethnic ones, between the Central Asian countries. In particular, the regional powers have every incentive to prevent any major war in Central Asia, for war could have negative security implications resulting from their shared long borders with that region. Moreover, they could even be dragged in such a conflict that would endanger their economic and security interests, potentially even pitting them against each other—a scenario that all want to avoid as long as there is a U.S. military presence in the regions along their borders.

Furthermore, the membership of the Central Asian states (except Turkmenistan) in the Shanghai Cooperation Organization (SCO) and the Collective Security Treaty Organization (CSTO) would invite mediation by these organizations in any escalating conflict with the potential for a war involving their members. Ties of the three regional powers to the SCO as members, or, in the case of Iran, as an observer bidding for membership, would make such mediation more likely. Russia's CSTO and SCO membership suggests that likelihood for those organizations. After all, the SCO, and particularly the CSTO, which have mandates for security cooperation among their members against various sources of instability, could not possibly remain idle in the event of a looming threat of war between their members. The CSTO, having had since October 2007 a mandate to deploy its peacekeeping force in its membership's territories to quell security threats and prevent "any outside interference," could and most likely would use force, if necessary, to end any war among its members, as well as defending them in the event of aggression by a non-CSTO country.

There are enough irritating issues between and among the Central Asian states to instigate armed conflicts should certain conditions arise. However, the likelihood of a full-scale war between any two of them is small in the foreseeable future unless major changes in the status quo set them on a collision course.

SCENARIOS FOR POSSIBLE FUTURE ARMED CONFLICTS IN THE CAUCASUS

The Rise of Armed Extremist Groups

When compared to Central Asia, the Caucasus has a lower probability of facing armed extremist groups capable of challenging the authority of the Caucasian states in the near future. Among the three Caucasian states, Armenia and Georgia are the least likely candidates to face such phenomenon, for their governments are more tolerant of political dissent, even though they have yet to become truly democratic (despite having some democratic aspects). This reality decreases as a factor the formation of armed extremist groups, which are a "natural" reaction to authoritarian and totalitarian regimes that leave no room or hope for political change, including change of government, through peaceful and democratic means. Yet, this greater tolerance does not totally eliminate the possibility of the rise of such groups in Armenia and Georgia, since other contributing factors exist, such as rampant poverty and the emergence of extreme forms of nationalism and xenophobia in reaction to deteriorating ties with other countries. Nevertheless, Armenia and Georgia will not likely experience such groups with a strong social base as a source of instability in the near future. However, anti-Russian extremist groups could well emerge in Georgia. Their raison d'être would probably be to defend their country in case of war with Russia, or to retaliate against the Russians and their Abkhazian and South Ossetians allies through small-scale operations when the Georgian military is unable to engage in armed confrontations, with them because of predictable dire consequences for Georgia.

As experienced in many other countries facing a much stronger enemy, the formation of such armed extremist/nationalist groups and their activities could well be supported by their governments. The Georgian government's main objective would be to impose a small-scale, but agonizing war of attrition on Russia, not just to retaliate for its defeat in August 2008, but also to force Russia to leave Abkhazia and South Ossetia by increasing the cost of its continued stay. It is quite possible that at some point the Georgian government could lose control over these groups, resulting in their becoming a source of threat to law and order, as has occurred in many Latin American countries.

In the case of Georgia, the activities of armed organized crime involved in a wide range of illegal activities, such as drug trafficking, have been a source of lawlessness and of the weakening of the central government's authority since independence. There is no evidence that the Saakashvili administration has been successful in dealing with this problem, inherited from the preceding Shevardnadze administration. Nor is there any indication of a decrease in organized crime in the foreseeable future. Should the current trend continue, this phenomenon will be a concern for the Georgian government for its ability to destabilize the country, but it will not be a major threat to the survival of the Georgian government.

Azerbaijan does not currently have armed extremist groups strong enough to pose a threat to its security. In fact, it does not have any armed opposition group of any significance. However, its prevailing political environment makes it prone to the emergence of such groups. The domination since 1993 of the political and economic life of the country by the Aliyev family, known for extensive corruption, has created a fertile ground for the expansion of extremist ideologies and groups, including the armed ones. This is the result of the Aliyevs' extensive abuse of power to ensure their domination, and the continued rule of the Yeni Azerbaijan Party. In particular, the undemocratic succession of President Ilham Aliyev, who turned the Azeri republic into a royal republic, and his administration's misuse of power to ensure the Yeni Azerbaijan's victories in parliamentary elections, have practically removed the possibility of a peaceful change of government through elections. Azerbaijan is heading toward a dangerous social polarization characterized by the concentration of wealth in the hands of a small social stratum facing a majority of the Azeris, who suffer from poverty or low income because of the extremely uneven distribution of oil-generated income. The resulting political fragility will create a suitable ground for the expansion of extremist groups capitalizing on the frustration of the people, who are burdened with a political system that denies them the right to peaceful change while depriving them of a fair society and a prosperous life.

Intrastate Wars

The outbreak of civil wars in Azerbaijan and Georgia are quite possible in the near future. As discussed in the following sections, the frustration of the Azeris with the deadlocked issue of Nagorno-Karabakh and the occupation of a large part of their small country by the Armenian Karabakhis, fully backed by Armenia, will probably push them toward a military solution. The practical reluctance of the international community to find a peaceful settlement to the stalled territorial dispute and to restore Baku's sovereignty over its lost territory will further increase the plausibility of a resort to arms to end the unacceptable situation. Although the military weakness of the Azeris vis-à-vis their adversaries is well known, their resort to war could be justified not by an expected clear victory, but by its effect, revitalizing the international community's interest, especially that of the regional and nonregional powers, in ending the territorial dispute.

Similarly, years of unsuccessful and fruitless negotiations to settle the dispute between the Georgian government and the breakaway republics of Abkhazia and South Ossetia have frustrated the Georgians. Their frustration was at least one of the major factors prompting the Georgian military attack on Tskhinvali in August 2008. In particular, Russia's backing of those republics and recognition, since that month, of their declared independence, on the one hand, and of its maintenance of 8,000 troops in their territories, on the other, have made the separatist leaders confident in staying their course. Added to increasing disillusionment about a possible peaceful settlement to restore Georgia's territorial integrity, as evidenced by the resort to arms in 2008, the Georgian government's enjoyment of American backing and its outright hostile relations with Russia will likely encourage it to resort to war one more time to end the frustrating loss of its territory. At minimum, the Georgians could hope that such a plan would force all concerned with stability in the Caucasus to intervene to end the armed conflict—which could pit Russia and the United States against each other—and also to settle the dispute behind it. Settling the underlying dispute would be seen as necessary to avoid any future resort to arms by the Georgians, out of concern, at minimum, for the implications of a Russian-American military confrontation in the Caucasus.

Meaningful efforts by all the regional and nonregional powers with stakes in the Caucasus to find an acceptable settlement of the territorial disputes of Azerbaijan and Georgia is the only scenario capable of preventing the outbreak of another round of civil war that could quickly escalate to an interstate war in those countries, especially in the case of Georgia. However, there is no strong evidence of such efforts, nor does the possibility of a settlement requiring the restoration of the full sovereignty of Baku and Tbilisi over their lost territories seem realistic, largely because of the interests of the Armenian Karabakhis and Armenia in unifying the occupied land with Armenia and the declared independence of Abkhazia and South Ossetia as a first step toward their unification with Russia.

Interstate Wars

Interstate wars in the Caucasus are a distinct possibility in the predictable future. In fact, compared to Central Asia, their outbreak is more likely, although not inevitable.

Within this context, armed conflict between Georgia and Russia is a feasible scenario, as discussed earlier. There are many issues in the post-Soviet era capable of developing into armed conflicts. However, they are not inevitable, for efforts on the part of Tbilisi and Moscow to address their unsettled issues or, more realistically, efforts to find a compromise with which both can live could prevent ongoing disagreements from developing into major crises, and subsequently armed conflict. However, if the history of Georgian-Russian relations since 1991 is any indication, addressing these issues in a mutually satisfactory manner, especially after the 2008 war, seems highly unlikely in the predictable future unless dramatic changes occur in either or both countries that make compromise feasible.

Certain issues are the most important sources of conflict in Georgian-Russian relations with the potential for escalation to armed conflicts. They include Russia's heavy military presence in Georgia's breakaway republics, Russia's backing of these republics and their declared independence, the expansion of the U.S. military presence in Georgia, Georgia's growing ties with NATO and its bid for its membership (now backed by the American government), Georgia's dependence on Russian gas exports and Moscow's use of this to pressure Tbilisi (unless the Georgians find alternative suppliers), and the continued deepening of hostile Georgian-Russian relations in the aftermath of the August 2008 war. In all these cases, a resort to arms, or threats of doing so, by either Georgia or Russia to settle the conflict or to prevent the situation from getting out of hand could well escalate to a war.

Georgia and Russia could also enter an armed conflict as a result of the intensification of the current hostile relations between Georgia and its two breakaway republics, Abkhazia and South Ossetia. Pressure within Georgia to end these regions' declared independence could well push the Georgian government into a war to end this unacceptable status quo. Among other factors, such independence, now recognized only by Russia and Nicaragua, undermines the territorial integrity of Georgia and weakens the authority of the Georgian government. Additionally, it provides ground for Russia's permanent military presence in those republics, its interference in Georgia's internal affairs, its attempts to squeeze the Georgian governments for concessions, and its eventual integration of those republics into its own territory once more.

In the post–Georgian-Russian war era, it is now a sure bet that Moscow would not confine itself to helping the Abkhazians and South Ossetians in the event of war initiated by the Georgian government. It would certainly engage in such a war directly to defend its protégés, to settle scores with Tbilisi, and to send a clear message to other countries on hostile terms with Moscow. Tbilisi's resort to a military solution to restore its sovereignty over Abkhazia and South Ossetia will certainly develop into a military confrontation between Georgia and Russia, involving the United States in some form.

In all the aforementioned scenarios, the form, length, and intensity of the armed conflicts would be determined by the specifics of the situation in Georgia and Russia and in the region. Furthermore, the attitudes of other powers having interests in the Caucasus—the United States, Iran, and Turkey—as well as their ties with Russia and Georgia, would be two determining factors.

War between Azerbaijan and Armenia over the disputed enclave of Nagorno-Karabakh and its adjacent land is probable if the two sides fail to find a peaceful settlement to their conflict. The failure of mediation by a variety of regional and nonregional states and organizations has practically eliminated the possibility of a durable peaceful settlement to the conflict. The expectedly unsuccessful talks of the Armenian and Azeri presidents since 2006 have proved once more the absence of a ground for peaceful settlement of the territorial dispute because of the incompatibility of the two sides' interests, as discussed earlier. The regional and nonregional powers with interests or influence in Armenia and Azerbaijan and in the Caucasus in general, added to Iran's, Turkey's, and Russia's proximity to the region, do not favor a war between the two Caucasian states. This has been a major external factor explaining the reluctance of these states since their 1994 cease-fire agreement to opt for a military solution to end the unacceptable status quo, apart from such additional internal factors as the heavy cost of another round of war and the need to address numerous transitional economic, political, and social problems.

Yet, there is no certainty that these factors will be strong enough to dissuade Baku and Yerevan from resorting to arms in the foreseeable future. This is especially because the Armenian Karabakhis, frustrated with their uncertain status, could seek to provoke a war in concert with Armenia to finalize their separation from Azerbaijan and make official their de facto unification with Armenia. This would certainly lead to a war between Armenia and Azerbaijan. Furthermore, the growing frustration in Azerbaijan over the occupation of 20 percent of the Azeri land by the Armenian Karabakhis will likely force the Azeri government to seek other solutions to the deadlocked territorial dispute when the uselessness of trying to settle it through negotiations has become evident beyond any doubt. In fact, Baku could resort to war not even with the conviction of its ability to restore its sovereignty over its lost territories, but simply with the intention of putting the mainly forgotten territorial dispute on the agenda of all influential forces, whether regional and nonregional powers or international and regional organizations. In this case, its hope would be to force them to intervene—not just to end the war, but also to settle the issue in its favor to prevent another war in the Caucasus.

Moreover, the fragility of the social basis of the Azeri government and its lack of legitimacy in the eyes of many Azeris could well incline that government to instigate a war. Such a war would likely address its legitimacy weakness, at least for a while. It would provoke Azeri nationalism and motivate the Azeris to rally around their government as it waged a war to liberate their occupied land.

In all the mentioned scenarios, Azerbaijan's initiation of a war would be notwithstanding the predictable defeat of its armed forces, which are militarily inferior to those of Armenia and the Armenian Karabakhis. In such a case, the reaction of the regional and nonregional powers to the armed conflict would be a major, but not *the* major, factor determining its shape, extent, and outcome.

WAR OVER OWNERSHIP OF THE CASPIAN OIL FIELDS

The absence of a legal regime for the Caspian Sea could well pave the way for armed conflicts between the Caspian littoral states. In particular, this is a stronger possibility in the southern part of the lake, where, unlike in the northern part, no bilateral or trilateral agreement has been signed by Iran, Azerbaijan, and Turkmenistan providing an acceptable manner of dividing it among them. As discussed in the previous chapters, they all have claims to certain oil fields, which has damaged their bilateral relations to a varying extent. Iran and Azerbaijan, Azerbaijan and Turkmenistan, and Iran and Turkmenistan have not yet reached any agreement settling their ownership disputes, nor is there any indication of any workable plan to that effect.

Because the conclusion of a legal regime acceptable to all the Caspian littoral states seems unlikely, at least in the predictable future, the absence of such a regime will leave no widely acceptable peaceful means for settling the ownership disputes among the mentioned states. In such a situation, unilateral moves to establish one state's ownership over its claimed oil fields would be a conceivable scenario. Efforts by another side to reverse the move and establish its own ownership claim would likely lead to some form of use of force appropriate to the situation. Hence, small-scale armed conflicts are a possibility and could escalate to larger ones should a losing side view its loss as totally unacceptable. As long as Iran and Turkmenistan continue to enjoy extensive, growing, and tension-free multidimensional relations, unilateral moves and a resort to arms to settle conflicts are highly unlikely between the two neighbors. Although the relations of Iran and Azerbaijan have been tension-free since 2001, their limited ties, the existence of many sources of disagreements since 1991 in their bilateral relations, and the presence of the American military in Azerbaijan all increase the possibility, but not inevitability, of such a scenario. Yet, the likelihood of the escalation of an ownership dispute between Iran and Azerbaijan to a full-scale war is not very strong, for neither side would benefit from it.

Unilateral moves to settle ownership disputes in the Caspian Sea between Azerbaijan and Turkmenistan are also possible, especially in light of the poor state of relations of the two Caspian neighbors and the importance of the Caspian oil fields to the economic prosperity of both. Their relatively small amount of proven oil, not enough to secure them long-term oil exporting status, will only increase their stakes in any future dispute over their offshore oil field.

In view of the military weaknesses of both sides, particularly the fact that their small naval forces are little more than coast guards, small-scale armed conflict would be the most likely form of armed conflict. Major steps by either or both sides to build strong navies and air forces could bring about the possibility of larger-scale armed conflicts, an unlikely scenario for the short term.

THE POSSIBILITY OF A PREEMPTIVE WAR

The growing military presence of the United States in the Caucasus could provoke a preemptive war by Iran. It is conceivable that Iran's fear of an imminent attack by U.S. forces or U.S.-led forces from Azerbaijan, where the U.S. military is present, could convince the Iranians to prevent such attack. They could also do so to discourage other neighboring or regional countries who are hosting the U.S. military (Georgia, Turkey, Iraq, Pakistan, Afghanistan, and Persian Gulf Arab countries) from letting the U.S. government use their territories to attack Iran. In these cases, escalation of unrelated conflicts such as over the disputed Caspian oil fields could also be justified for a preemptive war designed to make impossible the use of the Azeri land for an attack on Iran.

Ultimately, it should be stressed that these scenarios are not inevitable. In fact, efforts to settle those issues that create grounds for armed conflict of different forms and kinds could eliminate their outbreak altogether, or at least help prevent their escalation to the point of conflict until a time when changes in circumstances could make settlements possible. Nonetheless, in the absence of such efforts, these scenarios will likely be realized sooner or later, engulfing in a destructive state of affairs both Central Asia and the Caucasus—two regions that have experienced more than their fair share of destruction since independence.

Nazar, Khan Haq, 123
Nazarbayev, Nursultan, 6, 125, 126, 189
Nejad, Saed Hadi, 76
Neka, port of, 68
Nineteenth century
   Russification policies, 237
   Soviet Union, rule in Azerbaijan,
      248–249
Niyazov, Safarmurad, 7, 31, 176, 182
   assassination attempt on, 187, 188
   building monuments, 187
   death of, 96, 182, 184, 188
   dissatisfaction with European Union,
      181
   policy of constant dismissal and, 182
Noghaideli, Zurab, 73, 74
Nomads, 122

Odyssey (Homer), 268
Oghuz tribe, 174
Oil prices, 12, 91
Opium, 94, 150
Organization for Democracy and
      Economic Development (GUAM),
      262
Organization for Security and Coopera-
      tion in Europe (OSCE), 47, 243
Osh Province, Kyrgyzstan, 196, 204
Ossetian Popular Front (Ademon
      Nykhas), 281
Ossetia, South, 69
   conflict in, 281–283
   declaration of independence, 53
Ottoman Empire, 129, 144, 197, 231,
      235. *See also* Turkey
Ottoman-Persian Wars, 232

Pakistan, 150
Pankisi Gorge (Valley), conflict in,
      285–286
Parliamentary elections of 2005, Tajik-
      istan, 167
Partnership for Peace Program (PFP), of
      NATO, 273
Pasha, Mustafa Kemal, 231

People's Democratic Party of Tajikistan
      (PDPT), 160, 161, 167
Persia. *See* Iran
Persian language, 131, 158, 162, 193
Persian script, 159. *See also* Cyrillic
      alphabets
Peter the Great, 178
Petro Kazakhstan, 136
Petrosyan, Leonard, 241
Pipeline projects, 70–71
   pipeline to Armenia, 71–72
   pipeline to Georgia, 73–75
   pipeline to Ukraine, 75–77
   South Caucasus Pipeline (SCP), 77
Pompey the Great. *See* Gnaeus
      Pompeius Magnus
Poverty, failed transition and, 32–35,
      88
Presidential election of 2003, in
      Azerbaijan, 260–261
Presidential election of 2007,
      Turkmenistan, 184
Presidential election of 2008, 61, 242
Privatization program, of Armenian
      government, 239
Prostitution
   and crimes, 14
   drug addictions and, 40
Putin, Vladimir (President), 18, 208,
      276, 280, 285

Rabbani, Burhanuddin, 162
Rahmanov, Imomali, 18, 159, 164, 167
Rahmon, Imomali. *See* Rahmanov, Imo-
      mali
Red Army, of Soviet Union, 175, 237,
      269, 274
Republican Party, Armenia, 241
Republic of Azerbaijan, 248, 250
Republic of Kyrgyzstan. *See*
      Kyrgyzstan
Rice, Condoleezza, 19
Rose Revolution, 50, 51, 278
Round Table bloc, 282
Ruhnama, 182